DATE		

THE MAKING OF A
Conservative
Environmentalist

THE MAKING OF A
Conservative
Environmentalist

*With Reflections on
Government, Industry, Scientists,
The Media, Education, Economic Growth,
The Public, The Great Lakes, Activists,
and The Sunsetting of
Toxic Chemicals*

GORDON K. DURNIL

INDIANA UNIVERSITY PRESS
Bloomington • Indianapolis

The paper used in this publication meets the minimum requirements of
American National Standard for Information Sciences—Permanence of
Paper for Printed Library Materials, ANSI Z39.48–1984.

Manufactured in the United States of America

Library of Congress Cataloging-in-Publication Data

Durnil, Gordon K., 1936–
    The making of a conservative environmentalist : with reflections
on government, industry, scientists, the media, education,
economic growth, the public, the Great Lakes, activists, and the
sunsetting of toxic chemicals / Gordon K. Durnil.
        p. cm.
    Includes bibliographical references and index.
    ISBN 0-253-32873-X (alk. paper)
        1. Great Lakes Region—Environmental conditions. 2. Environ-
mental policy—United States. 3. Environmental policy—Canada.
4. Durnil, Gordon K., date. 5. Environmentalists—United States—
Biography. I. Title.
GE160.G75D87 1995
363.7'0092—dc20   94-24989

1 2 3 4 5 00 99 98 97 96 95

To Lynda.
She is always there.

It is the duty of government
to make it difficult to do wrong,
easy to do right.
  William Ewart Gladstone

Contents

❧ Contents ❧

Preface

A Conservative's View of Environmentalism

THIS IS A BOOK ABOUT THE PERCEIVED conflict of an individual's being a conservative Republican and, at the same time, an environmentalist. I do not see the conflict. I am both. For nearly forty years I have developed and practiced my conservative philosophy. I have been an environmentalist for only five years, but even so I have become convinced that current environmental policies are putting our children in harm's way.

My first broad exposure to serious environmental concerns resulted from my service as the United States Chairman of the International Joint Commission. As I began to meet with scientists, environmental activists, and industrialists, I intuitively applied my conservative philosophy and my experience as a political decision maker to resolving problems of the environment. My technique drew great resistance from those who did not want to change their way of doing things, but it worked. My willingness to form conclusions from the weight of evidence and to enunciate those conclusions also drew resistance.

Preserving our natural resources should be a conservative tenet. Restoring degraded natural resources to something close to what they used to be surely should be a conservative goal. But contemporary environmentalism is much broader; it has to do with the prevention of adverse health effects, not just preservation or restoration.

I have never met a conservative who prefers dirty air to clean air or fouled water to healthy water. Nor have I met conservatives who want to expose their children and grandchildren to toxic substances. Conservative friends of my age (nearly sixty) often reminisce about fishing in streams so clean they could drink from them, or about the beauty of a clear blue sky in summertime. They would like to see those conditions once again. Active environmentalists might find it hard to believe, but these same friends, and most members of the public for that matter, have not yet faced the possibility that some of our actions might have adverse effects on future generations of humans. If they were presented with that evidence to the extent that it is now known, they would act. But so far, neither the governments nor we concerned environmentalists have done a very good job of communicating. That is why communicating the message is a main topic in this book.

I am concerned that one of the largest barriers to achieving environmental protection is the artificial labeling of those who seek a clean environment as liberals and the labeling of conservatives as antienvironmentalists. It seems to me that the philosophical debate should take place on how we solve environmental problems, not on whether they should be solved. And it is at this point that I, as a pragmatic problem solver, contend that the environment should be an issue promoted by people with a conservative ideology. I delve deeply into these thoughts in the pages that follow.

I am convinced that the goal of environmental protection cannot be divorced from morality. I am also hard pressed to understand how morality can be divorced from basic religious teachings. I find myself, in this book, dealing with issues of political philosophy, moral values, and religion, all in an effort to come to grips with how we as a society can resolve our continued pursuit of environmental degradation. Because I believe that governments alone cannot fight the global battle against pollution, I conclude that solutions to such gigantic problems are the responsibility of us all. That being the case, ethics in industry, in government, and in the home must be at the very core of any sustained movement toward true environmental protection.

A few friendly reviewers of these chapters felt that morality and political philosophy were subject matters for one book, while environmentalism should be the subject of a different book. I disagree. I believe that the segregation of environmental activism from real-life motivations could reduce environmental protection to a disingenuous concern among policy makers in business and government. I fear it has already done so. On the pages that follow I will try to convince you that I am correct.

Many people mistakenly associate the International Joint Commission only with the Great Lakes. So it is important to point out that this book does not set out to detail the importance of the Great Lakes, though they are an outstanding resource. From an economic standpoint, if the Great Lakes Basin were a country, it would be one of the top seven industrialized nations in the world. I write this book with the presumption that you know something of the geography, the history, the nature, and the worldwide importance of the Great Lakes system, which contains 20 percent of the world's freshwater. I write with that premise while knowing that few of the nearly 300 million persons living in the United States and Canada really know these things.

Being such a huge area of surface freshwater shared by two great nations, the Great Lakes provide a laboratory for learning unequaled in any other ecosystem on Earth. What human has done to human there has been researched and documented as a learning laboratory for use by all the world, should the people of the world be wise enough to care. That is why the Great Lakes are an important subject of my reflections.

There are a number of players in the chronicles of international pollution. I try to reflect on each of the major actors in that ongoing saga. Who are they?

Obviously, governments are major players, whether they be federal governments, local governments, state or provincial governments, or the local prison, school, or wastewater treatment plant. And it is these government entities that tend to be among the more careless dischargers of pollutants into the water, ground, and air. Industry is commonly thought to be a prime polluter. That may be true, but in almost every situation, industry's pollution is legal. Businesses pay a fee to governments for permission to do it. But the term *industry* encompasses a lot—big, medium, and small operations—and it is not really fair to squeeze all under the same tent.

The organized environmentalists are certainly players, and they became more and more mature and responsible as my time on the commission stretched on. Scientists are extremely important players. Regulators certainly have meaningful roles. Educators are critical. What about the news media? Do they have a role? You bet your life they do! But they really have not been players to the extent they should be. The health care professions obviously contain necessary players, but they are coming slowly to the idea of prophylactic care for environmental health effects. And even more obvious than anything I have said so far in this dissertation, each and every member of the public must be a player.

My purpose in exploring the major environmental players is to give you my perception of how each of these interests reacted to the discussion of persistent toxic substances. My reflections may surprise you a little, or they may just confirm a preexisting belief that you harbored long before coming across this attempt at literary logic. You may agree with my reflections or you may not. But read on, and let's see what you think. But as you do, consider these words from the most widely read writer of the French Renaissance, the essayist Michel de Montaigne: "Nothing is so firmly believed as what we least know."

This book is not written as a scientific treatise, because a scientist I am not. I am a conservative Republican politician, a lawyer, and an environmentalist. If science cannot provide you with absolute proof of my fears, you might wonder, how can I? I can't. I will share with you what I do know and feel. I will admit what I do not know, which is enormous in scope. And I will ask you many questions in the hope that perhaps one of them will spark an interest for you to pursue on behalf of us all.

In 1989, President George Bush put me into a position of international diplomatic importance, with duties that required a reordering of my comfortable thought patterns. It was a responsibility that required a great deal of personal learning, understanding, evidence weighing, and decision making. The environmental well-being of the United States and Canada, the actions of each upon the other along the longest unguarded, and most peaceful international boundary in the world, encompassed the subject matter of concern. The task was to see problems of large magnitude from a binational perspective and, not being bound by unilateral policies, to suggest what I believed to be the best possible solutions to the governments of the United States and Canada. I left this high position with one overriding thought relative to the potential effects of persistent toxic substances on the sustainability of the human race: we need to change our way of thinking and acting. We just cannot keep on doing what we have always done.

I write this book as a reflection on my observations of the international environmental scene. In so doing, I couldn't help but include personal reflections that have caused me to see things as I do. Please forgive me for that.

THE MAKING OF A
Conservative
Environmentalist

I

The Early Years

The Acid Pond

"COME ON, SHADDY," I WOULD OFTEN YELL to my young friend, "let's go play in the Acid Pond." Sounds a little mindless now, but during the World War II years it was a frequent refrain through my neighborhood. I was the only member of my family of six children to be born in the city. My siblings were from the country. I came along during the Depression, seventeen or so years after the end of World War I. I entered the first grade one month after the Japanese attack on Pearl Harbor. I entered high school six months before the North Korean attack on South Korea. Many of my early memories are gauged by milestones of war.

At age eight I began delivering the *Indianapolis News,* and later I delivered the *Indianapolis Times,* both afternoon newspapers. And let me tell you, 1944 and 1945 were great years to be a paperboy. Before television, newspaper "extras" were the quickest and most complete source of news—and a good source of money for a young boy. D-day in 1944, the death of FDR and V-E day in the spring of 1945, V-J day in the summer of '45, and many other days of war are memorable to me as not only exciting but also profitable. The regular weekly subscription rate for the *News* was twenty cents, for the *Times,* eighteen cents. But "extras" were a nickel, and I was able to keep one penny of the selling price of each newspaper.

For a penny per paper, I did in fact walk up and down the streets of my neighborhood yelling at the top of my lungs, "Extra, extra, read all about it." I made enough money to put in layaway at the local dry goods store a toy six-shooter, with holster, just like the one Roy Rogers wore. Each week I took my pennies into the store to pay an installment and to admire that gun and holster set. After seven or eight weeks of payments, it was mine. Toy guns might not be all that politically correct these days, but the lesson learned then was that if I wanted something badly enough, and if I knew no one was going to give it to me, I had the option of working for it and getting it. Both of those things, guns and working for your reward, seem to be held in some disdain by many today.

My dad bought our house on Albany Street in Indianapolis for one thousand dollars, then set about fixing it up. He finished an upstairs to sleep the kids. Turning on and off the electrical ceiling light he installed in the bedroom where my brother and I slept was an experience to remember. It took a couple years for Dad to get an on-and-off switch, so we would hook and unhook the bare wires to turn the light on or off. We were told, at a rather young age, to always grab the wires where the insulation was, that touching the bare wires could kill us. We never touched those bare wires, but each night one terrific argument occurred between my brother and me over whose turn it was to unhook the wires. In recent years, my brother and I have calculated that a light switch then probably cost somewhere between five and ten cents. We still wonder why it took so long. Maybe light switches had gone off to war with Lucky Strike green.

My father dug a basement under the house to create a place for a modern central heating coal furnace and a gas water heater that would explode in your face for no reason at all. Seeing a kid without eyebrows was not unusual during those times of new inventions. Central heating was a wonder. The furnace would be banked before bedtime, but it never lasted through the night. Mornings were cold as we waited for Dad's efforts at restoking to take hold. There were no fans pushing the heated air through the ducts then, just nature. The first register (as the heat outlets were called in my family) to heat up was the one right above the furnace. Such is the way of nature. My siblings and I would fight with our dog, Buttons, for the first hint of heat to emerge. Dog Buttons, with sharp teeth and bad temper, usually won.

Dad also put in a modern kitchen. Electrical outlets were installed to replace the lone octopuslike light cord hanging from the ceiling with all those other electric plugs stuck to it. Before the improvements, if you weren't careful you could easily hang yourself on the cord leading from the new electric toaster on the kitchen table to the dangling source of electricity at ceiling's center. The toaster warmed only one side of the bread at a time. It was important to remember to turn over the slices of bread so they could be toasted on both sides by the new electric miracle. Something else new, asbestos tile, was on the floor to be waxed weekly, and to avoid the need to constantly paint the exterior, my dad covered our house with asbestos siding. For a working-class family, we were thoroughly modern.

These modern facilities were put to best use for Sunday dinner, which was served at noon. At my house in the forties, we ate breakfast, dinner, and supper. I was introduced to "lunch" when I started high school, where the cafeteria had such delicacies as red jello squares with macaroni in it. High school was also my first experience with cafeteria-style eating. I quickly decided that I preferred dinner to lunch, especially on Sundays. Because very early on Sunday mornings, my mother would start dinner by wringing the necks of live chickens, twirling them around until their heads came off. Then, always to our childish surprise, they would run around for a while like chickens with their heads off.

The kids had the job of plucking the feathers off those dead chickens. We would scald them in hot water and singe them with a burning newspaper to get the fuzz off. It was not a job that was easy, quick, or fun. The smell was repulsive. During the summer, an additional chore before Sunday dinner was cranking the ice cream maker for what seemed like hours. The results were good. Fried chicken, thick and greasy dumplings, fresh green beans with bacon grease, wonderful cobblers and pies, homemade ice cream, and even hickory nut cake. Now, on my low-fat diet, even if I found someone to make things taste as good as my mother could, not one of them can pass my lips.

One block south of my childhood home ran Troy Avenue, which marked the Indianapolis city limit on the south side of town. Across the railroad tracks was a place we shied away from called Dogtown. Now this whole area, though still somewhat dogtownish, is more like midtown, as the city limit has moved five or six miles south. At the corner of Shelby Street and Troy Avenue stood a steel mill, not very big, really. But at the time it seemed enormous. During the war, the steel mill ran day and night.

The boys in my neighborhood, and an occasional girl, would sit on the north side of Troy Avenue and watch the lights, see the smoke, and hear the noises of the steel mill. In that era, boys' parents kept a pretty loose rein; not so the parents of girls. It was a time before air conditioning, before television, a time when few automobiles roamed the streets, what with tires and gasoline rationed and nearly impossible to come by. Roller skating at Roller Land with sister Carol was a pretty exciting event. With open windows and few distractions other than the frequent whistles of the many wartime steam engines from the railroad just west of Allen Avenue, our neighborhood often went to sleep to the rumblings of the steel mill a block or so away.

But the real feature of the steel mill, the one that provided joy for adventurous youth, was the Acid Pond.

It was almost a daily activity to float our raft on the Acid Pond, a small body of water with surrounding fence in constant disrepair. The pond was just west of the steel mill and just east of the cow pasture. Holes in the fence made access easy to the area where we kept our raft on the bank. The cows kept the weeds down in the cow pasture, but inside the fence weeds were abundant, except on the bare bank, near the water, where nothing would grow. Tar was a necessary accessory for our trips, because we needed to fill the cracks between the boards of our raft to keep the furtive waters from seeping through. For the life of me, I can't remember where we obtained the tar. I have not had my hands on any tar for decades. But it must have been an easily available commodity then, for we always had the needed supply. It was great fun, and I have many fine memories of rafting on the Acid Pond on warm summer days fifty years ago. I now wonder who named it the Acid Pond? Why did they name it that? Was the acid toxic? I am sure it was. Was it persistent? Biocumulative? Was it a collection point for early discharges of PCBs? Did the managers of the steel mill concern themselves with the children playing there? Did the governments know enough then to care?

We didn't tell our parents when we went over there, because we knew they would worry about our drowning. And acid was a scary word, even then. Both of my parents were born in the nineteenth century, and they could not have begun to conceive of a worry about the subtle adverse health effects that we suspect and fear at the end of the twentieth century. If you doubt the inference about my parents' ability to conceive contemporary maladies, consider this. My father's father (born in 1852) had to take over the running of the Durnil Farm, in Washington and Harrison counties, because his father had been wounded in the Civil War. I am the sixth child of a sixth child. Just three generations, from me to my grandfather, takes us back to a time before the first Republican was elected as President of the United States. Not only was Abraham Lincoln the President when my grandfather was a child, but communications were slow and infrequent. Communications remained slow until the arrival of electricity and the radio, both of which came along in southern Indiana after my parents were married in 1915. Communications did not really become instantaneous until my high school years, or even later. And even now, much of our contemporary knowledge about potential environmental maladies is not being communicated on a broad scale.

But, I wonder, would I be smarter now if I had not played on the Acid Pond? Would my sperm count be stronger? (Hey, Shaddy, my sperm count can beat your sperm count!) Would my reproductive prowess have been heightened? Would my immune system have been more protective? Would my children and grandchildren have been different in any way? Would I want them to be? I don't know. But time passed and we stopped going to the Acid Pond. I wonder why. Maybe it was because of that guy in the cow pasture who shot at us with a small-caliber rifle when we tried to ride his horses. He really didn't want us to do that, or so it seemed.

One day, brother Al and I and dog Buttons were in the cow pasture. We were hovering on low tree limbs waiting for a horse to walk by, so we could jump on its back and "ride 'em cowboy," as we were wont to say in those days. Actually, it was my brother and I who did the hovering. Throughout his life, dog Buttons never once climbed a tree. Suddenly the farmer (or whoever that guy was) began shooting at us with his rifle. Looking at us now, you might think my brother and me incapable of speed. But on that day in the mid-1940s we were as fast as Mercury (not the heavy metal), and fear had so elevated our capacity for speed that we were confident we had even outrun our dog. Winded and glad to be alive, we struggled up to the friendly confines of our front porch, sure that dog Buttons had bought the farm, only to find him waiting there on the porch for our not-so-certain return. His fear and his speed had surpassed even ours.

That first decade of my life so long ago brought with it my first experiences with recycling. Oh, I do it now. I have an orange box in my garage into which I place papers, plastics, and glass. The recycling guy charges only three dollars a month and had been coming on Fridays, the same day as the trash collector. But the city fathers decided that was too easy. The trash collector now comes on Thursdays (without telling us about the day change, causing piles of trash to accumulate at the end of my driveway), and the recycling guy picks up on Tuesdays. I can foresee a real challenge to my dedication to the environment. Do I have the fortitude to carry waste to the curb twice a week? I don't know. I always hated to do it one day a week. I wonder why government likes to make doing the right thing harder? The wrong thing easier? When I wrote a letter to the mayor, a staffer called me with the new rules. All trash must be in plastic bags and not in big permanent containers, or so I was told. The recycling guy left a note saying newspapers in the recycle box must be bagged. Do these rules make doing the right thing easier, or do they just promote the sale of plastic bags? Bureaucrats tend to be bureaucrats wherever you find them. But back to the war years. The big one: World War II.

One of our favorite pastimes, besides going to the Acid Pond, was to go junkin'. Junkin' was fun. We would roam up and down the alleys of our neighborhood finding all sorts of neat and valuable things. I feel sorry for kids these days who grow up in suburbs without alleys, sidewalks, or large covered front porches. Alleys were indeed special places. During the war, rubber and metals were in short supply. Every ounce was needed for the war effort to make tanks, trucks, Jeeps, cannons, ships, and other necessities to preserve freedom. We would scour the alleys for scraps of metal and red inner tubes. Obviously you know that real rubber inner tubes were red, right? They were. And they would stretch forever, making great rubber guns. But we would forgo rubber guns for the war effort and deliver our scrap metal and old rubber to the corner collection site. We were paid for our collections. I don't remember how much, but it was surely something like a penny per Flyer wagon load.

We did all of our junkin' one year as a collective effort to raise money for camping equipment for my Boy Scout troop. We really worked at it. You had to get there before the junk man came along. Oh I know, it is probably not politically correct now to refer to a junk man as a junk man, but that's what we had then. With a horse and wagon, he would roll down the alleys singing in a loud voice, "Any old rags today?" If he got to the valuable stuff before we did, he would buy it from people for maybe a penny a ton, leaving nothing for me and my fellow scouts. That would mean no tents to ward off rain and cold, so we made sure to stay a day ahead of the junk man in the alleys on southside Indianapolis. A little later, when the Korean War came along, scrap metal was again in short supply. The old streetcar tracks were torn out to make guns and tanks, but I had lost my fervor for junkin' by then. I was in high school and a football player; I couldn't be caught junkin'.

Capons, John Dillinger, and I

Shortly after World War II ended, my friends' dad invented a new product, a pellet to caponize chickens. The chickens would be desexed and become plump, with more meat and less fat, bringing a better price at the market. The Japanese had done it with a scalpel. Then came a liquid formula that could be injected into young chickens. At about the time my friends' dad had his pellet ready for distribution, the liquid formula became suspect as a carcinogen. The introduction and subsequent sale of the pellet formula brought wealth to my friends' dad, a man who worked hard, took a chance as an entrepreneur, and succeeded.

As he was testing his pellet in the late forties, he needed my friend, me, and occasionally other eleven-, twelve-, or thirteen-year-old boys to help test the product. We would travel central Indiana a night or two each week, earning fifteen dollars by catching five thousand chickens a night to be caponized. After dividing the chickenhouse floor with portable fencing, we would grab five chickens in each hand, lay them on the table so our adult companion could implant the pellet under the skin on the back of each chicken's neck, and then toss them on the other side of the fence. Care had to be exercised in this process because even the slightest hint of a sudden noise would cause the chickens to stampede into a corner, piling on top of each other, suffocating hundreds at a time. Obviously the farmer who owned the chickens would become a little unglued whenever we suffocated his profits. Music calmed the chickens, we found, so a radio became a common tool by which Vaughn Monroe, Doris Day, and even Frankie Laine, "knowing what the wild goose knows," could soothe the avian beasts. We did that chore for several years and became quite expert at it. I learned quite a few new things, such as the cannibalistic nature of those nasty, awful chickens. Now, on my low-fat diet, chicken is a dietary staple. Ugh!

The stench of massive chicken flesh and feathers was difficult to cleanse away, but there was some excitement in the chicken-catching business of the 1940s. One of the regular farms on our forays through central Indiana was the childhood home of the famous outlaw John Dillinger. His father still farmed there, a pleasant individual. As a young boy on the edge of puberty while in the act of destroying the reproductive systems of unknowing chickens, I found it exciting being at John Dillinger's home. My barber claimed to be a Dillinger friend, and with each haircut at the Shelby Street Barber Shop I heard tales about John Dillinger being still alive in the 1940s, similar to our Elvis sightings in the 1990s. We always looked for John at the farm but never saw him.

Earlier, during development of the product, my friend's dad tested chickens in the basement and garage of his home. My friend's father's brother-in-law, a chemist who later became my father-in-law, did some similar testing in his home. For those of us who were children at the time, in and around those two homes and the business, exposure to synthetic estrogenic substances was easy enough and certainly not a matter of concern for anyone. We regular chicken catchers would often visit the little house in Cumberland, Indiana, where the pellets were made. White dust filled the air. Stories flourished, humorous at the time, about women whose breasts had become enlarged. No one knew why. No one thought about protective clothing. No one at the time, certainly not me, could conceive of future effects to humans from such activities. I was readying myself to enter high school at age thirteen.

Even though the purpose of the endeavor was to alter the sexual nature of those birds, to desex them, no one then even considered the possibility that a similar effect could afflict humans. That was more than forty-five years ago, and it is not fair to judge the actions of the forties by the knowledge of the nineties. But what has happened since then? Were there any resulting effects on humans? Well, I am not sure of the relationship, but my friend's dad suffered heart problems and cancerous large-organ tumors. He lived to a relatively advanced age. My friend suffered serious acne (chloracne?) as a boy and later, like his father, heart problems and large-organ cancerous tumors. He died at a relative young age. Just three generations of that family, fairly limited in size, had breast cancer, large-organ tumors, Alzheimer's disease, dermatomyositis, immune suppression, emotional problems, and learning disabilities.

The Fifties

I survived my duties as a chicken catcher and began high school at midcentury. That might not sound like a big deal to those of you too young to remember midcentury, but a big fuss was made when 1949 turned into 1950. My friend and I went to an all-night movie on New Year's Eve to celebrate the century getting over the hump. As a true and complete product of the fifties, I started high school in January 1950 and graduated from college in January 1960. That was four years of high school, two years in the U.S. Army (seventeen months in Korea), and four years in college. The year I started high school was the first year Negroes—the word *black* hadn't come into vogue yet—were permitted to attend the same high schools as whites in Indianapolis. It seemed to work out OK, at least from my point of view.

For me the fifties were a time of great excitement. They were not the liberal fifties recalled by David Halberstam. And they were not the boring fifties I often hear about from media and movie pundits. I remember the fifties as happy days. I have a hard time remembering being bored in the fifties. We went Halloweening, throwing corn on people's front porches and scraping their screens. We had water-balloon fights from cars. We killed our friend's goldfish, Popeye and Olive, as we experimented on the adverse effects of perfume in the goldfish bowl. We played football, basketball, and baseball. I even put the shot on the track team. We went to war.

In the late 1940s we prayed in school and struggled a little each morning as we added the new words "under God" to the Pledge of Allegiance to the flag of the United States of America. We had church school in our public schools. The local church would come to our auditorium to teach us about God. Then the Supreme Court did something that made us walk over to the church, instead of having the lessons in school. We thought that somewhat unreasonable of those black-robed old men, whoever they were. The church then brought in a little trailer just a few feet off school property. It was a good solution. Now we did not have to walk so far to learn the ways of God. We respected our parents and thought the Boy Scout motto about a good deed every day was not so corny. As kids, we had a lot of fun. There must have been something deficient in our psychic.

Maybe the political correctness pundits of today think we were boring in the fifties because it was so very difficult as a teenager then to get your hands on a condom. You had to convince a pharmacist that you really needed one, that you were old enough to have one, and that you knew what to do with it once you got one. It was a hard test to pass. But our friend Tony the druggist would occasionally see fit to sell us one of his "head caskets." As a freshman I played the French horn in high school band. We had a rather prim and proper female classmate who played the cornet rather well. For one recital, after she had warmed up and stepped away from her horn for a moment, my sinister buddies and I taped a condom inside her horn. We had visions of glee, thinking of the large bubble that would expand from the end of her horn as she puckered her first blow. But the tape didn't hold and the condom just sort of fizzled as it floated limply out into the audience. Who says we didn't know what to do with those things in the fifties? I had to give up playing the French horn in high school. I also played football and was in the ROTC. Both the band and the ROTC unit marched at halftime of football games, when I was supposed to be in the lockerroom finding out how many blocks and tackles I had missed. The band leader gave me the ultimatum of giving up one of the three, so I gave up the French horn.

Maybe people think we were boring in the fifties because there was never more than one girl in any high school graduating class who was involved in a controversy about whether or not a pregnant girl could march in the graduation ceremonies. We did a lot of fun things in school, a lot of things we should not have done, but we never carried guns to school as is today's fad. Maybe that made us boring. Maybe they think we were boring because they have heard Perry Como sing. But Nat King Cole was cool, as were Teresa Brewer and the Brothers Mills and Ames. We were taught character values in our homes and in our schools. We were taught self-pride and national pride. We were taught that our only limitations were the ones we placed on ourselves. Those are somewhat disturbing thoughts for those who believe that government should solve all problems and that all values should be neutral.

But then at age eighteen, I found myself in a war-devastated Korea. A teenage sense of duty to my country drove me to get there as quickly as possible, and I did just that. Climbing over the edge of a huge troopship on a rope ladder into a small landing craft at Inchon, even though no one was shooting at me, is a moment I shall not forget. I saw a lot of things in Korea that made lasting impressions on me. I saw firsthand the devastating environmental consequences of war. No trees were left standing. Green was absent from the landscape. Hunger and poverty were all around me for two cold winters and one hot summer. I witnessed an election in postwar South Korea which reinforced within me the burning desire to work to preserve freedom in America. It was a national election. Soldiers would come to the shacks, some of straw, some of flattened GI beer cans, some of cardboard, where the Koreans then lived. The soldiers, being the official vote takers, would ask the residents for their vote. If they voted wrong they were beaten, then given a chance to vote again. How widespread those actions were, I don't know. I did, however, see such instances in my limited area of the Korean Peninsula.

I saw a lot in Korea, life-and-death kind of things, things that made an impression on me as a teenager far from home. I saw the generosity of the United States when I was called upon to help unload a ship full of barley to be given free to the Koreans. We GIs spent the night unloading the ship, piling the barley into huge piles on the docks. The Koreans, with cloth bags, waited for an opportunity to garner their share of the barley. I wondered then, and wonder now, if Koreans really used barley. The bureaucratic rules were such that Koreans could not get their share until the next day. Overnight, a storm came up and blew all of the barley into Pusan Harbor. Another gesture of U.S. generosity I witnessed was the introduction of dairy cows, as a free gift, to provide the milk needed by young and old Koreans. The war-ravaged Koreans ate all of the milk cows within a matter of a few days.

When I arrived back in the United States from my tour of duty in Korea I found a different fifties from the one I had left. There had been a sharp dividing line, and that line was drawn by music. From the calm refrains of the early fifties, with the Four Freshmen and Gogi Grant, I discovered rock and roll with Elvis, Carl Perkins, Little Richard, and all the rest. From the Nelsons to the Cunninghams with just a small transition via Shaboom. With these impressions of youth and the GI Bill, I entered college and set off on an interesting course for the next thirty-five or forty years.

Developing a Conservative Philosophy

Living in a society where six or seven out of every ten children born to black mothers are born out of wedlock and where three out of ten children of white mothers are born similarly; and living in a society where the elderly, and the not so elderly, fear walking the streets of their neighborhood and also fear being alone in their homes; and living in a society where teenagers are armed and deadly, where weapon searches are conducted in the schools, where teenage girls hide the boys' guns in private places to avoid detection, where mothers defend the rights of teenage sons to carry guns for protection, where it is illegal to own a fully automatic weapon but the government will sell you a permit to do so for some amount of dollars, and where in my hometown, I recently read, only 16 percent of cases referred to the Juvenile Court involved kids that had both mother and father at home; and living in a society where reporters make fun of Vice President Dan Quayle for trying to focus the attention of the American people on the breakdown of the family structure, where it is illegal to poison the water or air unless you buy a permit to do so from government, where educators have failed to educate, and where mainstream clergy have run and hid while religion was under full-scale attack, I wonder, how do I apply my personal philosophy to problems of such magnitude?

Do we follow the failed example of communism, which, for a while, was able to contain criminal activity or at least hide it? Do we build more prison walls to keep bad people behind? Do we just kill off those who do things we deem to be wrong? Do we eliminate individual rights to protect the victims of crime? Let's take a look at the domestic tactics of communism. The communists eliminated morality from their society. Amoral and immoral leaders took control. The government-controlled media proclaimed as trivial any thoughts of God and morality. New generations were taught that immorality was moral. Abortion became the preferred method of birth control. Gun control was absolute. The use of alcohol became rampant. Health care became the province of the government. It all sounds similar to issues being debated in the United States during the 1990s, doesn't it? But please remember this: those authoritarian governments, unconcerned for the well-being of the individual, created the greatest and most heinous pollution the world has ever known.

All of this brings me to the development of my philosophy over the years, and why I am so disturbed with governments that seem to be leading us toward a greater breakup of the family, toward more crime, a softer attitude on drugs, juveniles without respect for themselves or others, a socialized society, acceptance of perverse life-styles, and a destruction of our ability to defend ourselves as a nation or in our homes as individuals. If our society can accept leaders who lack sufficient personal ethics to inspire good moral stewardship, is it any wonder that our society can simply ignore the fouling of our environment with chemicals that can unknowingly alter important aspects of life itself?

So why do I think the way I do about what I have now begun to discuss? Just where did I come from?

One of my alleged ancestors, John del Kay, was appointed Sheriff of London in 1201. I presume he was a conservative. My grandmother's maiden name was Kay. My middle name is Kay, a source of much ribbing as a youth. Grandpappy Kay (1814–1912) was my grandmother's grandfather. He was an early Hoosier settler and a legendary figure in my family. Just think of it, eight hundred or more years of Kays. Most of my ancestors were working their way into Indiana in the late 1700s and early 1800s. Many were active in the formation of the State of Indiana. Some were backwoodsmen, some were lawyers, many were politicians. Some were business and community leaders in the "Literary Center of the West," Salem, Indiana, where they owned the newspaper and woolen mill (providing uniforms to Indiana soldiers fighting for the North in the Civil War while much of the local sentiment favored the South). My great, great, great grandmother Hannah Levy Allen was one of the first people of the Hebrew faith in the "west." A fact my mother refused to believe.

My parents taught me respect for others, sometimes with gentle persuasion, sometimes with logic, sometimes with a belt. My dad had a really soft, well-worn leather belt and boy could he make that thing sing. A little childish disrespect from big-mouthed eight-year-old me would bring my mother's retort, "Wait until your dad gets home." Well, my dad, a mechanic, would arrive late in the day, dirty, looking for a bath, food, some rest, family interactions, and then mother would say, "Gordon did blankety blank today." It could be Gordon said a bad word, Gordon broke the neighbor's window with a baseball, Gordon was gone all day without telling me where he was, Gordon told a lie, Gordon sassed me (a biggie fifty years ago), or Gordon got into trouble at school.

With Dad just a few steps into the door, my mother would say, "Gordon did so and so." Off came the belt and the chase began. He always won! The chase would end. My butt would burn. It was on those days that you needed to be smart enough to get your bibbed corduroy pants off before Dad got home and unleashed his belt. Those little ridges of corduroy could easily be transferred to the pink skin of a young buttocks and hurt like the dickens. In those days, you had to be nearly twelve years old before you could wear pants with a belt, instead of those dumb shoulder straps that hooked to the bib of your corduroy and denim pants. My dad was not a cruel man; he was gentle. But he did believe in discipline. With a third-grade education he became one of the earliest automobile and motorcycle mechanics in Indiana. He found highway work during the Great Depression as he worked himself and his family toward the city where hopefully employment would be more plentiful. In the city he became successful as an automobile mechanic and later as an entrepreneur in the ornamental iron business.

I tell you all this because my philosophy is reflective of parental teachings and actions. We didn't have many rules in my childhood home, but the ones we had, patterned pretty much after the Ten Commandments, were to be obeyed. If you violated a rule, such as disrespect for a parent, or stealing a comic book from the local drug store, or telling a lie, or violating someone else's property, you knew what punishment to expect. You knew it would be swift, you knew it would hurt, and you knew it would cause you to think about your actions in advance of knowingly violating one of those rules again. We were never sent to our rooms to play with our toys as a form of punishment. We were not told to sit in a corner, although I did that at school a few times. No timeout chairs. Just a butt spanking, which, by the way, I also experienced a few times in elementary school.

My parents had a simple set of workable expectations for a child:

1. Know the rules
2. Violate the rules
3. Expect real and swift punishment
4. Don't wantonly violate the rules again

It worked then. It might just work now! Is punishment punishment if it doesn't hurt? I wonder.

So it was early in life when I was taught respect for others and taught to follow the rules. And, as I have described, I was taught that there could be adverse consequences to my acts. My siblings and I were taught, in words and by example, to be self-reliant. "Your only security is you," my dad would tell me as I grew into manhood.

As a young man when motorized vehicles first came along, he taught himself how to repair them. When World War I came along, he already had a child and did not have to go to war. Later, during World War II (as we younger kids sat on the floor circling the big radio, staring at it), he painfully listened to news reports for possible information about two of his sons in Europe. Later (without youngsters left at home) he would listen for news about another son during the Korean War. He built a nice business for a young man in the early years of the twentieth century. But after World War I he lost it all to cover the mortgage on his father's farm. He then struggled his way to success again for a second and third time. From nothing to success, several times. The American dream. But, as he learned and as he taught, you can depend upon no one else for your success. His example was that your best route to success is hard work, confidence, and self-reliance.

My dad never had a credit card. He was leery of banks. He would not buy anything he could not first inspect. No pig in a poke for him. He didn't really trust people in white shirts and ties. He worried about the practice of giving pieces of paper (checks) to pay bills. He never bought anything unless he had the cash to pay for it. He and my mother did without a lot. Oh, for the last thirty years of his life he was accumulating capital, but it was not to be spent for something that he thought he could do without. On my parents' fiftieth wedding anniversary in 1965, the siblings chipped in to buy my mother an automatic washer and drier. At age sixty-eight she would no longer need to run the clothes through the wringer and carry them wet up narrow and steep basement stairs to the backyard clothesline. An extravagance for my parents, a necessity for their progeny. My conservative parents always conserved energy, something I had never thought much about until I began writing these words.

Those were lessons of my youth. Lessons of respect, especially for your elders. Lessons that indicate society does need rules to live by, and that the Ten Commandments are as good as any ever devised. My parents were right. Their concept of raising a family worked. They raised six children, all of whom were self-reliant, none of whom became criminals, and all of whom were successful within their individual definition of success. All of whom supported themselves and their families. None of whom ever expected anyone else, especially government, to take care of their needs. My parents bred four sons who all voluntarily served their nation in times of military need. A pretty basic youth environment for developing a conservative philosophy, don't you think? But have I not described the basic beliefs of those who founded and built this great nation, whether as laborers or managers, generals or privates? Male or female? Black or white? Native born or foreign born?

Home from my tour in Korea where I had a firsthand opportunity to view governmental waste and environmental degradation, I entered college ready to learn how to correct the ills of society. Obviously I had just come from a military environment where rules were clear and their violation brought swift retribution. Some of my fraternity brothers had not yet learned such clear lessons, leaving clothing strewn around the rooms and dormitory. We veterans, though, knew how to keep our act together. Discipline had taught us to do so. It was then, at age twenty, when I began to ponder some differences between the thinking of men and women. I still have not mastered that subject. One night at dinner with some lifelong friends in the spring of 1994, three women in their mid-fifties thought it quite all right to not punish a wife for cutting off her husband's penis. The three males, in their late fifties, thought she should hang.

In the army it was always a rule that my shirts be hung in the locker with the left sleeve out. You learned to do that. If you didn't do it that way you received an immediate punishment. And the punishment could be harsh. For example, having your shirt hung so that the right sleeve was out could send you outside marching at night, in the rain, in the cold, with everything you owned strapped onto your back. Your pack, your extra pair of boots, your helmet, your rifle, your entrenching tool, everything. It probably all weighed half as much as the guy carrying it. And you might have to do that for two hours or four hours, depending upon the mood of the sergeant who found your right sleeve wrong side out. In that circumstance, you soon became one with your environment as the raindrops pitter-pattered off your helmet. But in civilian life women hang everything with the right sleeve out. They get upset when men do it the other way. Even their buttons are put on the opposite side. And this isn't just a male-female dispute, because every darn laundry in the country does the same thing. Every time I go into my closet I expect to be punished.

In 1958, at age twenty-two and the first year I could vote, I observed voters in Indiana sending Vance Hartke to the United States Senate. I wondered how they could make such a mistake. His Republican opponent was in midterm as governor and he was burdened with a scandal that had not occurred during his term. I decided then that I should find time in my life to participate in political activity. So I became involved as a volunteer law student in the 1960 elections, and I have been involved in every election since. In law school the big men on campus were those students who worked for the Democrat governor. Some were elected to the legislature while still in law school. But several of my friends and I became very active, as a minute minority of law students, in the conservative philosophy. It was hard because Democrats in the early 1960s were in control of everything in Indiana. We young conservatives read everything there was to read. We were founders of Young Americans for Freedom in Indiana, a conservative youth group. We were early supporters of Barry Goldwater. We even wrote about our exploits as conservative youth in a liberal world.

For the December 1961 issue of *New Guard*, the national magazine of Young Americans for Freedom, I wrote a lengthy article on the picketing of an Indianapolis automobile dealer for selling communist-made cars, the Skoda from Czechoslovakia. Prior to the picketing, we met with the owner and told him "we are opposed to the sale of communist-made goods in the United States and feel that you are, perhaps indirectly, assisting the communist in his goal of world conquest." He thought we were nuts and ignored us. We then, on October 28, 1961, gathered a good-size group of young conservatives to march in front of the dealership on a Saturday. We carried signs with slogans such as "Why pay for Soviet bombs?" It was on that day that I had my first experience as a newsmaker, with a variety of media interviews. It was an experience that would be repeated many times over the next several decades. One reporter who interviewed me that day was Gerry LaFollette, a dedicated public servant seeking truth. The likes of him, in his profession, have pretty well disappeared.

We young conservatives were also concerned with the sale of Easter candy made in communist countries. We would find it advertised as some sort of premium product, but we wondered what in the world did the communists know about Easter? Candy celebrating the resurrection of Christ being made by slave labor in an atheistic society. Hypocritical. Strange times then, strange times now. In the January 1963 issue of *New Guard*, I wrote about another experience of picketing when President John F. Kennedy came to town to support the liberal Birch Bayh for the United States Senate. We carried signs proclaiming, "Give Red China a Seat in the United Nations—Ours." The article goes on to describe the beatings to which several of our young conservatives were subjected by those not much interested in our freedom of speech.

My thoughts about the United Nations went back to my service in Korea. We were there under the United Nations Command. The U.S. troops didn't pay much attention to that circumstance until after the truce took effect, when the United Nations tried to flex some muscle. One day the U.N. honchos decided the U.S. and British troops did not need live ammunition. As a teenager, on guard duty on a mountain, in a foxhole, along the demilitarized zone without bullets, knowing armed communist infiltrators were all about,

I decided the United Nations just was not an appropriate authority to command United States troops. I have seen nothing since then that would cause me to change my opinion.

From my speeches in the early sixties, I find such comments as these:

Conservatism should be clear to all Americans, because all Americans are essentially conservative.

When the government assumes the position of employing, supervising and remunerating the citizens to do whatever the government may bid them to do, not only an obvious moral sin has been committed, but also a disastrous economic error. The past is demonstrative of this, in that whenever a government takes control of the economic system in a particular country, that economic system becomes less and less efficient.

It seems the real purpose of the New Frontier is identical with the ambition of the central planners of the New Deal and the Fair Deal, . . . to control the way we do business and the way we live.

Man, as created by God, has certain inherent God-given rights that are not for any government to take away.

The requisite for happiness is freedom. The requisite for freedom is courage.

Never doubt that I can do anything that another can do, . . . perhaps not as well, or as fast, but never cease to believe I can do it.

I seemed to have written a lot in those days prior to my thirtieth birthday. I find nothing in my writings about the environment.

I find notes from those days wherein I wondered why some in the conservative movement of the early sixties thought race was an issue within conservative doctrine. The media tried to paint conservatives as racists then and still do now. But what does race have to do with a political philosophy? The media sure seem to see a connection. It is still strange to me, as an example of generic media conduct, that whenever someone like Senator Ted Kennedy offers platitudes about the plight of minorities, he is proclaimed to be a deep thinker by the media, but when people I might admire speak to these issues and offer up prospective real solutions, they are vilified by the press as racists. Why is that? Why is the majority opinion deemed to be the wrong opinion?

There are more and more black conservatives. Public opinion surveys indicate that one-third of voting black Americans consider themselves to be conservatives. Hopefully their numbers will continue to grow, because liberal governmental programs have nearly destroyed opportunities for success for many blacks in America by setting groups of people against each other and by creating a permanent underclass dependent upon government. But in exploring a conservative philosophy which dictates that it is the individual who is supreme, how can that same philosophy include racism? It cannot and it does not! By the same reasoning, how can the environment be an issue of only one political philosophy or the other? Conservative or liberal? Republican or Democrat? To conserve our natural resources is not a liberal philosophy; it is a conservative philosophy. To protect the individual from assault on person and property also fits within a conservative philosophy.

To prevent or remediate the damage created by those who intentionally or unintentionally fouled our natural resources or invaded our bodies is not a matter for a political philosophy. It is just something that needs to be done. How much of such prevention and remediation is the responsibility of government and how much the responsibility of industry or the public is a matter for philosophic debate, but not the goal of an environment acceptable for fostering life.

The same is true for some other issues. How can abortion be a conservative or liberal issue? Some conservatives favor choice, while some liberal Democratic Catholics, for example, think that choice is a sin. Is that not a morals question, instead of a question of political philosophy? I think abortion is wrong and cannot see how a nation that aborts one and one half million babies per year can succeed morally. I believe those who abort babies will at some time need to answer to their God. I also believe that whether a person does or does not have an abortion is absolutely no business of the government.

Or how about gun control? Is gun control liberal or conservative? In high school I was on the rifle team. In the army I qualified pretty doggone well with rifles and pistols. I served time as a machine gunner in the Korean mountains along the Thirty-eighth Parallel. I have great respect for such weapons. But I never, ever, want a gun in my house. Even more important, I also don't ever want my government, or anyone else, telling me I cannot have a gun in my house. Having a gun is a right guaranteed to me by the Constitution. Not having a gun is a matter of personal choice exercised under the freedoms granted to me in that same Constitution. Conservatives respect the strict interpretation of the Constitution that has kept us free, while liberals seem to prefer a looser construction to solve the problems of today. The media like to paint one side as right and the other side as wrong on various issues. Normally, if the media believe one side of an issue, they then tell us that those on the other side are conservative. People in the national media like to define things for us.

So how did those formative years bring me to the point that I decided to dedicate much of my life as a Republican campaign manager and party chairman, to the effort of electing the best qualified people to public office? Well, in the 1960s I saw changes taking place that I thought would cause irreparable harm to a free and democratic American life-style. I saw the Supreme Court making law instead of interpreting the Constitution. I saw prayer removed from the schools as the beginning of the move toward an amoral society. I saw new math and other trendy teaching techniques being employed that would deter the learning of our children. I saw busing destroying neighborhood schools. I saw discipline being discouraged where it is most needed, in the schools and the homes. I saw courts giving too many rights to the criminal and too few to the victim. I saw high schools too large to give a majority of the students the opportunity to be involved in team sports, plays, or band, or whatever other group activities that can teach kids how to work together as adults.

I saw the end of a longtime requirement that young men give some military time, two years' active duty in my case, in service to their nation. There was a benefit to mandatory military service. If you had not learned respect and discipline in the home or in school, you would learn it after being drafted into the army. If you had not learned the benefits of teamwork, of working together, you learned it in military service. And I saw the birth of television and the growth and development of television news and network centralized entertainment programs, all of which promoted a valueless agenda and dependence upon government. I saw all of those things happening and I protested them and worked against them. Evidently I failed, because the same governmental elitism continues today, now even including a frontal attack on Christians reminiscent of the Roman Empire.

All of those societal disruptions have happened. Many of them in the sixties, as some in the nation were rebelling against the morality of the time. Children have not been the same since, and as they become adults, they are without knowledge of what was or what could be. Victory may be on the way, some conservatives believe, but big-government bureaucratic thought is still prevalent amongst us. We must continue to be vigilant. For example, one day when I went to the health club to exercise, I found workmen installing speed bumps in the parking lot driveway. Speed bumps are a symbol of societal paternalism at its worst. I hate them. My bank installed some. I told them that if I had to drive over speed bumps to do business with them, I would find a new bank with which to do business. The offensive speed bump was removed.

Consider the philosophy of speed bumps. One person, or a few people, do, or may, drive too fast through an area. The response is to put in speed bumps to punish the 99 percent who do the right thing and do not speed through the area. Why is the majority punished to control the minute minority? Is there not another solution, like a stop sign, or a guard looking for the bad guy? Why is it the easiest answer to drag down the majority, to damage the shock absorbers of responsible drivers, to punish the people who do not deserve to be punished? It's become the bureaucratic solution to all problems. Punish everybody. As a conservative, speed bumps really tick me off.

So that's my upbringing. That is how my thought processes were molded. And here I was, a conservative Republican politician, a lawyer, ready to serve the President of the United States, ready to be a diplomat, ready for my first real exposure to a set of environmental facts that could put into question the well-being of the human species.

2

The
International Joint
Commission

ON JULY 21, 1989, THE PRESIDENT of the United States of America formally nominated me to be a commissioner on the International Joint Commission, United States and Canada, by officially forwarding my name to the United States Senate. My Senate confirmation hearing was pretty much a nonevent. Not nearly as dramatic as reading about the process in the Federalist Papers or the Constitution. Article Two of the Constitution provides that the President "shall nominate, by and with the advice and consent of the Senate, shall appoint ambassadors, other public ministers and consuls. . . ." It was just another of those wise checks and balances conceived by forefathers who were rightly suspicious of large government. In the Federalist Papers, Alexander Hamilton wrote, "It is not easy to conceive a plan better calculated than this to promote a judicious choice of men for filling the offices of the Union; and it will not need proof that on this point must essentially depend the character of its administration." If he could come back for a few days, I wonder what Hamilton would have to say about some of the characters confirmed in recent years?

I had pretty well known that President George Bush would put my name forward since his inaugural ceremony in January of that year. Certainly since April I had been engulfed by many, many bureaucratic forms from the Office of White House Personnel. I had been interviewed several times by the FBI and others, and was well aware that I was moving toward new experiences on the international scene.

The commissioners and staff of the International Joint Commission are compensated by their respective governments. For the six commissioners to do a proper job, however, they have not over the years considered themselves to be employees of the government of Canada or of the United States. It is the job of the commissioners, with the aid of staff and volunteer experts, to arrive at the best solution for any particular problem the commission has before it for consideration. To find a best solution, the commissioners of the International Joint Commission cannot be bound by the policies of their own individual nation. That practice of operating as a unitary international problem-solving entity has served the commission well since early in the twentieth century, and that is especially true today when environmental matters are the prime issues of concern.

The commission was created by the Boundary Waters Treaty. This treaty was signed on January 11, 1909, by representatives of "the United States of America and His Majesty the King of the United Kingdom of Great Britain and Ireland and of the British Dominions beyond the seas, Emperor of India, being equally desirous to prevent disputes regarding the use of boundary waters and to settle all questions which are now pending between the United States and the Dominion of Canada involving the rights, obligations, or interests of either in relation to the other or to the inhabitants of the other, along their common frontier, and to make provision for the adjustment and settlement of all such questions as may hereafter rise. . . ." The signatories were U.S. Secretary of State Elihu Root, on behalf of President William Howard Taft, and the Right Honourable James Bryce, O.M., Ambassador Extraordinary and Plenipotentiary at Washington, on behalf of his Britannic Majesty George V. It was then formally ratified by the United States Senate on March 3, 1909; ratified by Great Britain on March 31, 1910; ratified by President Taft on April 1, 1910. Ratifications were exchanged at Washington on May 5, 1910, and the treaty was proclaimed official on May 13, 1910.

The treaty, crafted by a few visionaries, contained a purpose and specific provisions that most people agree would be impossible to conclude today. The treaty dealt with the flows and the uses of boundary waters, with limits placed on the diversion of waters. It required approval of the International Joint Commission before anyone could engage in construction that might affect the levels or obstruct the flows of boundary waters. The most visionary provision of the 1909 treaty is the following wording: "It is further agreed that the waters herein defined as boundary waters and waters flowing across the boundary shall not be polluted on either side to the injury of health or property on the other."

The very noble purpose of the treaty is to "prevent disputes regarding the use of boundary waters and to settle all questions involving the rights, obligations or interests to the inhabitants along the common frontier." To implement this heady purpose, the treaty called for the creation of the International Joint Commission, made up of six commissioners, three appointed by the President of the United States and confirmed by the U.S. Senate and three appointed by the Governor General of Canada in Council.

The commission generally provides for the regulation or approval of obstructions and diversions in boundary waters, waters flowing from boundary waters, or transboundary waters below the boundary, if such obstructions or diversions affect the levels and flows across the boundary. Some examples of commission authority have been to approve the development of hydropower projects in the St. Mary's and St. Lawrence rivers (including the St. Lawrence Seaway). The exercise of these IJC responsibilities is managed through the International St. Lawrence River Board of Control, the International Niagara Board of Control, and the International Lake Superior Board of Control. Members of these boards are appointed by the commission, with equal representation from each country. These attempts to control nature in a way that suits all can create a pretty good migraine for the commissioners and staff. I will delve more into that matter in my discussion of water quantity. Headquarters offices are located in Ottawa and Washington, D.C., where advisors and staff are on hand to assist the commission in fulfilling its treaty responsibilities. The Great Lakes Water Quality Agreement of 1972 added an office in Windsor, Ontario, with personnel from Canada and the United States working there. In addition, the International Joint Commission relies greatly on the services of individual experts from the various governments, industry, and academic and public organizations.

Another principal function of the commission is a study and report responsibility. The two federal governments from time to time refer questions or differences arising between them to the International Joint Commission. While the commission's recommendations to the governments are advisory only, the track record is quite good in terms of having recommendations implemented, sometimes even in advance of when they are formally communicated. The study and report responsibility has included a substantial number of questions on water-quality, water-quantity, and air-quality matters along the common boundary. Many people tend to regard air pollution as a relatively new phenomenon. In reality, major commission studies involving air quality started in the late 1920s, when the commission was asked by the

✻ *The Making of a Conservative Environmentalist* ✻

two governments to assess the transboundary implications of air emissions from the Trail Smelter in Trail, British Columbia. The smelter was alleged to have caused significant economic damage on the United States side of the boundary, and the commission was asked to verify if in fact damage had occurred, and, if so, the extent of the damage and ways such damage might be mitigated. The commission's Trail Smelter report is often cited as an international precedent regarding state responsibility in environmental matters, and the commission's experience with this reference established working principles for the IJC that continue to this day: operating as a unitary binational commission and decision making by consensus.

The first principle is for the commission to work as a binational fact-finding body rather than one which works as two separate national sections with individual national interests and agendas. It is a principle easier said than done, and easier for Canadians than Americans. Americans like to tell Canadians, "You are just like us." The American thinks he or she has just offered the highest of compliments. The Canadian thinks he or she has just been insulted. There are differences in the cultures of Canadians and Americans. We are not the same. But keep in mind that pollution knows no boundaries, recognizes no cultural differences. The people of Canada and the United States must work closely together if we are to win the pollution-prevention wars on the North American continent. We must, therefore, know and accept the cultural differences between us. We Americans must know, as Canadians already know, that we are not just alike.

Many of us have the same basic heritage, especially if our heritage is English. Even so, two hundred plus years ago a drastic split occurred. I am sure you read about it: the Revolution, the Boston Tea Party, Crispus Attucks, the Boston Massacre, Paul Revere, Betsy Ross, George Washington crossing the Delaware? Remember? Some of the folks living then in what is now the United States did not agree with our desire to separate from England. They remained loyal to the King and off they went to Canada, where they could continue to serve him. While Americans were demanding life, liberty, and the pursuit of happiness, Canadians (Englishmen then) were calling for peace, order, and good government. Americans wanted government off their backs and out of their way. Canadians were looking to government to provide order and peace so they could live an orderly life.

Even the English language is used differently, at times, north and south of the U.S.-Canada boundary. Canadians *take* a decision. Americans *make* a decision. Early in my experiences I would find myself confused at binational meetings. Canadians would suggest *tabling* a subject I wanted to talk about.

I would think, "What nerve, that guy knows I want to talk about that." My experience in parliamentary procedure tells me that to table an issue is to agree not to talk about it; to take it *off* the table. For Canadians, to table an issue means to put it on the table and talk about it. Americans describe people as being aggressive from a positive point of view, Canadians the negative. There are, of course, many more examples.

Even the word *government* has different meanings and connotations for Americans and Canadians. In Canada, government is something of a monolith. The majority is in complete control of the parliamentary system. The ministers of the majority party are the government. It is one. It is, therefore, very difficult for Canadians to understand the diverse nature of government in the United States. If these words stimulate an interest, I might suggest that you read *Why We Act Like Canadians*, by Pierre Berton (see bibliography). Berton is a prolific Canadian author, and his books were very helpful to me in understanding my diplomatic duties.

A second principle, strengthened by the commission's work in the Trail Smelter study, is that of arriving at decisions by consensus. Neither government was totally content with the findings of the commission in the Trail Smelter case, but because the commission was able to achieve unanimity in its conclusions and recommendations, it became difficult for either government to ignore the findings. That principle of consensus decision making continues to this day. Indeed, to my knowledge there have been few occasions in the history of the commission, and the commission has taken many hundreds of decisions, when consensus has *not* been reached. Every decision during my tenure was by consensus.

In the realm of environmental protection, where uncertainty seems to be the norm, consensus decisions are extremely important. But collective decision making was something new for me. My normal decision-making process was to check the facts, check with my colleagues, make a decision. I doubted that substantive decisions could be made by consensus. I was wrong. It does work, but maybe only if reasonable people are involved. I served with ten different commissioners during my tenure; all were thinking people, decent people, caring people. Together, unanimously, we made some major decisions.

In the commission's *Fifth Biennial Report*, submitted to governments of Canada and the United States as part of our water-quality agreement responsibilities, we, by consensus, concluded that there was a threat to the health of our children emanating from our exposure to persistent toxic substances, even at very low ambient levels. The Great Lakes Water Quality Agreement has a policy and philosophy uniquely developed to address that threat. It is the policy of the agreement that the discharge of toxic substances in toxic amounts be prohibited and that the discharge of all persistent toxic substances be virtually eliminated. The philosophy of the agreement is one of zero discharge of persistent toxic substances. This policy and philosophy makes a tremendous amount of sense to me. I think anyone who has worked in government and has engaged in this troublesome issue of what to do about toxic substances has come to understand that the attempts to *regulate* such substances have not resulted in a terribly efficient or successful set of programs.

Environmental regulations tend to be inconsistent, owing to the differing national, provincial, and state jurisdictional standards. Regulatory standards tend to find room for exceptions. And, of course, regulation is an expensive endeavor for the regulators and the regulated. It is also a perceived infringement on the personal and business lives of our citizens. A regulatory standard implies that such standard sets a safe level of human exposure for the discharge of whatever substance is being regulated. Regulatory standards imply that a safe standard exists, when more recent information would suggest that even one exposure to dioxin by a pregnant female may be enough to cause an adverse effect on the adult or the progeny. It is also important to realize that many of the chemicals to which we are exposed have never been tested for safety as they relate to living things. Regulatory standards tend to be excuses which enable governments to set exceptions for the discharge of various poisons into the waters of North America through the collection of fees and the issuance of permits.

In its *Seventh Biennial Report* in 1994, the commission said:

> The characteristics of persistent toxic substances make them much less amenable to traditional pollution control efforts such as discharge limits to set acceptable levels in the environment, end-of-the-pipe technology and disposal regulations. The idea of a non-zero "assimilative" capacity in the environment or in our bodies (and hence allowable discharges) for such chemicals is no longer relevant. The Great Lakes Water Quality Board supports this view, concluding that there is no acceptable assimilative capacity for persistent, biocumulative toxic substances. It states, therefore, that the only appropriate water quality objective is zero, even though interim objectives may be needed. . . .
>
> Within the environment's carrying capacity for human activity, there is no space for human loadings of persistent toxic substances. Hence, there can be no acceptable loading of chemicals that accumulate for very long periods, except that which nature itself generates. Moreover, conventional scientific

concepts of dose-response and acceptable risk can no longer be defined as good scientific and management bases for defining acceptable levels of pollution. They are outmoded and inappropriate ways of thinking about persistent toxics. . . .

The production and release of these substances into the environment must, therefore, be considered contrary to the Agreement legally, unsupportable ecologically and dangerous to health generally. Above all, it is ethically and morally unacceptable. The limits on allowable quantities of these substances entering the environment must be effectively zero, and the primary means to achieve zero should be the prevention of their production, use and release rather than their subsequent removal.

So surely it is time to ask: do we really want to continue our attempts to *manage* persistent toxic substances, or, to the extent possible, do we want to begin the process of *eliminating* such onerous substances in the first place? If you have a chemical or a suite of chemicals that qualify as persistent and toxic, it makes more sense to me to do as the Great Lakes Water Agreement demands: get rid of them. Why not just get on with the important business of creating a process to *sunset*—that is, to end in an orderly fashion—the manufacture, distribution, storage, and use of persistent toxic substances? Why continue the charade?

By consensus, we made the decision that the health of humans was at risk. This decision fostered other decisions, such as the recommendations to sunset the most onerous of toxic substances. These were major decisions, made by consensus. I still find it remarkable that such a collective decision-making process really did work.

How I Saw the Job

One of the first things I perceived in my dealings with those involved in international environmentalism was the stereotypical nature of many of the players. Environmentalists, scientists, and physicians and others in the health care field tend to have as their foremost generic trait compassion. Such folks tend to be soft-spoken. They are considerate of the words and ways of others. All admirable human characteristics. But such passions do not translate into good leadership, if leadership is defined as making the decisions and taking the actions necessary to resolve the particular environmental problem of concern. Needed, I think, in the environmental movement are people with proven leadership qualities, people who can move decision makers to action. Not just the traditional liberal Democrats but also conservative Republicans, leaders of industry, and others who know how to bridge the gap between concern and action.

Few people truly have the opportunity to exercise real leadership. Few ever find themselves in a situation where the idea they believe to be correct becomes the position of others, then policy or law, then a way of life for masses of people. It was truly fascinating to me as chairman of the International Joint Commission when two great nations would accept as policy an idea that had sprouted from my mind. That has happened. I have pondered the concepts and meanings of leadership for decades now. I wonder why some people have leadership ability and opportunities, while most do not. Is it genes? Is it arrogance? Is it the discipline in which a person was trained? Is it ego, or false pride? Do I think I have something I don't really have? Is it just the ability to create perceptions of leadership ability? The compassionate nature of an environmentalist finds the necessity for this discussion mundane. If we have a problem, why doesn't some leader, somewhere, just fix it?

It is hard to find many others to share in a serious discussion about the demands of leadership. There are, of course, many people in leadership roles. Many who find themselves in leadership positions, however, really do not exercise leadership. And they often seem to be the ones most anxious to discuss philosophies of leadership. Often people think management is leadership. It is to a degree, I guess, but it is providing leadership in the realm of ideas that fascinates me most. Leading people in a direction I conceived, not being a manager carrying out the policy of others.

Decision Making

To me the crux of being a good leader is the willingness to make decisions. I look around and find people most every day in a quandary. Should I do this or should I do that? If they ask my advice, I say do that. They become excited and think I have some extraordinary talent. Most people do not focus on what decision they should make; instead they focus on the fear of making the wrong decision. My way of thinking when coming to a Y in the road is to gather the available facts, weigh them, trust my instincts, make a decision and go on to the next problem. If you make the correct decision 80 or 85 percent of the time as you should, you are perceived to be one hell of a leader. A tremendous success. That seems odd to me. I ponder it often.

Someone once said, "The successful person is not the person without problems; it is the person who does not have the same problem he had yesterday." I found that quote early on in life when I was engrossed in reading everything I could find about conservative philosophies. I don't even know who first said it, but I have held onto it as a sort of philosophical guidepost. I try to solve today's problems today. I thought of that old saying when I began to realize that few of the most serious environmental problems that we are experiencing today in North America were not with us yesterday. They have been with us for fifty years or so.

I see people struggling through life never quite ready to decide if they will change jobs and take a chance on a new career, if they will or will not become a candidate for public office, if they will or will not make a firm decision on what it is they stand for in the campaign platform, if the new clothes they want to buy should be orange or fuchsia (easy for me with many blue blazers and lots of gray slacks), if they should buy a new car or one that has been used, if they should jeopardize their jobs by expressing their true feelings about the dangers of a specific chemical discharge, and on and on. Most of these examples are easy, but I see folks struggling mightily over them. My advice is to just make a decision, hope you are right, live with your decision, and go on. Easy for me, not so easy for others. I wonder why? My generic observation of Canadians is that they tend to be like that, loving unresolved conflict (witness the debate over their constitution).

My wife sees my decision-making ability as a boring way of life. If she decides, finally, to buy a certain make and color of living-room furniture, I agree, we buy it, and it is delivered. Fifteen or twenty years later, as I am just starting to notice the colors and becoming accustomed to them, she is tired of them and wants something new. My reaction is "If you didn't like it, why did you buy it?" She says, "I liked it then; I don't now." Odd, I think. Boring, she thinks. But the ability to make mostly right decisions in an expedient manner (before someone else makes it for you) is at the very heart of effective leadership. Then the question becomes, how do you get others to follow you? How does the chairman of a local environmental group expand the group's concern to a broader public?

Listening

I have found listening to be one of the absolute best techniques of leadership. First and foremost, if you do listen, you just might learn something. There are a lot of good ideas floating around. Maybe one idea out of ten or one out of a hundred is an idea that, if heard, would be profitable to pursue. The debate over ideas is an essential element of freedom. An idea may have competing sides. Proponents versus opponents. There may be more than two sides. Hear them all. Weigh what you have heard and read, and make a decision.

I like ideas. I like to wrestle with them. Explore them. I like to throw out an idea, and wait for the retort from a colleague challenging my original thought, expanding it, developing it. Most people, however, don't like that kind of give and take. Most people develop an occasional idea and then fight to the hilt to keep anyone from changing it. If you suggest changes to such a proposal, these people tend to think you have taken an advocacy position, that you are against them personally for some reason or the other. My Canadian colleague E. Davie Fulton is an intellect who can originate an idea, develop it, then turn his idea into a meaningful result.

I came onto a commission whose job it was to bring together various people on an international basis to find solutions to binational environmental problems. It amazed me, therefore, to find that only selected views were to be heard at the major meeting held by the commission every two years. It was 1989 in Hamilton, Ontario, and we had just finished the preliminary events of day one of the meeting. It was late at night and our staff was insistent upon a late-night meeting with the commissioners. We were tired and ready for bed, but we reluctantly agreed.

The subject of the meeting was that the next day we commissioners were to hear from our Water Quality Board and Science Advisory Board. Staff evidently presumed we were too lazy to read the prepared written reports and too feeble mentally to grasp what was said in those reports so as to enable us to formulate our own questions to ask of the board members on the morrow. We were given papers listing questions to ask of each board, one list for the Science Advisory Board and one list for the Water Quality Board. We indicated that we really did not need a list, but we were told by staff that it was critical that we asked only the questions on the list and that we decide which question was to be asked by which commissioner.

After a great deal of quizzing, we discovered that what had been done in the past was presumed by staff to be the best way to proceed now. The reason we should ask only those questions on the list was that the board members had already rehearsed the answers to those questions. So here we were, set to go before nearly a thousand citizens with a rehearsed script of questions and answers. A complete charade. The Water Quality Board members are high-level representatives of federal, state, and provincial governments. They were not accustomed to public criticism. They were used to the charade.

The next day, some commissioners asked questions not on the list which created great dissatisfaction among some of the board members. The first to ask a question not on the list was Commissioner Don Totten from Illinois. He was accused of sabotage. We then put microphones on the floor to allow members of the public an opportunity to say whatever it was that they wanted to say to us. The time we allotted was insufficient, so we enlarged it and then enlarged it again. All one day into late night, and into the wee hours of the morning, and then again starting early the next day. We heard example after example of personal adverse effects of Great Lakes pollution. We heard from individuals representing agriculture, business, environmental groups, and government agencies, and we heard from many individuals representing no one other than themselves.

We did not respond to anything that was said during the hearings; we did not argue or agree, we just listened for hour after hour. As people from political backgrounds, we commissioners could see that a head of steam had built up and needed to be let off. We did that by listening. Members of the Water Quality Board complained that the attacks on their governments and governmental actions should have been refuted. But we knew it was best just to listen and hear what was being said. We did that.

In that case, listening opened a lot of doors. It gave folks from within government an opportunity to hear firsthand what the public thought of their environmental actions and progress. It gave the few from industry who were there a first opportunity to hear what real people had to say about their production and marketing processes. It highlighted the very real possibility that the commission could actually bring together various interests to discuss ways to achieve the goals of the Great Lakes Water Quality Agreement.

Commissioner Fulton announced at that meeting that the commission would be holding a series of scientific roundtables seeking good solid information. As a result of the public testimony, more of a public outcry actually, we invited members of the public to participate in a roundtable on roundtables in Toronto. Whereas we had several ideas in mind for the roundtables, the public had but one: the philosophy of zero discharge. We agreed and pursued this subject in a series of roundtables held throughout the basin for the next two years.

We tried to include all the interests in those roundtable discussions, but we were pretty much rejected by industry. We did get some participation from the Canadian pulp and paper and mining industries. For the most part, however, our invitations for industry participation were rejected or ignored. A representative from the American pulp and paper industry did attend the last of the roundtable discussions, in Thunder Bay. She stood up and announced that she was there to listen, not to participate, and that she did not want her name or affiliation to appear in any minutes or record of that meeting. Such was the attitude of much of industry at the time. Sort of an ostrich syndrome. Much of the scientific and economic information gathered at these round-tables on zero discharge brought the commissioners to their decision after the sixth biennial meeting in Traverse City, Michigan, to recommend the sunsetting of chlorine as an industrial feed stock, an action that brought unnerved industry representatives streaming into the seventh biennial meeting. It was good progress in just four years of listening, weighing, and deciding.

But back to that meeting in Hamilton, where we took time to hear what the public had to say about the effects of pollution and the failure of governments to meet the commitments of the Water Quality Agreement. I had read various reports from such nongovernmental organizations as the Sierra Club, the Rawson Academy, Great Lakes United, and Greenpeace and the really good work of the Conservation Foundation and the Institute for Research on Public Policy entitled *Great Lakes, Great Legacy?* So much of what we heard was not new, but it was personal and it was real. We heard from an eminent Canadian scientist, a pregnant woman, who said to us, "The child that I am carrying right now has probably and is currently receiving the heaviest loadings of toxic chemicals that it will receive in its lifetime." A sobering thought from a government scientist.

The experience in Hamilton was much like the many platform hearings I had conducted as a political party chairman. People from varying interests would come before me and my appointees to proclaim the virtues or the fallacies of an issue: the arts advocates, who always asked for more funding; the highway folks, who wanted new highways and just happened to be in the business of building them or who did not want new highways because they could destroy their property rights; the prison builders and those who thought bad guys ought to rot in squalor; those who thought abortion was murder and those who thought it was a right; those who proclaimed the constitutional right to own guns and those who wanted to abolish or control them; and on and on. The public hearing concept is pretty much the same whatever the purpose, but in a free society it is an essential element for problem solving.

In Hamilton in 1989, in Traverse City in 1991, and in Windsor in 1993, we heard a great deal of testimony about the adverse effects of persistent toxic substances. But seldom did we hear any testimony about the good that such onerous substances bring to the health of the ecosystem and the things that live within it. We heard denials from some that particular chemicals were as harmful as others had claimed them to be. We also heard that there was not enough evidence to make a conclusion of harm. But we did not hear that anthropogenic chlorinated industrial feed stocks were good for human or ecosystem health. I listened for that, but I never heard it.

Another thing I have found is that you can listen people into your way of thinking. Say you have a candidate for governor, or senator, or mayor. The candidate and three or four supporters come to you for assistance. They are trying hard to develop a position on an issue that will find acceptance among the voting public. One will say, "I really like X, I have been for X all my life. It is the right way to go." Another will say, "Wait a minute, it's Y that is best. Everyone likes Y." The candidate might say, "But what about Z? I personally believe in Z." You sit there and hear them all out. You ask questions about X, Y, and Z. You probe the proponent of each. You let each have his and her say. You take your time until they are all pretty well talked out. Then you can say, "I heard what all of you had to say. I heard a lot of good ideas, and I am really impressed with your knowledge. And you know what? It sounds to me like you are all really saying B, and if you are, that is a really good idea you have all come up with." They quite often will nod their heads and say, "Yes, you are right. B is our idea. We will go with B." But B was not their idea; it was yours.

Bringing People Together

Bringing people together as a consensus-building tool in the exercise of leadership is indispensable for success. Early in my duties on the International Joint Commission, I found that the failure to bring together people from various interests was (and still is) a real barrier to the virtual elimination of persistent toxic substances as called for in the U.S.-Canada Great Lakes Water Quality Agreement. Public groups were doing their best to get the attention of governments, to get the media to take them seriously, to get industry at least to consider the concerns that were foremost in their minds. Policy makers at the highest levels of government were not hearing about problems of urgency from their constituents or from the news media. Governments, at the midlevel, were doing what they had always done, regulating at levels that someone else had decided upon. And industry was trying to ignore the whole thing. None of these groups was having adequate dialogue with the others.

Here's an illustration of how bringing people together can be used as a leadership tool. My friend Bob Orr, as governor of Indiana, would quite often make a decision about a good idea: ways of improving public education, the creation of the Indiana Department of Environmental Management, ways to attract jobs to Indiana. He would then test these ideas on others. He would listen to many points of view. He would refine his idea, bring people together to build consensus and to make sure he had sufficient support. He would then announce his plan, and as soon as he did the media and his opponents would declare the futility of the idea and the impossibility of getting it done. Little did they know he pretty well had the idea sold before he went public with it. In the environmental world, no one has yet assumed the mantle of leadership to build the consensus necessary for change. Conservatives might be the appropriate vehicles to do just that.

One of the things that made an impression on me from the commission's meeting in Traverse City was the testimony of a person who said, "I know you are the wrong people to be saying this to, but you are the only ones who will listen to us." People with environmental problems still have great difficulty in finding not just a sympathetic ear but a meaningful ear. Should conservatives decide to listen to, and act upon, the words of the many individuals and small groups who believe they are suffering an environmental injustice, new voting patterns may follow.

At the commission, we tried many ways to bring all the necessary interests to the same table. We tried roundtables, but industry resisted. We tried putting public and industry folks on our boards and task forces in their personal and professional capacities. That was easier done, for some reason, for public group people and government people than it was for industry people. We tried putting nongovernment people at every level of a large study of the fluctuating water levels on the Great Lakes. We followed the same procedure with the Virtual Elimination Task Force.

We wanted industry at the table because no decisions would be workable without the participation of industry. We kept inviting industry participation, but industry kept ignoring or rejecting our invitations. Finally, by making recommendations to our governments that if accepted would affect industrial processes, we found a way to bring industry to the table. When it got there, its representatives complained bitterly that they had not previously been invited to participate. Had they not been listening? But now they are at the table, and we do have some reason for optimism.

Communicating

From the very beginning of my service I found that scientific and technical people had a real aversion to the idea of communications and environmental education. Many were mired in the mode of scientific inaction, more attuned to bemoaning the inaction of government than trying to prod government into action. The concept of public communications was looked down upon by the scientific community as an attempt to rewrite scientific ideas and conclusions. Few looked at communications as a way of highlighting their findings, of creating funding for their research, or of helping to solve the problems about which they were most concerned. In reality, if members of the public are unaware of the problem, they will not push their legislators to do something about it. If the legislators are not being pushed by their constituents, they will not fund the research that scientists believe is necessary. Nor will they write laws to ban or restrict onerous chemicals if they do not hear from the media or the people about the need to do so.

Commissioners who served before I came aboard had created a Public Information Committee, which met the day before any commission meeting. I went to the first such meeting when I was appointed. Some longtime commission followers thought I was wrong for going, wrong for wanting to encourage the drafting of reports that were readable and actionable, because, some evidently thought, if it is readable it must not be scientific.

I served as a spokesman for the International Joint Commission at national and international meetings of industry, public-interest groups, government meetings, congressional hearings, medical associations, engineering associations, and meetings of scientists, educators, sportsmen, and others. Communicating the environmental message was the goal of the speeches. I addressed the plenary session of the largest gathering of world leaders in history at the United Nations Conference on Environment and Development (June 4–13, 1992) in Rio de Janeiro. Of all the speeches I made while on the commission, I never solicited one. I often had the feeling that some of my Canadian colleagues did not believe that was so. And for a while, the Canadian commissioners would object when we tried to get the commission to be a catalyst for Great Lakes environmental education. Their concern had to do with education being a provincial prerogative, not a federal prerogative. I could never quite focus their attention on the fact that in the United States it was a local district prerogative and that I had thirteen school boards in my county alone. So far in my political life I had been wise enough to stay out of school politics, but our job on the commission was to find answers. Obviously education was an answer that could not be ignored.

We did prevail, however, and did some good work in the area of environmental education. It gave me a sense of accomplishment to leave the commission with an established priority to determine the Great Lakes environmental message that should be communicated, who the audience is for the communications, and how best to effect such communications. Considering the attitudes I found at the beginning of my tenure—that public communications were demeaning—we had indeed come a long way.

Involving the Public

This was really an oddball thing. I came on the commission as a person who believed deeply that the solutions to societal problems required public knowledge and public actions. If the public did not know they should care, I worried. If the public knew the problem but still didn't care, then that's their prerogative in a free society. But my experience tells me the public does want to know and does want to be a part of the action if they have reason for concern.

We began to involve the public by naming a member from a public environmental group and another member from industry to the Science Advisory Board. Then the great debate began. The environmentalists said it was harder to express their views when someone from industry was on the board with opposite views. We even started debating who was to be included as a member of the public. Certainly no one who worked for government could be a member of the public. Environmental groups did not think industry representatives could qualify as members of the public. Then we worried whether anyone who belonged to an organized interest group could be a member of the public. For some reason, few people were willing to accept the thought that we were all members of the public.

Having traveled extensively all across the boundary and throughout the Great Lakes region of North America, I attended meeting after meeting where people demanded public involvement on a commission board or task force. When I would explain that we did in fact have public participation, I was always told the person we had selected did not count. A member of the public from one shoreline on the lake would not concede that it was good enough if we selected someone from another shoreline on the same lake. If the person came from the south shore of the St. Lawrence River, that was not good enough for someone living a few miles upstream on the south shore of Lake Ontario.

But then when deserving members of the public were put on a study board, we would hear complaints about their costs, about lost income, and demands that the volunteers be paid for their services by government. We did pay travel expenses, but if a volunteer public member is paid by government, is that person then a volunteer or a part of government? Can you have paid professional public volunteers? I think not. One could conclude that the public is not always reasonable or logical. But be that as it may, from the beginning of my service as U.S. chairman of the commission, I worked to further open the commission's process to the public. Time was set aside at each biennial meeting under the Great Lakes Water Quality Agreement to give any individual the opportunity to make his or her environmental concerns known. All of the commission's boards and councils, all across the boundary, are now required to hold at least one public meeting annually, a suggestion of mine approved by the commission.

The large final phase of the study of fluctuating water levels in the Great Lakes required public involvement at every working level of the study. Non-government scientists and social scientists were added to the commission's Science Advisory Board, and task forces were created not only to make sure official board members were interacting on priority environmental issues but also to include participation by representatives of industry, academia, and public-interest organizations.

During my years on the commission there was greater public participation than at any time in history, and I am sure such participation will continue to grow. There remained many more complaints, however, about the lack of public participation than there were compliments about involving the public. Despite the problems, my suggestion to commissioners, governments, and, yes, to industry is that they keep trying to increase and improve public involvement in their deliberations, knowing all along that no matter how good their efforts, their efforts will never be good enough.

Using Tax Dollars Wisely

This whole subject of trying to use dollars wisely was a tough one. Few in the process, it seems, really want to cut spending.

The commission's office in Windsor, Ontario, occupied two floors, a floor and a half actually, with the best view of the Detroit skyline anywhere, and some of the highest square footage costs in Windsor. We eliminated the half floor, which housed the library and conference rooms. We donated the library to the University of Windsor, where it would receive better maintenance and have wider availability. We used the saved money for work required under the Great Lakes Water Agreement instead of using it for unnecessary overhead items. Doesn't that sound like a good idea? I thought so, but some Canadians went a little crazy. Members of the Federal Parliament attacked us, labor unions attacked us, environmental groups attacked us, and the *Windsor Star* reported one false rumor after another about the motives of the commissioners.

And then, one fiscal year, the regional office did not spend all of the funds that were budgeted to it. The officials let some funds revert back to the general fund of Canada, half of which then remained in the funds of the United

States Section of the commission. As a conservative, my thoughts were, great, we got our work done and had funds left over for taxpayer use elsewhere. But again, some Canadians were upset. Parliamentarians attacked us, the *Windsor Star* attacked us, unions and environmental groups attacked us. They said it was all a part of some large conspiracy. It was nothing of the kind, but even so the Canadian chairman of the commission was called before the Federal Parliament to explain how such a thing could happen.

I know that the public wants government to spend its tax money wisely and to turn back money it does not use. I know that, but it is hard to remember when you are under attack by those who should be praising such actions.

Dealing with the Issues

I wonder. How could you expose yourself to a set of facts that just might foretell the possibility of your species' having serious reproductive difficulty and then not act upon this evidence? What if you saw indications that children's ability to learn and to behave civilly was being affected by actions permitted by governments seeking additional sources of revenue? How could you not seek out more evidence? How could you ignore such grim facts without taking some responsible action? How could you not preach precaution, when precautionary measures were not being taken? How could you utter anything but truth when future generations might be at risk? I asked these questions of some people who thought I was too much of an activist in trying to prod governments and industry toward responsible action. I asked these questions of the people who thought staid, stodgy, unknowing, and uncaring would be the better order of the day for a commissioner on the International Joint Commission.

I just kept thinking about those little kids having trouble in school, trouble that they would not be having had their parents or grandparents not lived where they lived or ate what they ate. In that circumstance, it would take a pretty cool customer not to at least make an attempt to move the responsible parties to action. Conservatives are not without compassion.

3

Environmental and Economic Barriers

THE GREAT DEBATE IN THIS NECESSARY but often shrugged off concern about the well-being of the environment in which we must live centers on the attitudes of industry relative to its production processes and waste-disposal practices and the attitudes of organized environmental groups, which view the leaders of industry as calloused and uncaring. In the middle, willing to compromise most any principle, lies the government.

Should these three entities, industry, environmentalists, and government, decide at any time to work together, the environment could in fact be cured and protected. Jobs would not be in jeopardy. Profits and growth could occur. Our standard of living could increase. Future generations would be healthier and not so much at risk. And the reality of our quest for life, liberty, and the pursuit of happiness could be achievable. I can make that claim because I believe that economic growth and environmental protection are not mutually exclusive goals. They are mutually interdependent. I believe it is cynical to claim, as industry often does, that environmental protection must cost jobs. That need not be. A healthy environment should produce jobs. Just the cleanup industry itself creates jobs. The development of new ways of doing business will create jobs.

Of course, any transition from the way we now do business to a new way of doing business that tries not to foul the water or laden the air with toxics may cause some economic dislocations. The planning of such transitions to a cleaner society must include considerations that will not cause employees of industry to be the pawns of environmentally improved production processes. Consideration must be given to the socioeconomic plight that could befall working men and women as society tackles seriously the real task of cleansing itself. In the *Seventh Biennial Report*, the International Joint Commission phrased it this way:

> Economic and environmental sustainability are not only consistent but necessary to achieving healthy and vibrant ecosystems. Both can occur with a minimum of disruption by phasing in required changes to economic activity over investment cycles, reorienting product markets using normal mechanisms, and providing retraining and other programs to protect local communities and workers from sudden discontinuities. If short-term disruptions occur, they should be resolved by considering the environmental, economic and related social issues simultaneously and by consensus.

In my time on the International Joint Commission, industry began to take notice. I felt good that industry was coming to the table, because without the full participation of the business community, environmental protection will just be a pipedream. The alternative to a cooperative effort by industry is dictatorial government decrees, which would destroy business and put people out of work. I was somewhat distressed, late in my tenure, to learn that industry lobbyists, instead of changing their way of thinking, were at the White House lobbying for new Democrat commissioners to replace me and my colleagues who would be more sympathetic to industry's old way of thinking. My references to industry, environmentalists, and government are generic, of course. There are millions of these people out there, and certainly not all are alike in their thinking or demeanor.

From a global point of view, environmental considerations differ somewhat from those of the Great Lakes ecosystem, where research, prevention, and remediation are light-years ahead of the rest of the world. While in the United States and Canada we have won the battles against some of the more basic problems of pollution and worry now about the somewhat more subtle aspects of preserving the species by eliminating the causal agents of doom, most countries in the world are still worried only about such basic problems as population and poverty. A controversial world conference on population, sponsored by the United Nations in Cairo, was held in September 1994 to try to come to grips with world population control. The Vatican saw it as an effort to promote the "decadent and amoral notions of abortion, non-procreative sex and a diminution of the family's central role." Norway

Prime Minister Gro Harlem Brundtland saw the key issue of the conference as "giving power to women as the way to slow birth rates."

When I addressed the plenary session of the United Nations Conference on Environment and Development in Rio de Janeiro, it was the largest gathering of world leaders in history. Many of the world leaders who were there, bad guys and good guys we normally only read and hear about, roamed freely around the large meeting room. Fidel Castro reminded me of a political candidate, shaking hands and working the crowd. The Iraqi leaders were there with faces familiar from CNN coverage of the Desert War. I listened to speech after speech from world leader after world leader and heard little about what should concern North America most, toxic chemicals entering our environment. I heard little about the persistent and biocumulative nature of the substances that worry us so much. From all of those I heard, I believe Canadian prime minister Brian Mulroney, a minister from one of the nations of the former Soviet Union, and I were the only ones who even mentioned the subject of toxic substances.

Here are a few comments from a speech I gave just a few days after returning from the conference in Brazil, comments reflective of my firsthand thoughts.

I spent all of last week in Rio de Janeiro, Brazil, at the United Nations Conference on Environment and Development. It was an eye-opening experience. In my current job, I deal with the very serious environmental issues jointly facing the United States and Canada. But the conference was not so much about those serious matters as it was about world politics. The G-7 versus the G-77. The undeveloped world versus the developed countries of the world. And let me tell you, we are outnumbered.

All the leaders of the world were there. But too many people at that conference were more interested in destroying our free-enterprise system than they were concerned about the environment. They want our enterprise system, they want our standard of living, but they seem to think they can only gain those things by destroying what we have. And they seemed shocked that our President would not simply sign away those property rights that help keep us and our enterprise system free.

And let me tell you something else that I know from my current job. No other nation on earth has a better environmental record than the United States. No other nation has as tough environmental standards, no other nation has developed more clean technology, no other nation has spent as much money on environmental protection, in its own country or in other countries around the world. And certainly no other nations in the world work as collegially in transboundary matters as do the United States and Canada. Here in our own neck of the woods the Great Lakes are a good example.

There is a whole lot more that the two nations could be doing, but the fact of the matter is, the work and the money that has been put into the Great Lakes truly is a model that the rest of the world should be emulating.

I learned some lessons in Brazil as I sat and listened firsthand to the leaders of the world. Most of them don't like us. They don't like us because of what we have accomplished. They want what we have and, once more as a reminder, they don't think they can have it unless we lose it. The most worrisome lesson I learned in Rio is that just because the Berlin Wall has come down and we have won final victory in the forty-year Cold War does not mean that we in the United States can ignore external threats to our freedom.

As you begin to take a global view, one thing becomes clear. It is the free-market nations and not the socialist nations who are leading the way in environmental cleanliness. True, these industrialized nations may have been responsible for errors of the past, but there is good reason to believe that the ingenuity that got us dirty can best get us clean. Industry must do it. Government can't. Because you just do not find much ingenuity in governmental bureaucracies these days.

My reaction? Simply this. The world wants environmental sanity, but many, many barriers must come down. Just as the Berlin Wall came down as a barrier against freedom, attitudinal walls must fall if we are to prevent environmental decadence. The same is true locally. The residents of a community and the local factory can coexist in a peaceful and healthy manner if they would only remove the barriers and agree to work toward a common goal. Industry is not an enemy! The people are not always wrong! And governments should work more seriously toward bringing differing interests together through education and awareness activities instead of trying to find more and more tax monies to regulate and remediate.

So just how is it that a conservative should address the environmental problems facing our continent? Well, since ethics and environmental protection must go hand in hand, why don't we spend some time talking about what many of us believe is primarily responsible for the decline in ethics in our American society? We conservatives tend to believe that a lack of respect for the lives and property of others occurs because people are not held responsible for the consequences of their actions. Parents are not good about disciplining their children anymore. It seems they would like to be friends with their kids instead of being the parental authorities they need to be. Schools say it is not their job to teach values. Television tells us daily and nightly that bad is good. And, of course, many of our elected leaders are the epitome of the "if it feels good, do it" generation. We have generations of people now who have lost respect for authority, people who have been taught that anarchy is a good thing, people who now think they can do what they like without facing any consequences.

One of the things that really upsets most conservatives, of course, is the coddling of criminals. We read and hear daily about rapists, burglars, stalkers, and all variety of bad guys committing crimes while they are out in society on parole or bond. Why aren't the judges tougher on the people who do wrong? Why don't they lock those guys up the first time and throw away the key? As a result of the federal crime bill which attracted so much attention in the summer of 1994, we now give criminals three convictions before we consider them to be habitual criminals and therefore bad enough to lock away behind bars. It's sort of like a game: three strikes and you are out. Next it will probably be like basketball, with five fouls allowed before punishment.

When a child molester molests again, we ask, "Why was he out on the streets? Why didn't people keep him away from our kids?" But when the executive of some large conglomerate violates the laws by discharging some onerous substance into the water or air or onto the ground, we pay little attention. We don't ask why he wasn't kept away from chemicals. We don't ask why he wasn't required to keep those unmanageable substances away from our kids. Science tells us of bad effects that certain kinds of discharges can have on our children, born and unborn, but we don't seem to see the analogy between a perverted individual sexually molesting a child and an industrial discharge affecting the basic sexuality of a child. I wonder why.

If some industrial plant illegally dumps something into Lake Michigan, the company might receive a fine. If it does it again, it might get another fine. Does it get three strikes or five fouls before it's out? Is it ever put out of the game? It doesn't seem so. Where are we, in this example, with our concerns for our kids? I wonder why we don't demand that the offenders stop dumping the stuff. Why not criticize the government for being too lenient, as we do with molesters of children? The adverse mental and physical effects on our kids can be equally as serious. But we should consider the other side of this discourse, as I did in a speech to the Indiana Wildlife Federation in June 1994.

For some reason, we don't expect our Representatives in Congress to practice morality, although many do. We don't expect our teachers to teach morality; in fact, we prohibit it. We don't expect the entertainment industry to practice morality; in fact, we patronize most the movies depicting violence and sexual perversion. We watch in awe as television news cameramen in Somalia or Bosnia or wherever capture on film the death of an individual pleading for assistance, the cameraman more concerned with shock news value than with helping the dying person survive. We don't even expect the holder of the highest office in the land to practice morality. So why then do we expect it from those who discharge onerous waste products into our environment? Such expectations of just one segment of society, and not all the rest, seem hypocritical to me.

Occasionally the environmental protection agency of a federal or state government will levy a big fine, sometimes as much as thirty million dollars or more. You would think fines that big would get an industrialist's attention, but then later you hear that the same company is being fined again for illegal environmental activity. The violators will often enter into agreed settlements with the government agency, willing to pay a huge penalty every now and then to stay out of court. Is that a logical or reasonable or ethical way of doing business? Why aren't we yelling more about the illegal polluters when they are caught and then not punished sufficiently to keep them from doing it again? I suppose the problem is that most people just do not have adequate information about such environmental matters or any knowledge about how they might affect the average person's family. Or, as is true with most people, they do not trust government and presume that government is merely harassing another businessman, trying to put him out of business.

As a conservative, I am yelling (in print). I am as disturbed that governments are too lenient with those who violate laws against putting substances into the environment that might harm a child as I am that government is letting known child molesters roam the streets to ply their trade again. The intent of a businessman not protecting society from some onerous industrial discharge is different from that of a guy who goes out to commit a crime. I know that. The pernicious end results, however, can be very similar. One of the good ideas to come out of huge fines levied by the United States Environmental Protection Agency was the requirement that large amounts of the fines be used for cleanup of past mistakes or for retooling to prevent future abuses. Hopefully, the reality of that concept will match the theory.

It seems to me that the logical thing a good conservative should do in considering environmental matters is to gather the facts, weigh those facts, then make his or her own decision about what to believe and what not to believe, what to do and what not to do, what to be primarily concerned about, secondarily concerned about, or not concerned about at all. The crucial element in all of this is an honest exposure to facts. For some reason, too many people turn off their ears to an absorption of existing facts as soon as the word *environment* is mentioned. I wonder why that is. Perhaps it is because the thought that we might be doing something that could adversely effect our ability to reproduce as a species is beyond comprehension for most of us. Perhaps it is because we are so surrounded by bad news and predictions of doom that we can't separate the wheat from the chaff.

As a member of the 1994 Republican Platform Committee in my home state, I one day found myself in a discussion over a platform plank that would require a cost-benefit analysis for any environmental mandate from the government. I tried to explain that the parents of a child exposed to lead might understand the costs. Brain damage is a primary cost of their child's exposure. It is the benefit of that exposure to lead that the parents might have a hard time comprehending. But my colleagues argued, "No, no, we are not talking about health. We just think government should prove the necessity of environmental regulation before mandating it on small business as a cost of doing business." Of course, I agreed; why not say just that?

"Businessmen like to hear about cost-benefit analysis," they said.

"Parents of children with adverse effects from exposure to lead don't like to hear that the dulling of their child's mental ability is a benefit," I said.

"We are not talking about health," they said.

"Voters are," I said.

Then it struck me. Many of my friends and colleagues are unable to separate in their minds the differences between conservation and contemporary environmentalism as practiced by the small groups of individuals in community after community who believe they are being adversely subjected to involuntary exposures of toxic substances. The examples of environmental protection known to my Republican friends have to do with such things as bureaucratic harassment at their place of business or the loss of property rights to a farmer whose century-old dry lands are bureaucratically declared to be wet. They have identified what is wrong with environmental policies pursued by our governments, but they have not yet, with some exceptions, focused on the more serious concerns about adverse health effects from exposure to synthetic substances in the ground, air, and water.

But then, many of my conservative colleagues do not have easy access to environmental facts. That is not surprising, of course, because the dissemination of data concerning the effects of serious pollutants is just not widely practiced. We have not done a good job of informing the public. Folks involved in environmental work tend to communicate with each other; we preach to the choir.

In a similar vein, I noticed several congressional heads come alert, however briefly, during my congressional testimony on May 24, 1994, when I said, "As a Republican and a conservative, I believe that humans probably

45

can manage wetlands, and maybe forests. There are a lot of things humans can manage, including some pollutants. But one thing humans have not been able to manage over the past fifty years is chlorine." It is difficult for some people to discover that some things are not manageable by humans. So the arrogance of humans becomes a barrier to overcome.

Another barrier is the lack of data relative to the effects of persistent toxic substances on humans. We humans don't like to use other humans as guinea pigs. As 1994 began, there was a big stir about the federal government using unsuspecting individuals back in the 1940s (and up to the 1970s) as human guinea pigs for the testing of radioactive substances. It was even alleged that plutonium was implanted into the bodies of eighteen unknowing victims while they were in the hospital for other reasons. We hate hearing such stuff. We don't understand why such things happen. Whatever the motives, humans should never be subjected to such involuntary risks.

So if we do not test humans for the effects of life-altering industrial chemicals, are we not left with making linkages between the results of research on animals and the probable adverse effects on humans? We know what PCBs do to mammals in the wild. Since the physiology of all mammals is similar, should we not presume a similar adverse result on the human mammal? Is that not the best thing we can do, short of injecting the poisons into humans? You would think so, but lobbyists have been successful in getting the public, via the media, to pooh-pooh linkages between laboratory animals, wildlife, and people. I am reminded of a remark supposedly first made by my hometown friend Bill Ruckelshaus, the first administrator of the Environmental Protection Agency: "Laboratory mice are like prisoners of war. If you torture them long enough, they will tell you anything you want to know."

We live, however, in a highly complex world. Uncertainty abounds, and the demand for certainty in today's world, on either side of an environmental question, is not always intellectually honest. In the face of such uncertainty, it becomes easy for some to presume that the environmental movement is the last haven for those of a socialist bent. But so what? That is primarily because conservatives have not yet joined the battle. It seems to me that there are right things to do, environmentally, as well as wrong things to do. My way of thinking tells me that we should look at the facts and do the right thing, no matter who is saying what or which political philosophies are held by the crowd that is the noisiest. Socialism has failed nearly everywhere it has been tried; it will continue to fail. Why not strive to solve the problems of the environment and not be distracted by other thoughts?

For thirty years of my life, I was a psephologist. Should you be unfamiliar with my area of expertise, let me explain. Back when the Greeks first conceived the idea of voting for their leaders, they cast their votes by the use of colored stones. A red stone for one candidate, a blue stone for another candidate. A psephologist is one who studies stones. In contemporary usage, or at least in my contemporary usage, a psephologist is one who studies how and why elections are won or lost, then applies that knowledge to winning the next contest. I became pretty good at the practice of psephology.

As a campaign manager and state Republican party chairman, I needed to know a little bit about everything. That makes it very hard to know a lot about any one thing. In most every campaign year, some limited discussion centered on environmental issues. Also, in almost every campaign year, few voters cared. Even when environmental issues were faced, they almost always had to do with waste and what to do with it. I remember the late mayor of Evansville, Russell Lloyd, saying, "Everyone wants me to pick up the trash, but no one wants me to set it down."

Never in my decades of knowing a little bit about everything was I ever exposed to the term *persistent toxic substance.* I heard about the potential for cancer as an endpoint of environmental exposure, but I did not know whether or not I believed such theories, because most all of my information came from the news media. News stories, as I mention elsewhere, usually give you equally weighted reasons to disbelieve as to believe. But then suddenly, upon becoming a commissioner on the International Joint Commission, I found myself surrounded by facts that were hard to refute. The truth is, in the beginning of my tenure, I wanted to disbelieve. But being a good conservative, with the ability to think for myself instead of being told how to think, I was willing to change my way of thinking. Evidence is evidence and facts are, indeed, facts.

Consider these facts: when my wife and I were married in 1963 it was expected that one woman in twenty had a lifetime risk of breast cancer. In the 1980s (my wife had her double mastectomy in 1982) that figure rose to one in fourteen. By the mid-1990s one woman in eight or nine was at risk for breast cancer during her lifetime. What kind of statistics will the next decade bring, or the next? When will our society concentrate on preventing breast cancer, instead of putting all the emphasis on curing it?

Thinking conservatives will accept facts if the facts are available. Having accepted a set of facts, the conservative mind will likely think first of stopping the problem before spending the money to remediate past actions. What good does it do, if logic is applied, to clean up the results of past discharges if we continue to discharge those same substances? Should we not stop doing bad things before we waste resources to clean up the results of those bad things? A conservative most likely thinks so. Any thinking person should think so. Prevention is not only safer from a health standpoint than is remediation, it is also much less expensive to business and to society as a whole. But the discharges continue. I normally do not buy into conspiracy theories, but I sometimes wonder if it has been a deliberate plan by someone unknown to me to put all the emphasis on the tail end of the environmental process. By emphasizing what we do with something after we use it, we take the heat off the folks who are authorizing it, making it, and using it in the first place.

How do we stop doing those things we should not be doing? Do we have a dictatorial government order demanding that we stop all discharges tomorrow, putting people out of work unnecessarily and causing great social disorder? By such an order, do we cause a factory to move from Toledo to Arkansas or Mexico? Or do we have an orderly procedure to phase a substance out of existence, doing the most good with the least amount of harm? Do we sunset the substance, allowing industry and labor organizations, as well as government and the public, to be involved in setting a timetable for the removal of the substance from the total environment? I favor the orderly process. Lobbyists' tactics would indicate they might prefer holding out for as long as possible awaiting the dictatorial government order—a bad choice.

Obviously, industry can set timetables, find alternatives, and adapt to change better than government can. As a conservative, I accept that fact without debate. Sunsetting is a conservative theory. The needs of all involved, including society as a whole, are considered and accounted for. Sunsetting is the sure way to get to zero, to prevention, all the while recognizing the importance of profit and work as motivating factors in a free society.

So now my conservative mind has acknowledged a problem and accepted a responsible method to prevent that problem from occurring in the future. What next? I would then look to see which problems of the past need remediation. I would consider which remedial actions will so benefit society that they are worth the resources needed to accomplish that purpose. A conservative should believe that industry executives, as well as individuals, are responsible for their actions. A question to consider up front is, after spending the zillions of dollars necessary to clean up contaminated sediments, will the environment be better off, worse off, or no different? Why not answer that question before the money is spent?

It also seems to me that a conservative would set environmental priorities, recognizing that everything cannot be done at once. Some things are just more important than others. Some facts are more compelling than others. It is also important to recognize that some things need not be done at all.

My somewhat limited exposure to the facts causes me to reflect that maybe too much time, money, and effort is being consumed chasing trash, hugging trees, and worrying about such esoteric theories as global warming. I have seen modeling projections that might predict a warming trend, but I am not yet convinced. I also believe that it just might be possible to manage our forests. And, obviously, the way to handle trash is to offer incentives (or at least publicly communicated reasons) not to create it in the first place.

The scientific evidence confirming problems with human reproduction, learning, behavior, and the ability to ward off disease is now becoming broadly accepted. Those are serious concerns. So instead of a multitude of government inspectors, thousands of bureaucrats, and a multitude of laws and regulations, all harassing us about trash as we try to go about our business, why not try setting some priorities to deal with the truly serious environmental effects? Why not prevention as the first order of business? As I said in a speech before the Indiana Wildlife Federation annual meeting:

> Why do I think it important to set environmental priorities? Human nature is the primary reason. Let me give you an example of how an average person, already quite cynical about the ability of government to perform its most basic of duties, might react to the news of a new environmental problem. That average person might say, "Okay, I have heard enough about lead to agree that it is probably harmful. I want to protect my kids from exposure to lead. And I might believe that dioxins (whatever they are) and pesticides are bad for me, if you did not also tell me that moviehouse popcorn, eggs and bacon, smoking tobacco, coffee, product packaging, landfills and incinerators, meat, whole milk, hormones injected into cows, methane excreted from cows, radon, electromagnetic fields, ozone, forestry management, nuclear energy and carbon-generated energy, hot dogs, herbicides, automobiles, plastic, asbestos, vinyl, breast implants, and Mexican food are all bad for me. It is just too much to worry about, so I will worry about none of it."
>
> Successful environmental protection depends upon public pressure. When the public hears one side say everything is bad and the other side say nothing is bad, the thought is mentally excused from their concerns. No pressure is exerted. It is easier to believe that nothing is bad, rather than to believe that everything is bad. So we need to set priorities. We need to attack the problems before they happen, and we need some consensus on where to start.

Conservatives should be leading that debate.

4

Water and Air—Quality
and Quantity

The Great Lakes Water Quality Agreement

I NOW WANT TO CONSIDER for a moment the International Joint Commission's role under the Great Lakes Water Quality Agreement, and describe the kinds of things the commission does under the agreement and, just as important, the kinds of things it does not do. For over two decades the Great Lakes Water Quality Agreement has been a model international effort. It is in many ways a visionary document, predicated as it has been from the beginning on an ecosystem approach to environmental stewardship. It is the commitment "to restore and maintain the chemical, physical, and biological integrity of the waters of the Great Lakes Basin Ecosystem" that has made possible the many successful initiatives undertaken by many dedicated professionals for more than twenty years and has made the agreement the envy of many other nations.

The International Joint Commission has been a full participant for all of those years in monitoring and assessing the progress made by the governments under the agreement, in assisting governments in the implementation of the agreement, and in conducting a public information service on Great Lakes issues.

In my address to the plenary of the United Nations Conference at Rio, I described the International Joint Commission as a model for use by nations sharing common resources throughout the world.

> As an established organization, the International Joint Commission provides a mechanism and an accumulated body of knowledge that are available instantly to assist governments in preventing and resolving issues that may arise along the boundary, within clearly defined parameters.
>
> One of the major successes over the years has been our process of bringing together the best available expertise to develop a consensus on the fundamental data to describe a particular problem and its practical solutions. This process has also resulted in the development of a large cadre of international experts who know and respect each other.
>
> One other factor has been crucial to the International Joint Commission's ability to influence through its process. It is direct public involvement. The commission has always placed considerable importance on an informed and involved public. It was one of the first bodies with a strong mandate and procedural rules requiring public consultation. Under the treaty and under our rules, all interests have a right to be given a convenient opportunity to be heard, a requirement that is subject to cultural realities and to which we are continually seeking to be responsive.

The Great Lakes Water Quality Agreement is not a creature of the International Joint Commission, as many people seem to think. Terms in the agreement such as *virtual elimination, zero discharge,* and *ecosystem* are frequently referred to as IJC wording. Many persons, especially industry lobbyists and some government regulators, refer to such words and concepts as if they were made up by an obscure commission, instead of being the words and commitments of two separate agreeing nations. At a public meeting in Toronto, a consultant hired by the chemical manufacturing industry accused me of working against the policies of the United States and Canada when the commission urged the governments to continue the movement toward virtually eliminating the discharge of persistent toxic substances into the Great Lakes; in fact, the two nations agreed in the Great Lakes Water Quality Agreement that such is the policy of the United States and Canada.

The agreement was originally signed by President Nixon and Prime Minister Trudeau in 1972. It has since been updated twice by the governments, in 1978 under President Carter and again in 1987 under President Reagan and Prime Minister Mulroney.

The implementation of agreement provisions are the obligation of the federal governments, not the commission. The commission has been given an important responsibility under the terms of the agreement. In its simplest form, the commission has been asked to monitor and report on progress being made by the federal, state, and provincial governments as they work toward implementing the agreement. The formal obligation of the IJC to monitor is what makes it different from nongovernmental organizations that have taken it upon themselves to critique governmental performance. The commission's role is also different from that of the executive agencies in both countries that do the day-to-day work in implementing agreement provisions.

In short, the commission's task is to look at the evidence of the work the governments have undertaken, then make an independent assessment of that work. The results of this assessment are formally made known to the two federal governments, the state and provincial governments, and the public every two years in biennial reports. There is often a lot of confusion about whether the commission, commenting as it does on governmental performance under the agreement, is an environmental advocate or a governmental apologist. It is neither. To the extent the parties are not meeting agreement obligations, the commission says so, and to some persons that makes the IJC look like an environmental advocate. To the extent governments are meeting their obligations under the agreement, that is reported, and to some persons that makes the commission look like a governmental apologist. In truth, the obligation and the efforts are aimed at assessing as fairly and accurately as possible the progress the United States and Canada are making to meet the stated purpose of their agreement.

One agreement responsibility is to report to the governments and to the public at least biennially. In its *Fifth Biennial Report*, the commission told the governments and the public that based on available evidence, it had concluded that there is a threat to the health of our children emanating from our exposure to persistent toxic substances, even at very low ambient levels. The word *toxic* is used so often these days that it has become too easy to forget the real meaning of what we are talking about. The United States and Canada in their agreement said that "toxic substance means a substance which can cause death." The dictionary defines it as "poison." Surely *toxic* is a word that should arouse our concern.

As we further our understanding of the frightening effects of exposure to persistent toxic substances, especially the danger posed to women of childbearing age, we realize how important it is to make people aware of where the dangers are, which foods to avoid, and the consequences to humans if they do not abide by such measures as fish advisories. The IJC suggested in its *Fifth Biennial Report* that governments that stock fish into the Great Lakes and then issue warnings to humans not to eat them may want to reevaluate such policies.

As we begin to talk seriously about pollution prevention in the Great Lakes–St. Lawrence River Basin, we need to look again at the Great Lakes

Water Quality Agreement and the commitments of the United States and Canada. The two nations agreed "to restore and maintain the chemical, physical and biological integrity of the waters of the Great Lakes Basin Ecosystem." They agreed that it was their policy that "the discharge of toxic substances in toxic amounts be prohibited and that the discharge of any or all persistent toxic substances be virtually eliminated . . . in order to protect human health and to ensure the continued health and productivity of living aquatic resources and human use thereof." The United States and Canada also agreed that "the philosophy adopted for control of inputs of persistent toxic substances shall be zero discharge."

How have the governments done in the first twenty or so years of the Great Lakes Water Quality Agreement? In fact, a great deal of progress has been made, beginning with the problems of phosphorus. The federal, state, and provincial governments have been hard at work over the past two decades to meet the purpose of the agreement. Billions of dollars have been dedicated and good results have been achieved. But in just the past few years, there has surfaced a new interest and a new dedication to restore and maintain the integrity of the waters of the Great Lakes.

In Canada we have seen the Green Plan. We have seen new Canadian resources and research directed at meeting the commitments of the Great Lakes Water Quality Agreement. A new comprehensive report by the government of Canada entitled *Toxic Chemicals in the Great Lakes and Associated Effects* was released. But then we have grown to expect a serious and ongoing concern for the quality of the Great Lakes by our Canadian friends.

What was truly gratifying to me was to witness the great flurry of activity in the United States that backed up the commitment of former Environmental Protection Agency administrator Bill Reilly by making water quality in the Great Lakes a priority of the United States government. In 1990 the Congress passed and President Bush signed commendable and extensive legislation relative to environmental concerns in the Great Lakes, as well as national legislation that benefits the Great Lakes ecosystem.

Included in those numerous acts were the Pollution Prevention Act, the Great Lakes Critical Programs Act which included many IJC recommendations, the Non-indigenous Aquatic Nuisance Prevention and Control Act which contained IJC recommendations, the Water Resources Development Act, the Clean Air Act, the National Environmental Education Act, and others. I was in Chicago for the signing of the Pollution Prevention Strategy for the Great Lakes, and a few weeks prior to that I was in Ottawa for the Bush-Mulroney signing of the U.S.-Canadian Air Quality Accord. And certainly the Great Lakes Initiative, in its various stages, has the potential for being the best effort yet to prevent pollution in the Great Lakes ever undertaken by either of the federal governments.

So we must acknowledge good work and dedicated effort. However, as yet we have not achieved virtual elimination for a single persistent toxic substance in the Great Lakes, and zero discharge is still just a philosophy. As a result, some children will never realize their full potential merely because they were born in the wrong place or their mothers ate the wrong Great Lakes fish.

Our emphasis must be on prevention; what sense does it make to spend billions of dollars in remediation if we continue to allow the input of persistent toxic substances into the environment as we now do? The governments will claim that we have tried bans on PCBs and DDT, but obviously they really were not bans in the literal sense.

In the IJC's *Fifth Biennial Report*, we recommended that the governments of the United States and Canada strengthen the principle of reverse onus in policies and programs concerned with the introduction of new chemicals, through appropriate legislation or regulations that include mandatory pretesting prior to approval for production and use—meaning that when approval is sought for the manufacture, use, or discharge of any substance which will or may enter the environment, the applicant must prove, as a general rule, that the substance is not harmful to the environment or human health. As it is now, thousands of untested chemicals are being released into the Great Lakes and throughout the North American continent.

In the *Seventh Biennial Report*, we suggested that all chemicals, new and in use, be subjected to the concept of reverse onus. Better legislation and enforcement of existing legislation is needed in both countries. Greater concern is called for, but the reality of the mid-1990s found that funding for Great Lakes projects was being reduced. So the snail-paced efforts to prevent the discharge of persistent toxic substances into the Great Lakes may be headed for a slowdown as the federal government puts its environmental priorities elsewhere.

Another of the recommendations in the *Fifth Biennial Report* was to ask that the United States and Canada designate Lake Superior as a demonstration area where no point source discharge of any persistent toxic substance will be permitted. We all hear the same old arguments, such as the one stating that the Great Lakes pollution problem is really a global problem, so zero discharge is just a pipedream. Or that zero discharge is impossible unless someone can ensure zero intake. Or that some substances are in nature naturally, so zero is impossible. Nonsense. Zero discharge doesn't include what is there naturally but the much greater amount that is added by human activity. It seems to me, as just one individual, that such arguments are dilatory excuses not to tackle the problem. That's why it made sense to me to test the philosophy of zero discharge in a somewhat pristine body of water such as Lake Superior. I thought we should try it somewhere and see if it is possible.

I was very heartened to hear that the United States and Canada formally accepted the Lake Superior recommendation. I was also heartened to hear that the United States Environmental Protection Agency and Environment Canada had launched a significant pollution prevention program in the International Great Lakes Basin, because the very first recommendation in our *Fifth Biennial Report* was that "the Parties complete and implement immediately a bi-national toxic substances management strategy to provide a coordinated framework for accomplishing, as soon and as fully as possible, the agreement philosophy of zero discharge." I wonder what happened to that binational pollution prevention program?

Whenever we start talking about pollution prevention, some voices will always be proclaiming that such a policy will put people out of work. That need not be true. We can have clean air and at the same time thriving economies. We can stop polluting the Great Lakes and still have plenty of jobs. The question is not can we do those things; the question is will we do those things.

If we are to be serious about pollution prevention, we are all going to have to pay increasing attention to the critical area of human values. Attitudes and corresponding behaviors are the root problem of pollution in our society. The IJC strongly emphasized the need for this kind of attention in its *Fifth Biennial Report*. Pollution prevention will be only as successful as our joint ability to begin to improve the values and attitudes of our children, as well as the behavior of the adults in our society. Once people get set in their ways, around puberty, it is not an easy task to get them to change. It is also not a popular approach, but unless we take this approach we are going to be constantly running into the problem of trying to legislatively and administratively alter adult behaviors, attempts which historically have been extremely difficult to accomplish.

I believe we are going to have to place our focus in the educational realm. We need to pay attention to the early educational process of children, where values and attitudes are created. By working with children we can begin the process of encouraging a society whose values and attitudes are consistent with environmental values and attitudes. It is important that we begin an educational process that will alter the way people treat the environment of which they are a part. Values are important. Among the values taught our young people must be a proper stewardship of the environment. A barrier to overcome here might be the reluctance of contemporary educators to teach values of any kind.

When I look at recent governmental pronouncements and at legislation on the environment generally, and legislation regarding the Great Lakes in particular, we are not about to go backward. Some lobbyists do not believe that is true. They believe they can continue the tactics of denial, diversion, and delay. But the effort I have witnessed is nonpartisan, and it cuts across all socioeconomic lines. Even other agencies of government are putting pressures on those in government responsible for cleanups to get on with the job. In the 1993 Report of the Auditor General of Canada, several deficiencies of governmental action were cited. One finding was that Canada has no federal strategy for water quality action plans. The need for multijurisdictional partnerships and public involvement was mentioned, as was the failure to provide Parliament with information on which it can act. The auditor general's report was reminiscent of recommendations made by the International Joint Commission. It appears the commission is no longer alone. Now even government is prodding government to do what it has committed itself to do. Interesting developments.

I predict that the nineties and the turn of the century will result in an increased attention on the part of individuals to the responsibility they have in their own households and of their own behaviors with regard to environmental integrity. I think we as a society are at a crossroads with regard to our environmental stance. We are going to have to choose between being seen as a society that chooses to delay environmental progress or one that insists upon specific efforts reflecting the kind of environmental care and sensitivity that will allow our two nations to do their share in making the world a better place for those who come after us.

Can We Manage the Unmanageable?

Communication and education are critical tools for success if we are going to finally accomplish broad-based pollution prevention as well as the goals of the Great Lakes Water Quality Agreement. The importance of communicating adverse environmental information to the public is obvious; environmental problems facing our society simply cannot be solved by government action alone. All parties, including governments, academia, industry, the professions, and the entirety of the public, must be informed and motivated to come to the table together, to set the agenda relative to pollution prevention and remediation. In North America the International Joint Commission is a logical catalyst to bring people together.

It is important to remember the goals of the Great Lakes Water Quality Agreement. I know I have given some of them before, but they are worth repeating. They are at the very heart of this overall subject matter. The two nations agreed that it was their policy that "the discharge of toxic substances in toxic amounts be prohibited and the discharge of any or all persistent toxic substances be virtually eliminated." The two nations defined toxic substance as "a substance which can cause death, disease, behavioral abnormalities, cancer, genetic mutations, physiological deformities in any organism or its offspring, or which can become poisonous after concentration in the food chain or in combination with other substances." Persistent toxic substances are defined as "any toxic substance with a half-life in water of greater than eight weeks."

Dire thoughts emerge from that definition. It was a forward-looking definition when written and continues to be forward-looking now. It is not a definition of *toxic* by some radical environmental group; nor is it a definition concocted by some remote commission. It is a definition agreed to by the governments of the United States and Canada. It should not be taken lightly.

The best minds in these two great free nations agreed that any substance that could become poisonous after concentration in the food chain is to be defined as toxic. They agreed that a toxic substance is a poisonous substance, that such a substance can cause harm not only to the exposed adult but also to an offspring. They defined one such harm as death. A toxic substance is a substance that can cause death, agree the governments of Canada and the United States. That sounds grave enough to me that perhaps serious attention should be given to eliminating the discharge of such substances. Who could humanely argue otherwise? What industry executive could argue that the discharge of such a substance is not a matter of concern, when the two greatest nations on earth agree that such an action can cause death? What government regulator or policy maker could possibly argue that issuing a permit to discharge a poison that could cause death is a reasonable thing for governments to do? Does any of this make any sense to anyone? Should we not be moving this debate to a higher level?

A toxic substance is one that can cause behavioral abnormalities. What were the definers from the United States and Canadian governments thinking about when they included behavioral abnormality as an endpoint of exposure to a toxic substance? Were they thinking about retardation or dulling of mental sagacity in our offspring? Were they thinking about unusual hyperactivity or anxieties among our children? Were they thinking about increases in juvenile violence? Were they thinking about abnormal sexual preferences? It is quite likely that they were thinking about all of those things and more. I am fearful of even trying to guess what the government definers were thinking about when they included genetic mutations as an indicator of exposure to a toxic substance. Then they listed physiological deformities as an end point to such exposure. In the long term, the most worrisome physiological deformity is a deficient reproductive system, but then a retarded immune system is nothing to sneeze at. Cancer is also included in the definition, but not as the most important end point, just one of many. And, of course, we are now seeing much more information relative to breast cancer as an end point of exposure to persistent toxics.

The highly educated and knowledgeable representatives of the United States and Canada, in a quiet and deliberative setting, with reams of good scientific data at hand, defined toxic substances (not just toxic substances in toxic amounts, but toxic substances) as substances that can kill, maim, retard mental ability, retard immune systems, retard normal hormonal activity, and retard the ability to reproduce. That definition can be read and reread as often as time allows, and nothing good can be found under the definition of toxic substances. Only bad things. Only terribly bad things.

My question as a lawyer, as a politician, as an admitted layman, is how can governments arrive at such conclusions as they put in their definition of toxic substances and not act definitively to sunset the existence of such things? Is it an anomaly or is it just the cynical way in which governments work?

Since the agreement was entered into, many lists of persistent toxic substances have been drafted. The Water Quality Board of the IJC came up with eleven really bad-acting persistent toxic substances several years ago. The eleven are so onerous that little debate is heard about the need to prohibit or virtually eliminate them. The list includes PCBs, DDT, dieldrin, toxaphene, dioxins, furans, mirex, mercury, lead, benzo(a)pyrene, and hexachlorobenzene. These substances are not only toxic; they are also persistent and biocumulative. Experts differ over which substances should be on a virtual elimination list, but most all lists include these eleven. The question is again obvious. Considering the implications of the definition of toxic and knowing that these eleven are even worse than most toxic substances, why are they still being discharged into the waters of the Great Lakes? Why do governments sanction their use by issuing permits to dischargers allowing official entry of such poisons? And why doesn't industry itself just say no?

I am proud to say that the International Joint Commission has formally asked those very same questions and has made serious recommendations to sunset human use of such substances as the surest method of achieving virtual elimination of their discharge.

It is the obligation of the commission to report and make recommendations under the Great Lakes Water Quality Agreement. It is, however, up to the two federal governments to decide whether or not they pay any attention to the words of the commission. One might wonder how the recommendations of the commission have been received by the governments of the United States and Canada. A General Accounting Office report indicated that about 50 percent of all recommendations had been acted upon in some fashion or the other. Many of the recommendations of the *Fifth Biennial Report,* along with recommendations from two special reports on exotic species and environmental education, found their way into law and regulation in one or both countries.

Sometimes the two federal governments jointly and formally adopt the recommendations of the International Joint Commission, as they did in the Lake Superior Zero Discharge Initiative. Sometimes the recommendations later become law or policy in one or both nations. Sometimes the recommendations are just a stimulus toward an action or activity off into the future. And, of course, sometimes the recommendations of the commission are simply ignored by one or both governments. One of the fun, or maybe rewarding is a better word, things about my role on the commission was the opportunity to affect the policies of two nations at the same time.

No matter what the reaction of governments, the commission's continued role is to monitor moves made toward achieving the goals of the agreement and to gather the best information that can be found to determine progress. As the commission gathered evidence from its boards and task forces, from government, from industry, and from other public sources, I would often ask myself some basic questions. Have the governments achieved the virtual elimination of the discharge of *any* persistent toxic substance into the Great Lakes? And how well have the governments pursued the philosophy of zero discharge as set out in the agreement between the two nations?

How are the two nations doing in restoring and maintaining the chemical, physical, and biological integrity of the waters of the Great Lakes Basin ecosystem? The answer is that good progress has been made, but the commitments of our two nations are far from being met. Compared with twenty years ago, there is a better ecosystem balance. But we have not virtually eliminated the discharge of persistent toxic substances into the Great Lakes. We are still doing it! The two nations have agreed to make Lake Superior a demonstration site to test the philosophy of zero discharge, which is encouraging. But they certainly have not restored the chemical, physical, and biological integrity of the waters. Improvement, yes. Restoration, no. These are important matters to debate. And for the debate to be successful, representatives of all the public must be at the table where decisions are made. If industry and labor are not at the table as full participating partners with government, success will be difficult to achieve.

My years on the commission were a period of intense debate and changes in perceptions as a result of the conversations we held with all sectors of the Great Lakes community. Some of the most profound changes have been in the words we use, the statements we can now make, and the confidence with which we make them. Much of this is reflected in the content and tenor of our fifth, sixth, and seventh biennial reports on Great Lakes water quality. I'd like to briefly trace the development of these changes in ideas, to put this discussion in a broader context.

Throughout the 1960s, the Great Lakes community was primarily concerned with the excessive amounts of nutrients such as phosphorus and nitrogen entering the lakes. These nutrients spurred on the eutrophication we experienced in many areas and most profoundly in Lake Erie. The 1964 reference from the governments of the United States and Canada to the International Joint Commission on the lower lakes resulted in the signing of the 1972 Great Lakes Water Quality Agreement, which focused on efforts to control the input of these nutrients from a variety of sources.

The decade of the 1970s was a period of intense action to reverse the eutrophication problem. At the same time, however, there was a growing awareness of the presence and effects of persistent toxic substances throughout the Great Lakes Basin. This awareness led to the agreement's expansion in 1978 and a reorientation from eutrophication to control and elimination of toxic and persistent toxic substances.

Ironically, we now hear concerns that perhaps the nutrient base for the Lake Erie ecosystem is endangered again, endangered as a result of the massive invasion of the zebra mussel and its even more voracious cousin, the quagga mussel, which is less fussy about habitat and is coating much of the lake bottom. These small mussels entered the lakes from European freighters, and they filter phytoplankton and other essential nutrients from the water. This again shows the delicacy of the ecological balance of the Great Lakes and how inputs of foreign substances or species can dramatically alter the system.

The agreement's policy on toxic substances, which stated that their release in toxic amounts be prohibited, was already well entrenched in existing water pollution control legislation and programs, such as the U.S. Clean Water Act, the Canadian Fisheries Act, and the Environmental Protection Act in Ontario. As a result of efforts under these acts and those accomplished under the agreement, the 1980s brought a marked improvement in Great Lakes water quality, particularly in the control of cyanide and heavy metal releases.

The agreement's policy concerning persistent toxic substances, however, was not familiar to most regulatory officials, because it was not included in any pollution control legislation. The broader Great Lakes community, including the regulators, did not realize the distinction between the two types of pollutants and the resulting controls needed until 1989. Few people in government, even now, acknowledge a difference between toxic substances and persistent toxic substances. I had one high governmental official tell me that persistence had to do only with the degree of exposure.

What caused this new realization to take seed? I think three things precipitated the change. First, the Conservation Foundation/World Wildlife Fund in the United States and the Canadian Institute for Research on Public Policy published the book *Great Lakes, Great Legacy?* The project was spearheaded by Dr. Theo Colborn, who pulled the latest research findings together to outline the full extent of damage that had occurred to fish, wildlife, and humans as a result of exposures to persistent toxic substances. Dr. Colborn followed that work by organizing the noted Wingspread conferences, where she brought together scientists from many different disciplines "to integrate and evaluate findings from the diverse research disciplines concerning the magnitude of the problem of endocrine disruptors in the environment." After the first conference in 1991, the participating eminent scientists released a consensus statement that, if read, should have caused a stir within our society. But hardly a ripple occurred at that time.

A second important thing that has happened over the past few years is that citizens became more organized throughout the basin as they began to recognize and understand the pollution issues facing the region and their effects on the health of all species in the ecosystem. They stated their concerns and findings clearly and defiantly at the commission's 1989 biennial meeting in Hamilton, Ontario, where the regulators, scientists, business and industry representatives, and the IJC commissioners clearly heard their call for greater action. They were back again at the 1991 biennial meeting in Traverse City, Michigan, and this time industry representatives appeared in stronger numbers. The public spoke, while industry representatives leaned against the wall in the back of the hall and listened. In 1993, at the seventh biennial meeting, a full complement of industry representatives attended as major participants.

Finally, and less well known, the commission's Council of Great Lakes Research Managers held a workshop on cause-effect linkages in March 1989. This workshop brought all the top researchers together and provided the scientific basis for taking a weight-of-evidence approach to reach conclusions about the role of persistent toxic substances in causing injury. That is, when the weight of all evidence on the impact of persistent toxics on the human and ecosystem health is considered together, it provides conclusive evidence that, indeed, we and every other species in the ecosystem are being injured by these substances.

These cause-effect linkages are what the regulatory community is requiring the scientific community to provide before they are prepared to take regulatory action against a substance. That is somewhat understandable, in that these substances are used widely in commerce and thus their prohibition could potentially result in significant economic disruption to industry and other segments of society.

One characteristic of science is that it is generally practiced by cautious and responsible people who believe that more information is required or another experiment is needed to obtain conclusive proof of harm. As a lawyer, I simply ask myself how much information we need before we ask an industry to change a process, or a decision maker to change a policy, or a citizen to change a life style. We can make the argument that there is never enough data and that there never will be, but that doesn't get us to solutions. The crux of the matter is, how does the regulatory community make decisions in the face of scientific uncertainty? The commission recommended the use of the weight-of-evidence approach in its *Sixth Biennial Report* and has essentially been using it to develop its recommendations about persistent toxic substances for some time. There comes a time when, despite the caution and responsibility of scientists and others, there truly is enough evidence to make a decision. Unfortunately, that point is often more than thirty years after the substance has been introduced into commerce and has already caused damage to a generation or two.

What kind of damage are we talking about? The remarkable thing is that we know far more about what happens to fish and wildlife than we know about effects on humans. Unfortunately, bald eagles and otters don't vote, and so the information on damage to wildlife tends not to carry sufficient weight with policy makers. The most pronounced effect from Great Lakes research is on the development of fish and wildlife embryos, but as every biology and medical student knows, all vertebrates have strikingly similar physiologies. In particular, human embryos are subject to the same exquisitely timed programming as other vertebrates during development, programming that is controlled by various hormones. Persistent toxic substances can disrupt this exquisite timing, resulting in subtle but devastating effects for society. What happens to fish and wildlife embryos also happens to human embryos.

We are being asked by the regulatory community to give the same level of proof for the documented effects on humans as was attained for fish and wildlife. Of course, we cannot test humans in the same way we test animals. The challenge here is to make decisions in the face of scientific uncertainty and, of course, with the knowledge of the enormous costs that these decisions could entail for industry and for government.

I don't want to leave the impression that governments have not taken any action to control and even eliminate persistent toxic substances from the ecosystem. There have been efforts at bans on either the use or the manufacture of some persistent toxic substances. But for the most part, the two nations have attempted to virtually eliminate these substances through regulation rather than by effective bans, phaseouts, or other proposals. These efforts have reduced the inputs and the loads. But regulation has not brought the levels of persistent toxics in the Great Lakes down to what can be considered safe. The attempt to regulate the most onerous substances out of existence has not worked. It cannot work!

The goal of the agreement is virtual elimination. The reality of the regulation of persistent toxic substances is that it is an effort to manage the unmanageable. As a U.S. commissioner, I believed that my society was already overregulated. Here is how things now seem to work. As new science emerges, new regulatory standards are set. As regulatory standards change, industry must retool and invest more and more capital to meet the new standards. Costs to the consumer rise. And each new set of regulations is, in my belief, a deterrent to new and existing jobs. It seemed to me that it was in the best interests of our Great Lakes community as a whole to rethink how we deal with persistent toxic substances. We need a new way of thinking.

The *Sixth Biennial Report* of the commission reflected the realization that regulation alone will never achieve the purpose, the policies, or the objectives of the Great Lakes Water Quality Agreement. The commission determined that the virtual elimination of toxic substances should be a priority of the commission, and we made it so. We created a Virtual Elimination Task Force, consisting of members of the public, of industry, of academia, and of governments, to devise a strategy which the commission could recommend to governments for the execution stage of the virtual elimination of persistent toxics into the Great Lakes. We sought advice from our boards and task forces. We considered information available from governments. We sought advice from scientists and researchers other than those from whom the commission had traditionally sought information.

We considered the past and pondered the future, and, as a commission, we came to the following decision in our *Sixth Biennial Report*: if a substance is so onerous that it cannot be tolerated by wildlife or humans, then let's set a time certain to phase such substances out of existence. Let's devise a timetable that causes the least interruption possible in economic activity, as well as in the quality of life of our citizens. Let's make sure the timetable allows ample time to search for an alternative substance or process. And let's make sure that all affected interests are at the table making proper decisions as to what and when. What I have just described is what we are talking about when we speak of environmental sunsetting.

In the *Sixth Biennial Report*, sunsetting is defined as follows:

> a comprehensive process to restrict, phase out and eventually ban the manufacture, generation, use, transport, storage, discharge and disposal of a persistent toxic substance. Sunsetting may require consideration of the manufacturing processes and products associated with a chemical's production and use, as well as the chemical itself, and realistic yet finite time frames to achieve the virtual elimination of the persistent toxic substance.

And, we said, "effective sunsetting also requires a cooperative approach whereby the traditional regulatory approach is blended with consultation and dialogue among all stakeholders, using a range of mechanisms and partnerships."

We advocated the sunsetting of PCBs. We knew that PCBs are no longer produced or imported into the United States or Canada, but we also saw reports that 30 percent or so of all PCBs manufactured in the past are already in the environment and that another 65 percent or so are still in use or storage available for entry into the environment.

We advocated the sunsetting of DDT, dieldrin, toxaphene, mirex, and hexachlorobenzene. We were aware that the use of DDT was supposedly banned but heard that it was still being deposited into Lake Superior and elsewhere. The Virtual Elimination Task Force Report of 1993 surprisingly indicates that DDT is still available for purchase in the United States. We know that use of some of these substances is declining, but some uses are still permitted.

We advocated that the governments, "in consultation with industry and other affected interests, alter production processes and feed stock chemicals so that dioxins, furans and hexachlorobenzene no longer result as byproducts." And knowing that we cannot completely sunset substances that are in the environment naturally, we advocated that the governments "review the use of, and disposal practices for lead and mercury, and sunset their use wherever possible."

All of the above raised the question of chlorine, in and of itself not a persistent toxic substance. In 1986 the Water Quality Board of the International Joint Commission developed a working list of 362 chemicals confirmed to be present in the water, sediment, or biota of the Great Lakes Basin. Approximately half of these substances are chlorinated organic substances. From this information and from information obtained following 1986, the commission concluded that the question about the standing of chlorine (the common precursor for the production of chlorinated organic substances) had been sufficiently raised.

We recognized that certain uses of chlorine were of special concern because of the overwhelming public health benefits from their use. Uses such as the disinfection of drinking water and sewage and the production of pharmaceuticals, as well as other uses to protect public health, required special considerations. We also recognized that socioeconomic and other consequences of banning the use of chlorine and the subsequent use of safe alternative chemicals or processes all must be considered in determining a timetable. And we then recommended that the governments in consultation with industry and other affected interests develop timetables to sunset the use of chlorine and chlorine-containing compounds as industrial feed stocks and that the means of reducing or eliminating other uses be examined.

We intentionally did not set timetables for any of our sunset recommendations but left that up to governments and affected interests. We recognized that the timetables for different substances would likely differ.

The reaction to the recommendation on chlorine was interesting and instructive to a person such as myself who has always been predisposed toward the views of industry and a free market. We found ourselves, as a commission, in the forefront of worldwide ideas to cleanse the environment of the most onerous of substances. Several international and domestic bodies have since reached conclusions similar to those expressed above, as we reported in the commission's *Seventh Biennial Report.* Examples of such international bodies are the 1992 Convention and the Ministerial Meeting of the Oslo and Paris commissions for the Prevention of Marine Pollution (OSPARCOM) representing fourteen European nations; the conclusions of the thirty-nation International Whaling Commission's annual meeting in May 1993; the Fifth World Wilderness Congress, Tromso, Norway, in October 1993; and the Barcelona Convention on the Mediterranean Sea (BARCON) representing twenty-one nations, Analya, Turkey, in October 1993. Various health professional organizations, including the American Public Health Association, the Michigan State Medical Society, and the Ontario College of Family Physicians, have also stated their concerns for the effects and management of persistent toxic substances.

In considering these matters, I realized that while the results of studies on the effects of persistent toxics to fish and wildlife may alarm and concern us, the results of studies on human health are what will enrage us and lead us to change. Thus we made human health a priority at the commission, and we focused on gathering additional information through an ecosystem health work group. We also joined with Physicians for Social Responsibility and other organizations to sponsor a physicians' roundtable, the first of its kind. Several physicians and medical researchers came together to help us learn how medical professionals communicate with one another and to design a continuing medical education course on the human health effects of Great Lakes pollution. The first environmental medical education course was sponsored by the Medical College of Wisconsin.

We also participated in a survey of Wisconsin pediatricians, obstetricians-gynecologists, and family practitioners to assess current views and experiences regarding the clinical significance of environmental pollutants. More than 86 percent of these physicians considered themselves to be somewhat uninformed about the risks of mercury and PCBs to human health. Fifty-six percent considered themselves very uninformed. Yet these same physicians in overwhelming numbers (90 percent) felt that it was appropriate for physicians to be a source of information for patients about environmental risks. Seventy-eight percent responded that physicians should also take public positions about issues that affect public health. The results of this study tell us that we must do a better job of getting the information out to the medical community.

The past thirty years of pollution research and administration in the Great Lakes Basin have been an exciting period of history, and it has been influential far beyond the boundaries of the basin. Governments and industry can have legitimate pride in their accomplishments, but there is much left to be done.

Air Quality

In addition to doing the study of the Trail Smelter already described, the commission has been involved in a number of other air quality studies. These have included questions on air pollution in the Windsor-Detroit area from smokestacks of vessels, several studies of air pollution in the Detroit–St. Clair River area, and a request from governments that the commission alert them to any emerging air quality issues along the common boundary.

It is for purposes of this alerting responsibility that the IJC maintains the International Air Quality Advisory Board. And most recently the commission has been given an ongoing responsibility to seek public comment on United States and Canadian progress under the recently signed Air Quality Agreement. The commission would probably have been given a larger role in the U.S.-Canada Air Accord had the governments not feared we would take such responsibility as seriously as we took our water quality responsibilities. The commission also studies and continues to comment upon the implications of air deposition for water quality in the Great Lakes.

Most perceptions of the International Joint Commission relate to the Great Lakes, to the attempt to control the quantity of waters flowing through the system, or to the studies and reports dealing with the adverse effects of end-of-the-pipe persistent toxic discharges into the waters. But let me touch just briefly on commission work relative to the quality of the air along the U.S.-Canadian border.

During my tenure I witnessed a dramatic increase in our knowledge about the role long-range transport plays in relation to the deposition of a broad range of contaminants. The commission's expert advisors on air quality matters have often found themselves at the forefront of this developing knowledge.

In 1979, for example, air quality experts working with the commission's Science Advisory Board found that lake trout in a small lake on Isle Royale in the middle of Lake Superior had PCB body burdens, the presence of which could not be explained by any phenomenon except the long-range air transport of this contaminant. I think it fair to say that the evidence compiled by the Science Advisory Board at that time resulted in a substantial increase in governmental attention to problems posed by long-range transport and consequently triggered the need for the development of models to establish sources and pathways of these contaminants.

I have spoken with enough experts to understand that the deposition of toxic contaminants resulting from atmospheric circulation is one of the most complex processes scientists have ever tried to model. I've also read enough reports and spoken to enough scientists to know how important the work of modeling the deposition of these contaminants can be to the general health of our society. And it is obvious that we need to get on with the important work of virtually eliminating the discharge of persistent toxic substances through the medium of air. We cannot get on with this important work, however, until we know a lot more about the sources of the chemicals and how they get into the air and the lakes in the first place. This is important business, and it is being addressed by a number of governmental agencies and other experts.

The International Air Quality Advisory Board, in cooperation with the Great Lakes Water Quality Board and the Great Lakes Science Advisory Board, has worked on the quantification of atmospheric loadings of certain toxic chemicals to a watershed of regional scale, specifically the Great Lakes Basin. What this work has yielded is the realization that neither country is equipped well enough in the way of comprehensive and complete inventories for the modeling that is needed.

The commission's interest in this issue of atmospheric transport of pollutants stems from its water quality agreement responsibilities. Annex 12 of the agreement addresses persistent toxic substances and strongly emphasizes the need to protect human health. The annex calls for intensified research to determine the pathways, fate, and effects of toxic substances so that we can better determine the strategies to be employed in protecting human and general ecosystem health. Annex 15 calls for research, surveillance, and monitoring to implement control measures for the purpose of reducing atmospheric deposition of toxic substances, particularly those that are persistent. The annex identifies the need for the establishment of an integrated atmospheric deposition network to determine atmospheric loadings of toxic substances. And the annex also states that the parties shall, when atmospheric conditions of toxics derive from outside the basin, notify the responsible jurisdiction and seek a suitable response.

The IJC's International Air Quality Advisory Board has the computer models and other tools required to provide a credible analysis of deposition to the Great Lakes. I find that the agreement contains specific language calling for the necessary programs to do the modeling work. So what is missing? The interest of governments at the policy-making level and resources, what else? Running models for the Great Lakes cannot be done without a complete and comprehensive emissions inventory. That would entail the commitment of substantial resources from our two governments at a time when resources are scarce and our economies fragile. But what is the alternative?

If anything, the evidence concerning the damage being done to children by persistent toxic substances is stronger than ever. Scientists for whom I have the greatest respect and who take great care in their pronouncements now tell me that a large number of manufactured chemicals that have been released into the environment have the potential to disrupt the endocrine systems of humans. They also estimate with confidence that some developmental impairments reported in humans today are seen in adult offspring of parents exposed to synthetic hormone disruptors and that large dysfunction at the population level is possible unless these synthetic hormone disruptors, such as DDT, PCBs, and dioxin, are brought under control and eliminated.

As we talk about cleaning up the air, it is important to remember that air is but a medium, a pathway. Air is not a source of pollution; it is a carrier of pollution. When we hear that all humans throughout the world are carrying an unnatural body burden of dioxin, we must think about air transport. We must also think about the effect that one isolated manufacturing process or one government incinerator may have on any person, anywhere in the world.

Water Quantity

Not all of the work of the International Joint Commission relates to the quality of the water or the air. Much of the work relates more to the disciplines of engineering and hydrology. It is the work of apportioning water in accordance with agreements between the United States and Canada. It is the more traditional work of the Boundary Waters Treaty. For some reason, more resources have been available to the commission for work on water quantity than have been available for water quality work. And, to my knowledge, the United States Congress has provided zero funds for air quality activities at the IJC relative to the required work under the United States–Canada Air Accord.

The Boundary Waters Treaty of 1909 requires the commission to approve certain uses, obstructions, or diversions of boundary waters if these operations affect the natural level or flow of the waters in the other country. In addition, under the treaty, Canada and the United States can ask the commission to conduct studies and make recommendations on specific problems along the common frontier. Examples of commission authority over the years have been approvals of the development of hydropower projects in the St. Mary and the St. Lawrence rivers. The commission relies on the services of government and public experts and citizens from both nations to conduct studies and monitor such operations as the regulation of Lake Superior and Lake Ontario.

The process that leads to the commission approval of obstructions or diversions is made up of several major steps. First, the entity interested in constructing and operating a diversion facility must apply to the commission for approval. The commission then conducts studies and in many cases appoints a study board, a binational panel of experts to carry out any detailed technical investigations. Public hearings are held to receive comments from the public and other affected interests. Through this process, the commission identifies what impacts the proposed facilities could have on levels and flows and, in turn, on various users of the waters. The commission can then weigh the merits of the application based upon a myriad of viewpoints and technical information.

When the commission approves an application, it issues orders of approval. Those orders may include conditions and criteria governing the construction and operation of the facilities. In some cases, the commission requires the establishment of a binational board to develop regulatory plans and to supervise the operation of such facilities in order to ensure that the conditions and criteria set out in the orders of approval are observed. Such orders are periodically reviewed and amended. Existing boards operate at the Lake of the Woods, Lake Superior, St. Mary and Milk rivers, St. Croix River, Souris and Red rivers, Columbia River, Rainy Lake, St. Lawrence River, Kootenay Lake, Niagara River, Osoyoos Lake, and Flathead River. From sea to shining sea.

In 1952 the commission issued an order of approval to the applications of Canada and the United States to construct hydropower facilities in the international section of the St. Lawrence River, extending from Lake Ontario to Cornwall, Ontario, and Massena, New York. The order gave the responsibility to construct and operate the hydropower facilities in Canada to Ontario Hydro and in the United States to the New York Power Authority. Apparently, at that time, the building and operating of the works by one of the interested users was not of such concern to the public as it seems to be today.

In 1956, during construction of the project, the commission amended its order to include regulation criteria designed to reduce the range of levels experienced on Lake Ontario, to facilitate navigation in the St. Lawrence River, and to provide protection for riparian and other interests downstream in the Province of Quebec. The order also established the International St. Lawrence River Board of Control to insure compliance with the provisions of the order by the operators of the works. The board undertook its duties when the project was completed in 1960 and continues today to advise the commission and the power entities on the regulation of Lake Ontario. A similar but a smaller board operates the Lake Superior controls.

From my personal experience, it was the spring of 1993 that tested the fabric of this detailed process on Lake Ontario and the St. Lawrence River. Record supplies of water to Lake Ontario were recorded for several months. Then in April all-time high recorded supplies of waters to Lake Ontario required releasing water through the St. Lawrence works above those granted in the order of approval. This high-water situation followed the winter floods in southern California, which severely damaged the Mission at San Juan Capistrano, and preceded the great Mississippi floods of the summer.

A relief valve in the commission's regulatory order for the St. Lawrence River was criterion K, which, if enacted by the commission, gave precedence to riparians, upstream and downstream, over the other interests. The commission enacted criterion K in February. But then, as often is the case with government, the board found that criterion K had never been defined. The board asked the commission if criterion K protection to riparians was to be accomplished even if it had adverse effects on other interests, such as shipping and hydropower. The commission said yes.

From that point the board increased the Lake Ontario outflow through the works on the St. Lawrence River to the point where shipping was endangered. At first the St. Lawrence Seaway authorities were concerned only about keeping the seaway open, lobbying IJC commissioners to hold the water back. Then, when the board announced its plan to release water at a level never before attempted whether shipping stopped or not, everyone seemed to acknowledge the seriousness of what was at stake and the resulting full cooperation among the various agencies, public and private, in two nations, created an atmosphere of solution finding. Shipping was halted for two days each week while water was discharged at velocities previously not imagined. The other five days of each week, water was discharged at high velocities, but at levels at which shipping could operate.

I am sure my former colleagues agree that the International St. Lawrence Board of Control proved its worth in the high waters of 1993. The board members did what no one before them had been able to do, and they protected riparians from water ravages experienced in other sectors of the North American continent in 1993. But during that time, at public meetings such as one in Greece, New York, I was accused, face to face, of being bribed by the shipping industry and taking favors from the hydropower industry as I let the high-priced homes of "little people" be flooded. Elected officials, including a United States congresswoman, urged the crowd on, playing to emotions instead of pursuing facts.

Past government actions became a barrier to the decision-making process. In past high-water circumstances, the governments had not assessed the damages to property along the waterfront. In the 1993 circumstance, official damage assessments were not available on which judgments could be formed and decisions made. The Corps of Engineers on the U.S. side did do some tentative work in 1993, but the Canadian governments did not even attempt to assess damages in the midst of the high water time. Obviously then, governments could easily say there was not enough evidence to declare a crisis circumstance. They could say that because they had deliberately not sought such evidence.

Accepting that humans cannot control nature is very difficult for some humans. Just look at Californians. More people live in California than in Canada, thirty million or more. But it is a land short on water and prone to major earthquakes, wildfires, floods, mudslides, and other events of nature. It is a land not naturally capable of supporting massive human occupation, but a massive human population dwells there. As a result, human disaster is a common occurrence in the Golden State, with taxpayers nationwide often picking up the tab.

Following the high waters and storms on the Great Lakes in 1985 and 1986, the governments of the United States and Canada referred a study on the adverse effects of fluctuating water levels on the Great Lakes to the commission. The emotions of riparians, people living on the waters, were similar to the emotions of the folks in Greece (near Rochester, New York). They live on a giant ecosystem of lakes and connecting channels. They know, deep down, that only God can control precipitation and evaporation, but they demanded constant water levels.

It is hard to imagine that people who love the beauty of the lakes so much really want huge works, billions of dollars' worth of concrete works, built in these waters so that these waters might possibly be controlled. The six-year study of water levels pretty well indicated that it was possible to build such structures and to control the levels to some extent, but doing so would have adverse environmental effects on the system and it would cost more than any imagined damages might cost over a long period.

The governments gave the commission twelve million dollars and six years to determine what we probably could have predicted in advance. That is not to say that there was not much good information provided by the study. There was. It was also an extremely successful experiment in public involvement at every level of a technical government study. It just seemed to me that the twelve million U.S. dollars might have been more wisely spent on what humans are doing to the Great Lakes rather than trying to correct what God is doing to his Great Lakes.

5

Health Effects

Human Health

I HAVE JUST WRITTEN A LOT about water and how we humans have fouled it. But there is something I did not mention. Life without water is not possible! But then, knowing that statement to be true, why do we continue to contaminate that which we cannot do without? Not only must we humans drink water daily; water provides us with a food supply, and water is the supplier of food to animal and vegetable life which then becomes food for humans.

Water is in the oceans, lakes, and streams of all sorts. It is in various states of precipitation or evaporation. It is under the ground and in the clouds. The amount does not change as years pass by. We have in the earth's bounds a constant amount of water. The same amount exists now as existed during the time of the dinosaurs. In fact, some drop of water consumed by a dinosaur millions of years ago may tomorrow come out of the faucet at your kitchen sink. Three and one-half to seven gallons of water departs your house each time you flush your toilet. In just the United States alone, we use 339 billion gallons of fresh water per day. The average American uses 100 gallons of water every day. Such examples can go on and on.

But consider this: most water is not available for human use. In fact, only about 3 percent of the earth's water can be used to sustain life, and perhaps two-thirds of that is frozen in the polar regions. Of all the water in the world, water so essential to life, maybe just 1 percent of it is available to sustain life as we know it. Surely, then, we humans, with all our knowledge and logic, would conserve water and not foul it. And isn't it logic, the ability to reason, that differentiates us humans from all other mammals?

But no, even with all of our knowledge and supposed logic, we have assumed that water, especially great bodies of water such as the Great Lakes, can assimilate any amount of garbage, pollutants, and poisons that we humans can dump into them. We also dump those same contaminants into the air, to be attracted into large water systems, just as magnets attract metal shavings in that little kid's game where the task is to put hair on a bald man's head. We dump those contaminants onto the ground in landfills, or just plain old dumps, to leach into the groundwater which flows to the larger streams and lakes. And we continue to salt the ground with pesticides, which eventually work their way into the great waters of the world. Where is the logic? Where is the reason?

But let's spend a little time here thinking about the effect all of this might have on humans. What do we know? What do we not know? What do we believe? How do we deal with our lack of knowledge if our beliefs cannot be proved absolutely?

First, it is important to point out that one barrier in dealing with human health effects is that traditional scientists, environmentalists, and ecosystem managers think it is wrong to isolate the human animal from all other living things. If a discharge of some onerous substance can be proved to be harmful to the otter, then we should alter the practice of discharging the substance, they say. We should not need the human example. All living things are deserving of equal consideration, and you must consider humans to be just one element of the ecosystem, those folks will contend. They remind you, always, that humans do not stand on the sidelines of the environment, that humans cannot really successfully manage the environment, that humans are not exempt from the ravages of nature.

All of those arguments are probably true, but so what? They end up being barriers to the goal of international agreements to virtually eliminate the discharge of such items. A congressman from the southwestern part of the United States probably will not express great concern over harmful effects to the otter on one of the Great Lakes, which is resulting from the discharge into the air of some poison in another part of the country. Funding for such studies probably will not be forthcoming. On the other hand, adverse effects on humans will attract attention anywhere in the United States and just might be the catalyst for obtaining the funds needed to see what's going on with the otter.

Second, the absence of human health studies is used as a barrier to progress in virtually eliminating the discharge of harmful pollutants. If it cannot be proved with absolute certainty that such a discharge will harm humans, then industry will not change its ways and politicians will not buck the industry lobbyists. Industry says it cannot prove the negative. But then, we do not have agreement on just what is the negative; is it that organochlorines are *not bad* for humans, or is it that organochlorines are *not good* for humans? Of course, if there are no human studies, there can be no proof of human harm. Time lags between exposure and effect are also a barrier. Cause-and-effect relationships are hard to prove when twenty or thirty years may pass between the time of exposure to a persistent toxic substance and the development of health problems in this generation or the next. Multiple exposures to many chemicals (and tobacco) over a lifetime also make it difficult to determine which exposure or accumulation of exposures caused the adverse health effect to occur.

Third among the many potential barriers we face in seeking environmental protection is the almost automatic denial by governmental officials. Official reaction to adverse after-effects to the health of Gulf War veterans is a typical reaction of governments and industry when confronted with adverse human and wildlife effects of persistent toxic substances. Many Gulf War veterans are suffering from mysterious diseases. Something like three-fourths of the soldiers in one unit suffered from similar diseases. Science cannot identify the commonality of those effects with the service of the men in the Persian Gulf area. But service in the Gulf is the only thing they have in common. In the face of scientific uncertainty, governments and industry too often officially presume the answer is the one best suited to their interests.

No matter how often the worrisome health effects of such persistent toxic substances as DDT, PCBs, lead, mercury, etc., are proved, governments and industry still do not want to admit that exposure to other like chemicals can cause similar adverse effects later in life to exposed adults or their progeny. Government regulators want conclusive proof before they begin to exercise caution. We then discovered from news reports at Christmas time in 1993 that thirty-six of fifty-four babies born to veterans suffering from the Gulf War disease had been born with birth defects. But because science cannot verify the linkage between military service in the desert, the illness of the adult, and the health defects of the babies, denial reigns supreme.

But what are the potential human harms about which we should worry? Let's take a look.

For years, cancer was preeminent among the known or suspected effects of persistent toxic substances on wildlife and humans. We heard that exposure to some substances could result in cancer. We believed those warnings at times, and at other times we did not believe them. We all heard stories about electric utility workers who used to stick their hands and arms down in PCBs and lived to be as old as dirt. But cancer was, and is, an adverse human effect resulting from the discharge of persistent toxic substances. So regulators took that information and set regulatory guidelines based upon the risks of cancer. Cancer studies dominated the research agenda. Compromises between scientists, regulators, politicians, and lobbyists caused standards to be set on the discharge of some of the poisonous discharges, standards that the public was encouraged to presume would protect it from cancer, with the public all the while not knowing that *safe* was a word subject to political compromise.

But then we learned that even more subtle disease and dysfunction outcomes occur from the exposure of living organisms to toxic chemicals, in addition to cancer. Those effects were neither carcinogenic nor mutagenic, but they were occurring in increasing numbers. They had to do with reproductive problems, severe metabolic changes, gross deformities, behavioral and hormonal changes, and suppression of the immune system. These effects tended to appear in the offspring rather than the exposed parent, as a result seemingly of maternal transfer. The threat was widely believed to be caused by such substances produced intentionally and unintentionally as PCBs, dioxin, furans, hexachlorobenzene, DDT and its metabolites, dieldrin, lead, mercury, and others.

The United States General Accounting Office, in an October 1991 report to the chairman of the U.S. Senate Committee on Governmental Affairs, reported:

> Reproductive and developmental diseases have a pervasive impact on our society. In 1988, about 250,000 U.S. children were born with birth defects, 600,000 women experienced a miscarriage or fetal death, and many young children were exposed in their homes and neighborhoods to chemicals that will reduce their ability to develop the intellectual skills necessary to function in the 21st century. There is growing scientific evidence that exposure to environmental chemicals causes a broad spectrum of adverse reproductive and developmental outcomes and that they are preventable if the exposures are better controlled.

Those are significant numbers indeed, and the overall deleterious effect on children is extremely worrisome. It would seem appropriate to mention at this point, for purposes of numerical comparison, that more than 1,500,000 fetal deaths occur each year in the United States due to voluntary abortions. That same General Accounting Office study found that "roughly half of the existing set of major regulations for the chemicals of high concern for their reproductive and developmental toxicities are of doubtful protection against those toxicities."

Later research brought evidence that chemicals that are persistent and toxic can disrupt the endocrine systems in fish, birds, and mammals, including humans. As we said in the *Sixth Biennial Report* of the International Joint Commission, "These disruptions can be profound because the endocrine system plays a crucial role in controlling the extent and pace of the development of the individual." We also said:

> Patterns of effects vary among species and compounds and are dependent upon the age of the individual at the time of exposure. Thus, the chemicals may affect the embryo, fetus or perinatal organism differently than the adult. Effects are more likely to become apparent in offspring rather than the exposed parent. The time of the offspring's exposure is crucial to the severity of these effects on character and future potential. Most troubling of all is the experts' conclusion that humans are being affected as well. Indeed, they estimate that levels of some of these chemicals measured in the human population are in the same range, and in some cases even greater, than those found in adversely affected wildlife populations. They concluded that the potential hazard to humans is great because of the likelihood of repeated and continued exposure to those chemicals known to disrupt the endocrine system.

The expert scientists at the Wingspread Conference expressed the following judgment in their Consensus Statement:

> The scientific and public health communities' general lack of awareness concerning the presence of hormonally active environmental chemicals, functional teratogenicity, and the concept of transgenerational exposure must be addressed. Because functional deficits are not visible at birth and may not be fully manifested until adulthood, they are often missed by physicians, parents, and the regulatory community, and the causal agent is never identified.

We learned from a U.S. Environmental Protection Agency draft report in late 1992 that "chemical manufacturing and processing workers with long-term exposure to some dioxins appear to have a 50 percent greater chance than the general population of developing certain cancers." And we learned from an EPA scientist that no place in the world today is free from dioxin, even though dioxin is not an intentionally created substance. Experts have also grown to believe that perhaps just one exposure to dioxin by a pregnant female may be sufficient to adversely affect the health of her unborn child.

And we learn from page 1 of the National Research Council's book *Pesticides in the Diets of Infants and Children* (1993) that "some pesticides can cause a range of adverse effects on human health, including cancer, acute and chronic injury to the nervous system, lung damage, reproductive dysfunction, and possibly dysfunction of the endocrine and immune systems." We also learn from that report that tolerance levels established by governments for pesticides are "not based primarily on health considerations" but rather on "good agricultural practices."

In the *Seventh Biennial Report* of the International Joint Commission, we reminded the governments of the United States and Canada of our previous declaration: "What we do to the Great Lakes, we do to ourselves and to our children." In that same report, we reiterated previous commission conclusions and said, "Little evidence has been presented, in the commission's view, to seriously challenge these earlier findings or the urgent need to address them." That is not to say that industry did not make noise; it did. Its denial was loud and broad, carried by lobbyists through the halls of legislative bodies. Industry did hire a couple of vendors to put a lot of preconceived words on paper. But real evidence in opposition—so-called good science— was noticeably absent, or at least in very short supply.

One of our recommendations in the *Sixth Biennial Report* really got the attention of the chemical manufacturing industry. We had recommended the sunsetting of a number of persistent toxic substances as the only sure way to rid the environment of them. Since the common precursor for many persistent toxic substances is chlorine, we recommended the sunsetting of chlorine as an industrial feed stock. We knew that many jobs were involved with chlorine and how disrupting, both socially and economically, a sudden ban on chlorine could be. That is why we recommended an orderly process. We knew that industry was best suited to determine a timetable to eliminate the industrial use of chlorine. So we did not set a timetable. We did discuss it informally among ourselves and thought fifty years might be manageable. At least there would be a time certain, off in the future, when such a formidable substance would be taken totally out of existence without a societal disruption. Industry came to us and told us how stupid we were, that a sunsetting of chlorine and finding a suitable alternative might take thirty years. Later they reduced that figure to twenty years.

In the *Seventh Biennial Report* we continued by saying:

> mounting evidence continues to reinforce concerns about the effects of persistent toxic substances. Long-term exposure of fish, wildlife and humans to these substances has been linked to reproductive, metabolical, neurological and behavioral abnormalities; to immunity suppression leading to susceptibility to infections and other life-threatening problems; and to increasing

78

levels of breast and other cancers. Available evidence also points to long-term reproductive and inter-generational effects. . . .

One growing concern has to do with effects on endocrine systems. Research has shown persistent chemicals such as PCBs, dioxins, atrazine, hexachlorobenzene, as well as other organochlorines and polycyclic aromated hydrocarbons (PAHs), to be strongly implicated in laboratory animals and in wildlife. The substances appear to act as artificial, external hormones that disrupt the normal balance of hormonal activity in animals. Studies have also shown similar effects in humans. Levels of these chemicals have been found in humans within the same range, or in some cases at even higher levels, as those found in adversely affected animals. The biological reactions are known to be similar. Furthermore, many of these hormonally active chemicals are found in fish, wildlife and human tissues in the Great Lakes ecosystem.

The National Wildlife Federation refers to this new pollution threat to the Great Lakes environment as "hormone copycats." In a report using that term as a title (August 16, 1993), the federation does a nice job of communicating the essence of the issue. It asks, "What is the issue?" and then says:

In short, some environmental pollutants are capable of mimicking the critical functions of human hormones—with dire and often unpredictable consequences to people and their offspring. These "hormone copycats" threaten all living things in the Great Lakes environment, including people. The increased risk of cancer from exposure to these environmental contaminants is generally recognized. But there is increasing evidence and scientific concern that people face other insidious threats from exposure to these pollutants. Moreover, the risks may be the greatest to those most cherished among us—our children. And these risks are not widely recognized or appreciated by the public. . . .

Researchers have suggested that hormone-like substances may result in numerous detrimental effects in humans including immune system suppression, thyroid dysfunction, decreased fertility, developmental and behavioral abnormalities and learning deficiencies. Furthermore, two of the most prevalent and costly diseases in older humans, prostate enlargement in men and breast cancer in women, are thought to be linked to hormone exposure and therefore be influenced by exposure to hormone-like environmental contaminants. . . .

Dr. Theo Colborn and her colleagues have documented that many chemicals in common use since World War II enter the bodies of humans, domestic animals, and wildlife, chiefly through contaminated food and water, and that these chemicals mimic hormones. The body mistakes them for natural hormones and reacts to them in ways that cause deep and permanent trouble, especially when exposure occurs during the critical period of development, before, and immediately after birth. Due to the role hormones play in human development and the ubiquitous presence of pollution, everyone is at risk from these effects. The most significant route of exposure, however, probably is from eating contaminated food, especially fish. The ability of many contaminants to be stored in the tissues of women and then be passed on to children during pregnancy and breastfeeding poses a particularly disturbing scenario, and one that is essentially impossible to prevent once the mother has been exposed. There is evidence that individuals exposed in the womb to contaminants stored in their mothers' tissues could have adverse effects for their entire lives. Further research indicates significant unfavorable consequences to learning potential and behavior is likely for children born to women living in polluted regions or who have eaten contaminated food.

In the *Seventh Biennial Report* we indicated that the effects of persistent toxic substance exposure are not found just in females. We said, "Various studies have indicated increased infertility as well as cancers and other abnormalities in male reproductive systems. Human sperm counts have been reported to have declined by fifty percent over the past fifty years. Sperm samples tested in one recent Canadian study indicated the presence of several persistent organochlorines." We also heard from key researchers in Great Britain and Norway that they are finding deformities among live spermatozoa. All of this leads one to wonder if the decrease in male sperm count and the increase in male genital tract disorders are a result of the mother of the male being exposed, and the male, as a fetus, being exposed in utero to environmental estrogens. It leads one to wonder if teenage behavioral problems are a product of such exposures. And to wonder about causes for the continuing increase in breast cancer.

Is the declining learning performance of our children the fault of the school system, or has their capacity to learn been affected by exposure to some onerous chemical, before or after birth?

In January 1994, at a conference sponsored by the National Institutes of Health, more than three hundred eminent scientists, cancer researchers, wildlife biologists, and physicians from around the world were in attendance. The reports from that conference were startling, to say the least. Rick Weiss, of the *Washington Post*, wrote an excellent feature article titled "Estrogen in the Environment" on January 26, summing up many of the concerns. Janet Raloff, in her article "That Feminine Touch" in *Science News* (January 22), also reported on the National Institutes of Health conference. Her article dealt seriously with the question "Are men suffering from prenatal or childhood exposures to hormonal toxicants?"

So again, with more scientists and more facts but still with uncertainty, we heard that it is plausible that some chlorinated compounds can mimic hormones, causing adverse effects on present and future generations. We heard about increasing cancers and malformations of the penis and testes. We heard that women exposed to chlorinated organic substances had sons with testicular abnormalities and smaller penises than boys of mothers not exposed. We heard that testicular cancer has increased 50 percent in the past twenty years. We also heard the concern of researchers over the role chlorinated substances might be playing in the increased incidence of endometriosis now affecting over five million women annually in the United States. We heard a strong suggestion that toxic substances in the environment may affect the early development of sex organs in males.

Scientific evidence does not now exist to prove absolutely that any of these effects are, or are not, caused by the exposures suggested. Such scientific certainty may never exist. The National Center for Health Statistics does tell us that at least one couple in ten now has an infertility problem, while the American Fertility Society reports that at least one couple in six experience an undesired fertility impairment. Monthly now, the weight of evidence is growing, and the weight is very much on the side of taking these health concerns seriously and on the side of precautionary actions, beginning now.

As a result of the discharge of some persistent toxic substances under permits purchased from governments, human health continues to be at risk. Is the exercise of precaution still premature?

New Science

During my time on the International Joint Commission, a great deal of new science sprang forward concerning potential harmful effects on humans and wildlife resulting from the discharge, past and present, of persistent toxic substances into the environment—at first yearly, then every few months until new findings were coming from all over the world at monthly intervals, or even less. Much of the new science was accompanied by proof sufficient to invoke caution. Some of it contained enough evidence to convince the scientists working in the specific areas of research, but not enough to convince regulators or policy makers. None of it was disproved during my tenure.

In the 1990 report of the International Joint Commission, we said that there was "a threat to the health of our children emanating from our exposure to persistent toxic substances, even at very low ambient levels." Since then, evidence has continued to mount indicating the correctness of that conclusion. I have seen no science to refute the statement that humans are in danger as a result of their exposure to toxic and persistent toxic substances, and the danger will likely increase with each passing generation. Detractors, those who would fight for the status quo, will say, I am sure, that they have seen no conclusive science proving the statement. The question again is, considering available evidence, how long should we wait before exercising caution?

Should not those who discharge prohibited substances (legal for a fee to some agency of government) be required to adopt a precautionary principle in conducting their activities? Does not good stewardship require, at the very least, caution? Is there not a place for ethical standards, beyond legal standards, in the discharge of these substances? Why not ignore the minimal government standards and just do the right thing?

Various government reports estimate that somewhere between 60,000 and 200,000 chemicals are being released into the Great Lakes. Some of these chemicals have been tested. Most have not. We just don't know what's out there, folks! If that makes you feel somewhat insecure, good! Go tell your elected official. The estimated 60,000-to-200,000 range of chemicals was used in the *Seventh Biennial Report,* but not until after much debate. One commissioner thought that the 70 percent spread between the low and high numbers was just too imprecise for use in our report. He was right, of course. But we did use those numbers because no one, not government, not industry, not the experts, knew any better. No one knows for sure which chemicals, in what amounts, of what persistence, and in what state are now in or entering our environment. No one knows!

Still, the two federal governments do not want to look at classes of industrial chemicals. They prefer to look at them one at a time, as do officials of the chemical manufacturing industry, who were quite upset with me over the commission's recommendation that governments treat chlorine as a class. As a general rule, I have found that government doesn't do things very well, but let's give it some credit. Let's say government can efficiently look into four such chemicals per year (if it can determine what and where they are). That would only take government somewhere between 15,000 and 50,000 years to accomplish its task. Ten chemicals per year would take only 6,000 to 20,000 years. And if we could look at 100 chemicals per year, one at a time, we might get pretty well along by the year 3000.

So the onus is on you. And on me. And on our unsuspecting neighbors. Under the present system, it is our personal responsibility as private citizens to know all there is to know about advanced chemistry. To know precisely how exotic chemicals react when they interact with each other. To know which chemicals are being used and discharged, and to know the potential effects all of that might have on us and our progeny. What nonsense! I can just visualize the last male baby born, working in some government laboratory trying to determine (conclusively, of course) which insufficiently tested chemical destroyed his ability to reproduce.

Does not logic demand precautionary actions? Should there not, at the very least, be a legitimate study of these substances of serious concern? Why would government oppose a legitimate effort to determine the truth about chlorine and other chemical substances? Is this an example of government gone amuck? It certainly is government making the wrong thing easy.

What should we expect, morally, of a discharger of an onerous substance, whether industry or government agency, when some new science is developed by credible scientists indicating present or future harm to humankind as a result of such discharges? Should there not at least be a requirement to do research and present credible science that the discharge is not harmful to humans or wildlife? Is it really good enough to ban swimming at the beach, or to place in a government fishing guide an obscure warning to fishermen not to eat the fish, as we now do? Why should the discharger not be willing to respond (voluntarily or involuntarily) to scientific evidence that indicates such discharges could affect generations of humans?

The dischargers say it is the American way of jurisprudence for an injured individual to prove not only the injury but also the causal agent of that injury, should recompense be sought. They can say that because in most cases science is not far enough advanced in the late years of the twentieth century to prove that a specific exposure or even multiple exposures resulted in a specific injury. Such proof would require circumstantial evidence, and that might be more plentiful. Science also cannot prove that such exposure did not result in the injury, but no one seems to care much about that side of the argument. And with such insidious chemicals, the involved parties may well be out of business and long gone before the effect ever surfaces, in the current generation or the next, or the next. The current standard does, in fact, require individual humans to prove in court that they were injured by a specific chemical discharge. The chemical is presumed to be harmless until proved harmful. Obviously, that is backward thinking. As someone at the 1993 International Joint Commission's biennial meeting said, "It is humans who are supposed to be innocent until proven guilty, not chemicals."

But what is this new science? By the time this book gets into your hands, whatever I say here will probably be regarded as old science because of the startling new discoveries that continue to come forth. The *New York Times* on November 2, 1993, ran a story by Natalie Angier about a study wherein the researchers "are learning precisely what hormonal signals impel males and females to pair up into cooperative units and assume the demand of rearing and protecting young." The article revealed that "studies of higher animals like humans suggest that the same hormones that shape the dynamics of rodent family life may also influence human social behavior, including the responsiveness of a mother to her baby, the affectionate bond between male and female and the capacity of a child to connect with the outside world and form friendships." And the article said:

> The two hormones that appear to be essential to family and other social relationships among mammals are oxytocin and vasopressin, small and structurally similar proteins produced in the brain that divide in their impact along roughly, though not exclusively, sex-specific lines, with oxytocin influencing female behavior and vasopressin stimulating monogamous and paternal behavior in males.

So, OK, I read that and now here come the questions to my curious mind. If the hormone that causes males and females to pair off together is replaced by a "copycat hormone" during fetal development, what happens to the natural pairing of male and female? Does it change? Is it changing? I read in the *Wall Street Journal* on October 29, 1993, that 1.2 million children were born to unwed mothers, nearly 30 percent of all births. Why are there so many fatherless children? Can we presume it is the fatherless children who are the prime movers of the escalating juvenile crime epidemic? Did something happen to destroy, to whatever extent, the monogamous and paternal behavior in males? Did the receptor cell grab onto a chlorinated substitute for vasopressin during fetal development due to some dosage from the discharge of a persistent toxic substance by the mother of that missing male?

What about the single mother? Was it a conscious choice to be a single mother? Was it the Murphy Brown syndrome? Why would a woman choose to go through life without a monogamous relationship with a male? Did Murphy miss out on the needed oxytocin owing to some sort of exposure that her mother (or grandmother) experienced at some point in her life?

Well, I don't know the answers, but those who are using persistent toxic substances and those who are permitting the use of persistent toxic substances have a moral duty to find those answers!

It is abundantly clear that wildlife exposure to certain substances causes disruption to the endocrine system, with consequent effects that include thyroid disruption, decreased fertility, decreased hatching success, gross birth defects, metabolic abnormalities, behavioral abnormalities, demasculinization (in males) and masculinization (in females), and compromised immune systems. We have also seen that the potential for similar effects on human populations is great because scientists estimate that levels of the culprit chemicals measured in the human population is in the same range as, and in some cases even greater than, those found in adversely affected animal populations. In some cases, injury may not be proved according to reductionist scientific methodologies, but given this sobering array of findings, any reasonable application of a weight-of-evidence approach, an approach that has now been accepted by both the United States and Canadian governments, leaves no alternative but to take action now.

In the waning months of my tenure on the International Joint Commission there were further findings strengthening the view that there is a need to ensure immediate action to stem and eventually reduce to zero the human-caused flow of persistent toxic substances into the air, water, and ground. Here are some examples:

- In 1992 a metanalysis that reexamined sixty-one sperm count studies resulted in the determination that worldwide human sperm count has decreased 50 percent since 1938. There is evidence to suggest that a reason for this reduction is exposure to elevated levels of estrogen during prenatal development. It is increasingly being suggested by research scientists that such elevated exposure may be related to environmental contaminants. Research also demonstrates an alarming reduction in sperm quality.

- Disorders of the male reproductive tract have doubled over the past fifty years. Some research scientists argue that a cause for such reproductive tract abnormalities are related to increased estrogen exposure in utero.

- In Yucheng, Formosa, prenatal exposure to PCBs and furans has been associated with significant reduction in penis size and other problems.

- We know now that one of every eight women in North America will develop breast cancer in her lifetime. We also know that many of the risk factors for breast cancer are related to a woman's hormonal and reproductive cycle, and scientists tell us that this relationship strongly suggests an association with estrogenic compounds. Most important is a report in the *U.S. Journal of the National Cancer Institute* stating that women more heavily exposed to the pesticide DDT may have breast cancer risk four times greater than women not exposed to the chemical. DDT is an organochlorine which is suspected of causing cancer by mimicking the effects of estrogen.

- On July 7, 1994, a study based on 371,933 women and published in the *New England Journal of Medicine* strongly indicated that where people live and work affects the risk of birth defects. In the study, women who gave birth to a defective child were likely to see the same defect appear in a second child. But the risk for the second child was decreased by one-half if the mother moved to a different town. The experts concluded that environmental factors in the household or in the workplace were more important than previously believed in the battle against birth defects.

- A U.S. Public Health Service study found that among pregnant women who drink or bathe in chlorinated tapwater, there is a 10 to 30 percent increase in premature births and low birth weights.

- The U.S. Environmental Protection Agency found in a report issued in the fall of 1993 that "children of women exposed to low levels of dioxin during pregnancy may suffer reproductive problems later in life," and that "there is a general implication that dioxin has the ability to interfere with certain responses that are hormonally controlled." As reported by Reuters news agency, "Dioxin is a chlorine by-product of chemical processing commonly found in fish and animals." Common it is. One EPA scientist says there is no place left in the world today where humans are dioxin free.

- An Italian study found that leukemia, lymphoma, and liver cancer are occurring at higher than normal rates in people exposed to a cloud of dioxin from a chemical plant explosion in Italy seventeen years ago.

- There is increasing evidence that exposure to certain persistent toxic substances, many of which are organochlorines, can alter human development and behavior.

- In the United States the incidence of testicular cancer has increased by nearly 50 percent in the past twenty years.

- Endometriosis, an overgrowth of uterine tissue, now affects an estimated five million women in the United States, affecting fertility, and is another problem where hormone copycats may play an adverse role.

- The sons of Michigan mothers whose breast milk contained an industrial flame-retardant chemical had a higher incidence of testicular abnormalities and smaller penises than the norm.

There are more examples, and the consequences to humans and their children cannot even be predicted. However, the increased risks of cancer to the exposed adult and, more worrisome, the effects on the unborn progeny of the exposed, are frightening.

It is not as if these things are not happening and not being reported. They are. So how can we ignore them, especially when they raise such serious questions about today's societal problems? Here are some ponderables.

- What if, as current research suggests, the startling decrease in male sperm count and the alarming increase in the incidence of male genital tract disorders are in fact being caused in part as a result of in utero exposure to elevated levels of environmental estrogens?
- What if, as current research suggests, the increasing numbers of breast cancer victims are being brought about in part by the great numbers and quantities of estrogenlike compounds that have been and are being released into the environment?
- What if the declining learning performance and increasing disobedience of our children in schools is not so much a function of the quality of our educational system but is, in part, related to the great numbers and quantities of developmental toxicants that have been and are being released into the environment, or to which these children have been exposed in utero?
- What if the breakdown of traditional values, such as two-parent homes and parental responsibility, monogamous relationships, and sexual preferences, are not related to the breakdown of traditional morality but instead to the governmentally permitted immorality of the unknowing or uncaring harm related to the discharge of persistent toxic substances into our environment?

What if?

What if?

New evidence continues to come forward. Its weight is accumulating. The question remains, just how much knowledge do we need before we act? Consider this item reported at the Estrogen Conference in Washington, D.C., in January 1994. An endocrinologist doing research on breast cancer cells that would not grow without estrogen found them growing even though no estrogen had been added. The breast cancer cells were getting an estrogeniclike compound from the plastic flasks being used for the experiment. The substance (nonylphenol) in the plastic was mimicking estrogen, making the cancer cell grow. How many such incidences are necessary to elicit some precautionary actions?

Wildlife scientists are very concerned about the low birthrates of alligators in Florida. They believe the problem was caused by a spill ten years ago of a chlorinated substance. The alligators that do hatch are predominantly female (feminized). In the few males hatched, phalluses were up to 75 percent shorter than normal.

Is a time coming when reproduction of the human species is a rare event? Will we discover then that precautionary measures really were not premature? Do we wait that long?

Weight of Evidence

It was in the fall of 1992, when I spoke to a group of scientists and governmental regulators in a hotel near the airport in Chicago. They were trying to come to grips with how to regulate certain onerous substances in the face of scientific uncertainty about the effects of such substances on wildlife and humans. Scientists and regulators were intermingling, trying to understand the needs and wants of the other. It was refreshing and was further evidence of the good that can be done by an international organization such as the International Joint Commission. Too often such technical people, in telling us what they do not know, are demanding more funds for more research, instead of acting on the knowledge at hand. Doing both seems to make more sense to me.

I often wondered, when experts on specific subjects came before me claiming that there was not enough data to form a conclusion on that subject, how those folks became labeled as experts? Their expertise seemed to be in clearly defining what they did not know. Normal for a scientist, I suppose, but certainly not conducive to action. Rightly or wrongly, to the generic population, lack of expert knowledge implies there is no reason for concern. It seems that regulators often arrive at the same conclusion. So, in my remarks, I spoke of change that had occurred during my short time of immersion in environmental issues:

> Some of the changes have been made in what we say and how we say it. For instance, we are now prepared to talk about persistent toxic substances as distinct from toxic substances. We are no longer hung up on the worry about definitions of such words as ecosystem, virtual and zero. We are no longer self-conscious when talking about injury, whether it be to fish and wildlife resources, or to human health and child development.
>
> Where in the past we only talked about potential effects, we now are prepared to make cause-and-effect statements based upon a weight-of-evidence approach. Our thinking has been reoriented from considering cancer as the most serious end point, to also considering the seriousness of reproduction and embryo development.
>
> The commission incorporated these ideas and changes in perception into its fifth and sixth biennial reports. These reports have been regarded as landmark documents by the public and by the scientific community, but they have also resulted in a serious challenge to the regulatory organizations in both countries in how to respond, within the limits of their legislated powers and economic resources.

Part of the challenge in implementing many of the commission's recommendations is that, in doing so, the often separate and divergent sectors of scientific research and the regulatory community must interact in intricate ways. Each is equally important, scientists must do the research, which should provide the causal statements, and the regulatory community must take some appropriate action, based on these and other findings.

Which brings me back to the question that drives the weight-of-evidence approach: How much information do we need, before we ask a policy maker to change a policy, . . . or an industry to change a process, or an individual citizen to change a life-style?

In a memo during the summer of 1993, I said to staff who were organizing a workshop on weight of evidence:

Critics often attempt to find flaws with individual studies in order to discredit findings and conclusions about persistent toxic substances. While limitations to study design may exist, this does not necessarily invalidate the findings and conclusions when considered in a weight-of-evidence context.

Those interests who do not like the findings of a particular study can easily find fault with the methods by which the study was conducted. Those interests who don't want to hear about pesticide in baby food can find fault with not just the conclusions, but the methods used, in such a study. The effects of dioxin can be disputed by some interests and we can keep restudying the effects of dioxin. There is no end of such examples. [This thought was not in the memo: technical people tend to think the potential flaw in a study is what should be expected and debated. Debates become barriers to needed action. I often wonder, in discussing such studies, why so much attention to the negative, and so little to the positive?]

Even though it is possible to pick holes in every study (especially on methods), doesn't a definitive time come when there is enough evidence to form a conclusion? Most all definitions of human risk refer to the *potential* for adverse effects. The standard is not absolute proof that risk exists, the standard is that there is a *potential* for adverse effects.

Do we just deal with scientific studies in applying a weight-of-evidence rule, or do we also consider what we can see, or smell, or feel, etc.? If a population of humans or wildlife in a specific community all suffer a common malady, even though scientific proof cannot be obtained to substantiate the malady, is not the fact that the malady exists among that population a matter of evidence to be weighed? What weight should such data be given in comparison to scientific studies?

Regulators want definitive conclusions from the scientific community before arriving at an acceptable exposure level. Many of the concerns (hormone mimickers, etc.) cannot be proven to the level demanded by regulators to regulate. How do we get the weight-of-evidence approach into this consideration?

My thesaurus gives me alternative words for:

Weight	*Evidence*
1. Heaviness	1. Confirmation
Mass	Data
Poundage	Proof
Tonnage	Testimony
2. Burden	2. Indication
Load	Sign
Pressure	Symptom
Strain	Token
Stress	
3. Albatross	3. Denote
Cross	Exhibit
Millstone	Illustrate
	Show
4. Consequence	
Emphasis	
Force	
Importance	
Significance	

My view of weight of evidence in the context we are using it for assessing potential risk to humans or wildlife, or for sunsetting, or for regulating, or for reversing the onus to the user, would lead me more to word combinations such as consequence of symptoms—or emphasis on symptoms, importance of signs, significance of indications—and not so much to words such as tonnage of data or mass confirmation.

The above are examples of what I would see discussed in a workshop of scientists, regulators, policy makers and the public. The question should not be how do we define weight of evidence. The question should be how can the weight-of-evidence tool best be used?

And then when the workshop actually occurred, I had the opportunity to challenge the assembled scientists, regulators, and representatives of industry and the public with the following words:

So what does that mean, weight of evidence? Is it Perry Mason terminology, understood only by lawyers? Is it the simple measuring of scientific reports? The tallest stack wins? Can it be identified by applying percentages? Fifty-one percent of scientists agree that brown is blue, therefore, the weight of evidence is on the side of blue. No, it is none of that . . . at least in my view, it is none of that. As a lawyer, I want you to pass out of your minds the way that lawyers use words. A preponderance of the evidence in civil trials, and beyond a shadow of doubt in criminal trials. Forget all that. In our use of weight of evidence we really are not looking for absolute proof, but rather for the potential for adverse effects on the environment, including humans. Note the word *potential*. It is critical to the weight-of-evidence debate. Most accepted definitions of risk relate to the potential for adverse effects.

The questions on my mind center around such things as: How do we know when there is sufficient evidence, or accumulated knowledge? Or how do we decide when there is enough potential for harm for a reasonable person to expect that scientists should sound the warning and that policy makers should act?

Do we look at each scientific study and weigh the nonquestionable conclusions with those that are questionable? Do we reject all conclusions in a study if one or some of the conclusions cannot be proven beyond some level of doubt? Even though it is possible to pick holes in every study, especially on methods, does not a definitive time come when there is (or is not) enough evidence upon which to act? On a broader scale, do we just deal with scientific studies in applying a weight of evidence approach, or do we also consider the perceptions of lay people in a specific community?

I attended the Presque Isle Remedial Action Plan Review Meeting, at Erie, Pennsylvania. During the afternoon we visited the bay, so we could see what it was we were there to discuss. Standing on the shore with representatives of state, provincial, and both federal governments, we watched as a couple of grizzled old codgers walked up to us and said, "Hey, you're standing on our fishing spot." So we moved.

One had on an orange hunting cap and some sort of fatigue jacket. The other had on a camouflaged hat and camouflaged jacket, so it was harder to tell what he looked like. Both had scuffed boots and scraggly beards. They looked like they might have been the grandfathers of some of the guys playing for the Philadelphia Phillies in the World Series going on at the time. We asked if they had been fishing there long. They said, "Yep, for over fifty years." We asked if anything had changed, and they somewhat angrily replied, "It sure has. There used to be a lot of fish, now it is hard to catch any, and when you do catch some, they have sores all over them and you can't eat them. The birds have gone. And nobody cares," they told us. When we asked what had caused the problems, they pointed out a coking plant and a couple of factories across the bay. I tell you this story, because it is obvious to me that those two old guys are part of the weight of evidence.

Another one of those questions that float around in my mind is, if the scientific community has grave concerns about the potential effects of a substance being introduced into the environment, but they do not have sufficient data (especially human data) to definitively declare a substance harmful, but they suspect they may have such proof when the next generation reaches puberty, should they not come forward with evidence they now have, even if such evidence is more suspicion than fact? If not, then how do we deal with preventive measures in the face of scientific uncertainty?

From all the questions I ask about weight of evidence, one might suspect I didn't know what I meant by the term. I do. Most individuals do. However, we don't always agree with each other on our meanings. But a time comes when weighing whatever evidence is available brings an individual to a decision point where action is or is not desired or necessary. But how do we deal with it collectively? As decision makers, as scientists, as regulators?

The workshop discussions were wide ranging and interesting. It became clear that many differing perceptions of what is meant by weight of evidence do exist among those trying to use it as a new tool. In law, the trier of fact is not always right, but certainly right in a vast majority of the situations. Is that good enough for science? I would suggest that it is, in fact, good enough for government work.

In the *Sixth Biennial Report* of the International Joint Commission, I agreed to the following language:

> The commission recognizes that scientific data are open to interpretation and that, notwithstanding the confirmed cause-effect link in some cases, unequivocal conclusions may be difficult to reach in others, especially if individual studies are considered in isolation. With low contaminant concentrations, subtle effects and potentially confounding factors, equivocal evidence of injury to humans by persistent toxic substances may be difficult or impossible to obtain.
>
> However, at some point, the emerging mass of data and information must be accepted as sufficient to prompt or, in the case of the Agreement, ratify action against environmental contaminants. Therefore, the commission has adopted a weight-of-evidence approach. Taking the many studies that indicate injury or the likelihood of injury together, we conclude that the evidence is sufficient that many persistent toxic substances are indeed causally involved, and there can be no defensible alternative: their input to the Great Lakes must be stopped. The urgent need is for effective programs to achieve virtual elimination.
>
> The confirmed cause-effect linkages and weight of evidence approach have profoundly altered how society perceives and is now responding to persistent toxic substances. This approach needs to be applied to other suspected substances to determine which of them are also persistent and toxic and should, therefore, be subject to the Agreement requirements of zero discharge and virtual elimination.

We then went on to recommend that the governments of the United States and Canada "adopt and apply a weight-of-evidence approach to the identification and virtual elimination of persistent toxic substances." And two years later, they responded. Canadian officials acknowledged support for the weight-of-evidence approach in evaluating contaminant impacts, in defending regulatory decisions in court, and in identifying and controlling persistent toxic substances. They almost got it. But not quite. If they did apply the weight-of-evidence approach, they would know that some persistent toxic substances cannot be controlled. The United States also acknowledged support of the approach, but did a much better job, in words, of understanding what the weight-of-evidence concept encompasses.

I found the following statement in the April 1993 *Concluding Report of the Carnegie Commission on Science, Technology, and Government*. It is pretty much on point.

> Scientists view their work as a body of working assumptions, of contingent and sometimes competing claims. Even when core insights are validated over time, the details of these hypotheses are subject to revision and refinement as a result of open criticism within the scientific communities. Scientists regard this gradual evolution of their theories through empirical testing as the pathway to the *truth*.
>
> In the legal system, however, all of the players are forced to make decisions at a particular moment in time, while this scientific process is going on. Given the indeterminacy of science, how can the judicial system make the best use of a scientific *fact?*

Those are two true statements and one good question. Both statements are valid methods of operating if you are a scientist or if you are a lawyer. But what if you are a bricklayer elected to Congress and many of your constituents are pressuring you to support the banning of an organochlorine that is being discharged by the local factory? As a member of Congress, you need to make a decision. You need to make it before the next election. You need to find out the economic effects of banning the discharge. You need to gather as much information as possible about the technical reasons why the stuff does or does not adversely affect humans. The scientists are sure it affects otters, but they do not have definitive proof that it has the same effect on humans, even though the physiology is similar. Your constituents keep pushing you. What do you do?

Do you wait for the scientific community to find its way down the neverending pathway toward the truth? Or do you weigh what information is available about the stuff and its effects, along with the socioeconomic impacts, and make a decision? The local factory will say, as industry always says, that you are being premature if you decide to introduce legislation to eliminate the stuff. What does that mean? Should you wait for another generation of injury before you do it? One thing you can do is ask the scientists for a personal, as opposed to a professional, view. You probably will hear that they do believe a precautionary principle should apply and that there is enough evidence to exercise caution. If your discipline is value neutral, your professional expressions can differ from your personal opinions, or so it seems.

I have learned, in my dealings with international scientists, that a panel of expert scientists looking at a specific issue will, in a majority of instances, find that there is no problem. They will look for definitive proof that there is a linkage between the alleged cause and the effect. They won't find absolute proof, so they will conclude that there is no linkage between the chemical and the effect. That does not mean there is not a linkage; it is just the way scientists are taught. That is the cautious way they operate.

A study was conducted by the National Institutes of Health and the Nutrition Foundation–International Life Sciences Institute on whether or not sugar contributes to hyperactivity, aggression, and mood changes in young children. I personally think it does. I can give my five-year-old grandson some candy and clearly watch him accelerate. The finding of the study, however, was that "it shows no evidence that sugar and sweeteners affect behavior or learning." Once again, scientists reduced down all the possibilities known to them in today's science, and since they could not find the positive, they found the negative. Did they find any evidence that sugar does not affect behavior?

We made an effort, over my last year or so on the commission, to determine how society can deal with such problems in the face of scientific uncertainty. The onerous substances in the Great Lakes and their suspected effects are similar to the Gulf War illnesses being suffered by the veterans, in relation to alleged chemical warfare; the only thing the vets have in common is where they were. Laypeople find it easy to know a truth. While scientists may suspect the truth of the public view, if there is no definitive scientific proof that those substances affect humans, they will publicly conclude no linkage. Scientists may not be able to find definitive proof that there is *not* a linkage between cause and effect, but they don't seem to be trained to deal with that side of things.

As in Agent Orange, leukemia clusters, other cancer clusters, clusters of babies born without brains, Love Canal, and on and on, it is a common scenario for the public to suffer an effect, see a potential cause, then tie the two together. Scientists who cannot find definitive proof will, however, deny the linkage. Government and industrial scientists and other bureaucrats will work hard to convince the public that its conclusion is wrong. Quite often, maybe fifteen, twenty, or twenty-five years later, the affected public is found to be correct. That doesn't happen because the scientists and bureaucrats are bad people; it's just that they are trained to operate within a framework of scientific certainty, when we live in a world of uncertainty.

An uncertain world is a world where decisions delayed may be a gamble too great to suffer. When we think in terms of children not doing well in school, in health, and, as they age, in reproductive prowess, we know that absolute scientific proof of harm is not the criterion for precaution. The potential for harm is a much more reasonable standard for decision making, when we are making decisions about the ability of our species, and others, to procreate. Too often the lack of absolute scientific proof is deliberately used as an excuse not to change our way of doing things. Too often it is my Republican colleagues who fall into the "sound science" maze.

Anyway, to me weight of evidence is like pornography. I know it when I see it!

Good Science/Bad Science

Early in my tenure on the International Joint Commission, I became very concerned when someone would say, "Your report is not based on good science." That claim would always cause a stir. The IJC scientific staff would review the report. We would then investigate all the findings of the various scientific workshops, roundtables, task forces, boards, councils, and all those many other group and individual sources considered by the commission before making decisions. We would consider evidence supporting a view as well as evidence refuting that view. We would be extremely careful, admittedly not always demanding absolute proof for just one side of an issue, and then we would issue another report.

Those who agreed with the conclusions of the report would be supportive and accept the underlying science. Some of those who disagreed with the report would tend to say, "Your report is not based on good science."

Now, I really don't want to spend a lot of time here attempting to distinguish good science from bad. I will say that you do need to put faith in experts who have no ax to grind, whether in agreement or disagreement with the prevailing views, and you obviously need confidence in your underlying science. Think about it. Who would want to make a decision based on bad science? I would just very briefly offer here what seem to be the definitions most often used by those who bring up the subject:

Good science: When the conclusions match those of the reader, the reader is sure the report was based on good science.

Bad science: When the conclusions disagree with the conclusions of the reader, obviously bad science has been applied.

Point of view seems to be the determining factor in this debate.

I would like to end this discussion quickly, because, as in the case of defining words and phrases such as virtual elimination, the good science/bad science debate is too often very much a dilatory tactic being deliberately practiced.

6

Reactions of Governments

THE REACTIONS OF GOVERNMENTS to new information are similar to the reaction of your lips after a shot of Novocain from the dentist—sort of numb, taking some time before they are able to get back to work in an effective fashion.

Governments are not geared for quick action. And when they do act quickly, normally they act wrongly. According to my friend Daniel F. Evans, Jr., government workers often confuse urgency with importance. He is right; they do. I have often received calls indicating that the urgency of something might require more resources, more effort, more time, more tax dollars. It would be at a point where the government folks were agog with excitement over such urgency. Thinking of my friend Dan and his words, I would always ask, "Is it important?" Usually, it was not. Canadians, by the way, are particularly prone to confusing urgency with importance. A typical situation might be as follows. At an Ottawa staff meeting one person might mention receiving an invitation to some event. The staff could discuss that letter for a couple of hours and someone might suggest that a response was required. A majority would agree. Then I would receive an international telephone call from a colleague saying we had an urgent matter to ponder. We needed a response to the invitation within a week. How were we to deal with such an urgent matter? My response would normally be that I didn't particularly care. However urgent it might be, it was not important.

Government workers may have the best of intentions, but they have difficulty in communicating concerns to their superiors. And, of course, for the first few months, or years, a great many people in government spend a great deal of time trying to decide whose job the new problem is not. Hey, man, it ain't my job; go see those guys at Agency X.

And then there is jurisdictional gridlock. In the Great Lakes ecosystem alone, you have two federal governments, eight state governments, two provincial governments, and many, many city, county, township, and regional governments. Each one of those jurisdictions has some degree of responsibility for the prevention and remediation of pollution. None has all of the responsibility. In the naive hope that you might find one jurisdiction with total responsibility for one problem, that jurisdiction won't have either the experience, the technology, the equipment, or the money (always the money) to deal with the problem.

I believe in political boundaries. How can we have pride of state or nation or city without them? And in my judgment, pride of self and community is essential to the effective and efficient resolution of societal problems. But jurisdictional gridlock is one of the great barriers to transboundary environmental actions by our governments. Among the various jurisdictions, it is estimated that there are over 60,000 environmental laws to which industry may be subjected. What nonsense that is!

A good question to ask about now is just who is government, anyway? Is it the public relations person who answers questions from the media and the public? Is it the scientist lost in a laboratory somewhere, who never or almost never sees anyone from the media or the real public? Is it the regulator who administers regulations which are set by someone else? Is it the top person at the United States Environmental Protection Agency or Environment Canada? Is it the lowest-level people at those agencies? Or is it the thousands and thousands of public employees in the middle of those vast bureaucracies?

Is it the many, many folks at the state and provincial level? Is it the mayor? How about the guy who runs the wastewater treatment plant? Or the prison warden who dumps untreated effluent into our waterways? Is it the person in charge of dumping chlorine into the water collection basin at the hydroelectric plant in an effort to kill off the zebra mussel? Or is it the school board president? Is it a guy named Fred whose job is to make sure his boss doesn't look bad? Or is it the elected boss who doesn't want to look bad—the member of Congress, the parliamentarian, the state or provincial legislator, or the member of the local council or assembly?

Or is it the president, the prime minister, the governor, the premier?

My experience has taught me to start at the top when I have a problem with government. But that is not so with the many, many people in the general public worried about the environment. They believe they are having meaningful dialogue with government when they are talking with regulators, to the midlevel management people of government—not to the people who make policy, but the people who execute policy made by others. To midlevel bureaucrats, change is anathema. They are comfortable doing things the way they have always done things. Lobbyists for industry, however, know the difference. They go to the top and get their way. And all the time, the worried members of the public are having a nice but ineffective dialogue with the midlevel people who are merely tasked with the job of carrying out the policy from above, policy that was influenced by the lobbyists.

Occasionally you will hear leaders from environmentalism bemoaning the access to elected officials available to industry lobbyists as opposed to access not available to random members of the public. They presume that elected leaders are available only to those who make big contributions. Not true. Oh, it may be a little difficult to walk into the Prime Minister's Office or the Oval Office, but every member of Congress and every parliamentarian is available to individual constituents. Most have home district offices. Most are home on a regular basis. Most are available to hear or read what any individual has to say. As is true in so many endeavors, persistence is the key to success.

Every two years, under the mandate of the Great Lakes Water Quality Agreement, the International Joint Commission reports to the governments of the United States and Canada with an assessment of how well those governments are doing in meeting the commitments of their agreement. The commission also makes a series of recommendations. Approximately two years later, after various meetings of bureaucrats, the midlevel people get their bosses to sign off on their bureaucratically agreed responses to the commission recommendations. In the intervening time, commissioners and staff, or others, have brought the recommendations to the attention of national legislators or their staffs for inclusion in law or regulation. The actions of governments at the top levels may not necessarily reflect what governments at the middle level have responded to the commission. All of this illustrates the futility of the formalized bureaucratic process. Realistically, that process has no meaning.

When government does decide to act, the action is not always what those demanding action were demanding. Often it is too little, too late. It can be reminiscent of the "Half Fast Waltz." Not too slow. Not too fast. Just half-fast. When action is taken, by law or by regulation, the result is quite often one law, or one rule, to solve one problem. We have laws relating to the various pathways of pollution. Laws for water. Laws for air. Regulations affecting runoff, or landfills, or groundwater, or whatever. The environmental protection agencies are divided into various departments relating to air, water, etc. Government funding to scientific endeavors is decided along the same individual mediums, which means new scientists, wanting government grants, are taught along those same narrow lines. While many government employees are promoting an ecosystem approach, government does not practice it. In fact, turf battles are often the order of the day.

As I write these words, Congress is rewriting the Clean Water Act. A couple of years ago, it passed the Clean Air Act. If the government was serious about an ecosystemic approach in its environmental endeavors, Congress would stop doing that. It would draft a Clean Environment Act, dealing with the concerns in a holistic manner. Former EPA administrator Bill Reilly used to lament the fact that the laws designed to clean up the environment often get in the way of the people trying to do so. Right he was. And too often those laws deal with errors of the past without advocating a serious move toward preventing the problems in the future.

The cynical among us can imagine that government, by putting its emphasis on the results of pollution instead of the cause, is only doing so to deceive the public into thinking the government is on top of the problem. We all know that you don't kill a snake by cutting off its tail. You cut off its head. And you don't stop pollution by attacking it at the end of its life; you attack it at the beginning. That would seem to be pretty basic stuff, but evidently it is all a little deep for government thinkers.

And then what about those laws or regulations? How do they work? Do they result in the removal from existence of substances that most all scientists and regulators agree are truly bad apples? No. Those laws and regulations usually set acceptable levels for discharge by industry. Exceptions are created, if industry provides some level of government with some amount of cash. The result is that a formal and legal method of discharging persistent toxic pollutants into the waters of North America has been established by the governments for the purpose of creating revenue-enhancing schemes.

I want you to recollect, once more, how toxics were defined by the United States and Canada in the Great Lakes Water Quality Agreement:

> Toxic substance means a substance which can cause death, disease, behavioral abnormalities, cancer, genetic mutations, physiological or reproductive malfunctions or physical deformities in any organism or its offspring, or which can become poisonous after concentration in the foodchain or in combination with other substances.

Those same governments that define persistent toxic substances in such dire terms are, for a fee, making exceptions and legalizing the discharge of substances which meet that definition and defy the policy agreed to, again by those same governments, in the Great Lakes Water Quality Agreement.

Now more questions are entering my relatively thick skull.

What is a reasonable fee for the industrial discharge of a substance that can cause death? Is it more or less than a fee to discharge a substance that can cause reproductive problems? Is death worth more, or less, than the inability to reproduce? Is this a chicken-and-egg question or a father-and-son question? Who developed this system? What were they thinking of when they did it? Who keeps this system going, and what are they thinking of as they do it? Did the public have input in deciding that a safe level of exposure existed for dioxin or PCBs? Did industry, through its lobbyists, have input? What about science? Were these decisions supported by good science or bad science? These are important questions now that science suggests that just one exposure to dioxin by a pregnant female may be enough to adversely affect her unborn child.

Are we polluting the waterways if, for example, the government, for a charge, says it is OK to do so? Industry says no. Government says no. The public says yes, because the regulatory standards are artificially arrived at by compromising science to meet the pressure of lobbyists, as well as government's need for hard cash. Are we polluting the waterways if the pollution is "nondetect"? If technology is not yet to the point where a substance can be detected coming out of the pipe, but it is biocumulating in the fish nearby, is it there? Industry says no, because it cannot be detected. Government shrugs. The public says yes, because how else does it get in the fat of fish?

These arguments tend to be enigmatic. The real question to be addressed is, since the governments of the United States and Canada agreed, as late as 1987, that such substances are so harmful that they should be virtually eliminated, why do these same governments authorize the issuance of permits to industry to legally discharge these substances? The answer is that it's simply a matter of government revenue! The answer does not deal with jobs or social disruption, because these serious concerns could be dealt with by a reasonable transition timetable in a sunsetting process. Are governments so hungry for a few more dollars that they should authorize the discharge of something that they agree can cause death, genetic mutations, and physical deformities?

Is anyone in government even considering such questions?

Do morals, in any way, factor into these considerations?

In my own state, the governor found himself in a funk because legislators would not grant him his wished-for tax increase in 1993. He decided to get even by cutting the budget of the Department of Environmental Management and trying to turn over the permitting process to the federal government. The claim, to pressure legislators to do his will, was that industries would not come to Indiana because they could not get permits to discharge various pollutants. Coming through the back door, and for all the wrong reasons, maybe my governor did the right thing. Oh, it is not right to give surrounding states a leg up on economic development activity because it is easier to license pollution in those surrounding states. But hopefully the actions of my governor just might give someone cause to consider the ethics of all this inanity.

It seems to me, as a relatively simple guy, that either the governments of the United States and Canada should keep the commitments they have made in the Great Lakes Water Quality Agreement and stop legalizing, through permits for a fee, the discharge of persistent toxic substances into the Great Lakes, or they should revoke the words by which they made those commitments. It is basically dishonest to pledge to do one thing and then, for a fee, do another.

Those were some of the thoughts in my mind as we commissioners of the International Joint Commission recommended to the governments that regulation alone would never get them to the virtual elimination of the discharge of persistent toxic substances. We said that a sunsetting process was necessary for the most onerous of these substances—a process that would set a time certain to take such substances out of existence. Then we heard from government regulators—who feared that a sunsetting process might remove a need for their jobs—saying that bans are part of a regulatory process and other such things.

Now you have to stop here and think about what was just said. You need to realize that for many in government, words either have no meaning or multiple meanings. *Ban* doesn't mean not allowing use in some instances. The United States says it has canceled DDT, but *canceled* does not mean that it is not available for purchase or use in the United States, as the Virtual Elimination Task Force found in 1993. People in government take words that they know have specific meanings within the public sphere and give them different meanings for their purposes. Then they start to believe that their definitions have real meaning—thus the argument that banning is a regulatory action. From my point of view, and I think the public point of view, if something does not exist, it would be pretty darn hard to regulate it.

It is easy to get lost in these debates over the meanings of words, while all the time trying to prod governments to action. *Virtual elimination* is a phrase that the two federal governments put into their agreement with each other. If they didn't know what that phrase meant, why in the world did they include it in a formal agreement between two great nations? They did know. They meant "to the extent possible." That's easy. What's the big deal? Well, either it is a big deal, or people, especially scientists, regulators, and industry lobbyists, just want to delay action by continually debating what is meant by *virtual.*

And how about zero? What does *zero* mean in relation to the zero discharge philosophy adopted by the United States and Canada? I have no problem in deciding that it means nothing. Scientists and regulators have spent years trying to come to grips with what *zero* means. And not only that, they would debate the very existence of zero.

Does nothing exist? No. I think not. And that is the goal for the discharge of persistent toxic substances: nonexistence. Even the dictionary gives differing and conflicting meanings, but all dictionaries agree on at least one definition of *zero* that we should all accept, and then forget about it. That definition is "nothing, nil."

And then we have *ecosystem approach,* another phrase the governments of the United States and Canada decided should be applied in their efforts to prevent or remediate pollution in the Great Lakes. Governmental employees can spend a career debating the meaning of *ecosystem* and trying to build frameworks and boundaries for it. Of course, boundaries and frameworks defeat the concept of ecosystemic thought. These officials also seemed to be more concerned about how to do it than what it is. *Ecosystem approach* simply means that all facets of the system are to be considered in trying to deal with any one facet, that everything is interrelated. That is why it is somewhat cynical for government to create separate laws for clean water and clean air.

I wonder how many years were wasted by scientists, by regulators, by bureaucrats, and how unnecessarily long the delay was successfully fostered by lobbyists, over the debate about the meaning of words formally used by their own governments?

I guess we also need to ask questions about the desirability of government action. What is the best way to foster the goals of the Great Lakes Water Quality Agreement or to achieve pollution prevention continentwide? Is it to have governments pass laws to force industry to do something? I think not. What does government know about industry? Industry should do the job for itself. It will do the job better in a process of its own, using the ingenuity of the free enterprise system. But how do we get industry to face up to the level of stewardship that it should be exercising on its own? That is a question for another chapter.

And when government does act, it is increasingly in the form of unfunded mandates. The higher level of government orders the lower level to pursue an environmental objective, but then does not give the lower level the resources to do what is mandated. Many people think unfunded mandates are unfair. They are. They are also a cowardly action by one level of government afraid to raise taxes, ordering something done at a lower level and forcing tax increases on states and municipalities.

On May 25, 1994, I testified before the Committee on Public Works and Transportation of the U.S. House of Representatives as it considered the Clean Water Act. The administrator of the Environmental Protection Agency was also there, along with several other experts and a few victims of environmental harm. Instead of quizzing those present on how to better their legislation, the representatives seemed to be more interested in speech making for their own benefit. I did find Representative Wayne Gilchrest of Maryland, whom I had not previously met, to be penetrating, perceptive, and sincere in his questioning. But all in all, I found this opportunity to give testimony to the highest legislative body in our land, relative to legislation important to our nation, to be pretty much a wasted effort. I could have spent my time better elsewhere. People seem to think contemporary government is not working. After days such as that one when major environmental legislation was under consideration, I think I must agree. At the very least, government is not working well.

I don't want to leave the impression that all government employees are without virtue. Some are great. A fellow named Tony Wagner, formerly with Environment Canada, is a highly dedicated, responsible, and serious career government employee who donates to society a great deal of his time on weekends and evenings in his personal and professional capacities. Salvatore Pagano, from New York State government, is another. On the commission staff, David LaRoche and Geoffrey Thornburn are caring, hard-working deep thinkers, with a great ability to communicate their thoughts. LaRoche is particularly forward looking in his concern for our society's future. Good examples of public employees who are gentle, competent, and caring would be Alan Clarke in Ottawa, Frank Bevaqua in Washington, and Sally Cole-Misch in Windsor, Ontario. James Chandler, in Washington, could be the model for integrity, fairness, and hard work. And Rita Kerner did yeoman service to get me to all the places around North America where I had to go for four and one-half years.

And I don't want to leave the impression that governments don't occasionally do the right thing. Sometimes they do get it. As I was leaving the commission early in 1994, the Canadian government issued a Priority Substance List Assessment Report on Chlorinated Wastewater Effluents. It determined that chlorinated municipal waste-water discharges were toxic. That decision came just a few months after the midlevel Canadian government folks had somewhat minimized a holistic recommendation from the commission on chlorinated substances. And even more important, on January 28, 1994, the Clinton Administration sent to Congress its proposals for the Clean Water Act update. Included were calls for a serious study on chlorine and chlorinated compounds and one to determine toxic chemical effects on sperm counts, breast cancer, and reproductive, immune, endocrine, and nervous system health effects. Those proposals came just a few months after midlevel U.S. bureaucrats had rejected the commission's holistic chlorine recommendation.

Like everything else, government shows us the good and the bad. The new developments indicate that some people, at the highest level of government in two separate nations, are considering the words and ideas put forth by the International Joint Commission from 1990 through 1994. The developments sound good. We will just have to wait and see if the federal governments really do create and enforce new laws.

Unfortunately, too often government shows us apathy. It is fearful to make waves, afraid that an innovative idea may be a hindrance to some official's career advancement, afraid that bucking the demands of lobbyists might make reelection more difficult, reluctant to enforce laws that might ruffle a feather or two. Just consider how one government deals with tobacco. The U.S. government promotes the growth and sale of tobacco through international trade negotiations and various domestic farm programs. At the same time, that same government labels the smoking of tobacco as harmful to our health, a carcinogen. And then that same government conducts multiple educational programs telling people not to use tobacco. But that same government does not classify tobacco as a drug or a food. For if it did, some standard of product safety would be required. Instead, through the imagination of lobbyists, tobacco is classified by the government as a "device of pleasure," with no attendant safety standards required. Such hypocrisy in government action is not unusual.

A new way of thinking is needed. But of course a new way of thinking is discouraged by a good many in the current crop of government thinkers. Let's not do anything different from the way we have been trained. Let's continue to do what we have always done, because we know how to do that so well. Let's treat all poisons in the same way we treated tobacco.

A federal government assistant secretary at a January 1994 meeting about estrogens in the environment said that it took forty years to get action on cigarette smoking and suggested that it would take even longer for the now worrisome hormone-mimicking compounds because of their important industrial uses. That old way of thinking has become a barrier to progress. Another tremendous barrier is the inability of government to enforce current environmental laws. These laws, some 60,000 of them, being single-medium oriented and normally not including target dates for compliance, also become barriers to success. In trying to achieve the goal of environmental protection, government has become one of the most troublesome problems: a barrier to environmental progress.

Remedial action plans in the Great Lakes are another example. The International Joint Commission recommended and the two federal governments accepted forty-three areas of concern. Once an area of concern was declared, a remedial action plan (RAP) was required, with the commission reviewing progress at three stages. Stage one is defining the problems; stage two is establishing methods of cleaning up the problems; and stage three is the actual cleanup.

The costs of cleaning up the forty-three areas of concern are astronomic—billions and billions of dollars, more dollars than almost any level of government will ever have available. But the beauty of RAPs is that they depend upon innovation. They depend upon public participation. They depend upon local governments, local industry, the professions, academia, not just on federal dollars. It was a new theory, a new way of thinking. My predecessors on the International Joint Commission deserve great plaudits for such an innovative idea, an idea that taps into the ingenuity of the free peoples of Canada and the United States.

But most government bureaucracies cannot deal with innovation. In some cases, as in Michigan before John Engler took charge as governor, the bureaucrats treated remedial action plans as just another bureaucratic regulatory activity, and they struggled. The Province of Ontario was not much better, except for the Hamilton Harbor RAP, which is an example of environmental remediation that should be emulated around the world. The binational RAPs, the ones that had one river separating two nations, with the pollutants not aware of the political line in the center of the river, have been problems. Those problems tend to be cultural and bureaucratic rather than technical. Obviously, when such things happen, government becomes a barrier to achieving success.

Government in the State of Ohio, on the other hand, has grasped the true potential of remedial action plans. Officials there have let the interested public take the lead and put state agencies in a supportive position. Ohio RAPs, being people oriented, are achieving the innovative funding and ingenuity that the conceivers of the original idea had in mind. But generally, contemporary governments are slow to act and slow to react. Officials lack the facts necessary to make decisions, or so they say.

Government leaders lately have spent a great deal of time debating what to do about, and how to treat, the growing number of homosexuals in our society. But they do nothing to try to learn why there might be a growing number of homosexuals. Could it be that doses of persistent toxic substances are affecting the sexual preferences of the progeny of exposed females? Was their hormonal future altered while in the womb? There is some science to indicate that possibility, especially with wildlife. Since some elected officials seem to be intent on debating the plight of homosexuals, why not also investigate environmental factors that might be causing the increase, instead of simply proclaiming its normalcy?

There are worldwide studies indicating that young men today have lost 50 percent of the sperm count that men around the world used to have. "A young man today is only half the man his grandfather was" is the way one leading scientist says it. That sounds serious. Should not some elected official, somewhere, sometime, be worried about that possibility? Does the continued discharge of persistent toxic substances have any connection with the decline of spermatozoa?

I personally expect very little from government. I am a firm believer in limited government. But the limits should be set based upon what a knowing people will accept, on what the people want. Those limits should not be expanded or reduced simply because of the limited abilities and concerns of many of the people we now have leading our governments, as so often now seems to be the case. Groucho Marx once said that "politics is the art of looking for trouble, finding it everywhere, diagnosing it incorrectly, and applying the wrong remedies." I don't know for sure when Groucho said that humorous line, or even if he intended it to be humorous. Today his words seem to be truer than ever before.

7

Reactions of Industry

THE REACTIONS OF INDUSTRY, specifically the chemical industry, surprised me most. Instead of joining in the environmental discussion, instead of making their case, instead of discussing potential solutions, industry officials built barriers to dialogue. They seemed to try very hard to live up to the reputation given to them by their nemesis, the organized environmental groups. That reaction was disturbing to me, because I had spent a lifetime in support of industry. My most basic philosophical beliefs include the thought that we cannot succeed as a free nation without a free market economic system. I expected more from the captains of industry.

I am a born competitor. Competition, I believe, must be an essential ingredient for individual freedom to flourish. Entrepreneurism is essential to the opportunity of a quality life-style for us all. I don't believe that all Americans should be equal; that would be boring and fail. I do believe that all Americans should have equal opportunities and equal protection under the law. And if an individual takes on the challenges of an opportunity and succeeds, then clearly that individual should be rewarded for the ingenuity and hard work that resulted in improved economic activity, job creation, and profit.

But with opportunity comes responsibility. An individual's efforts may be stimulated by a desire to better his or her own standard of living. But in carrying out that effort, in undertaking that opportunity, he or she should do nothing to harm anyone else. Such a person should be willing to take precaution, especially environmentally, when precaution is in order. That is what I found so disappointing in the reactions of industry in general when confronted with the evidence, or the suspicion, that a chemical feed stock used in a manufacturing process may harm an unsuspecting person at some point in time (whether that person is related or unrelated to the manufacturing process).

Oh, there are many examples of individual companies accomplishing great things in pollution prevention and in waste reduction. I don't want to imply otherwise. For example, the E. B. Eddy group is a large Canadian firm involved in forest products, sawmills, and pulp and paper mills. The company has developed a set of principles for a sustainable development, proclaiming that a forest products company:

- integrates environmental management criteria into the corporate decision-making process;
- recognizes that people and reputation are among its most valuable resources and that the education, training and motivation of its employees to conduct their activities in an environmentally responsible manner will ensure that its reputation is maintained;
- ensures that customers' expectations for service and product quality are met or exceeded while striving for excellence in environmental performance;
- works in partnership with customers to encourage the safe distribution, use, storage and disposal of products and also requires that the actions of suppliers be consistent with the concept of sustainable development;
- adheres to a forest management philosophy that focuses on the provision of a reliable fibre supply and conservation of biodiversity through forest renewal and integrated resource management;
- reduces pollution at source by incorporating process modification using the best available technology that is economically achievable;
- ensures that operations take into account the efficient use of energy and materials, the sustainable use of natural resource, the minimization of waste generation, and the safe and responsible disposal of residual wastes;
- develops products that have no undue environmental impact, are safe in their intended use, and can be recycled, re-used or disposed of safely;
- maintains open and honest communication on all environmental concerns, provides opportunities or input on the impacts of the operations, and reports on environmental performance and compliance regularly; and

- contributes to the development of public policy, through business, governmental and educational initiatives that will enhance the importance of sustainable development.

In my own hometown, the large pharmaceutical firm Eli Lilly & Company has developed a similar set of principles that should result in good stewardship.

In general, however, when presented with an unfavorable proposition, industry goes into a siege mentality. The predominant response is denial. And then immediately after denial come the tactics. Amateurish tactics. Industry lobbyists, like most all lobbyists, are just trying to make a buck. They know the positions of the people paying them, and to earn their retainer they work hard to make sure no changes take place. I suppose that is the classic definition of a conservative, someone who wants no change at all. That is the definition used by U.S. news media in describing the Russian Communists who like the old ways and try to get their followers to go on rampages to battle against change. Conservative is what the media call the bad guys in Somalia, Haiti, China, and elsewhere when it gives national reporters an opportunity to imply bad things about those who are conservative.

But in the United States, conservative has a different connotation. I am a conservative. I oppose large government. I favor limited government. I support wholeheartedly the free enterprise system. I believe the individual is supreme. I know that my fellow citizens and I know better what is good for us than does anyone in government. I believe that values are important. Right is better than wrong and there can be a clear distinction between the two. And I believe that I am responsible for my actions. I also believe that change is not necessarily bad. In fact, change is the only constant that we can depend upon in this modern society. Obviously, change just for the sake of change is of no value. Times of change, however, can also be times of great opportunity if, as a leader, you remain alert.

Change has been a normal occurrence over my lifetime. Each decade has brought new ideas, new thoughts, new products, new attitudes, new lifestyles. The 1990 census, however, brings us notice of change that is hard to believe for people of my age. We learn that the decade of the 1980s saw the United States population grow more slowly than in any decade in history, except the decade in which I was born during the Great Depression, with the number of children under age eighteen in decline. We learn that there are now more childless married couples than there are couples with children, with U.S. births just barely at the replacement rate as determined by demographers. We learn that more foreign-born residents now live in the United

States than at any other time in our history. How do we deal with change of such magnitude?

On my tour with the International Joint Commission I watched the chemical industry, through its lobbyists, fight any potential for change and then try to avoid responsibility for its actions. In fact, chemical industry lobbyists often tacitly deny that their benefactors do what they do. Analogous to administration officials appearing before congressional committees, the lobbyists use tricky, qualifying words to deflect truth. Rather than join the dialogue regarding the responsibility we all have to future generations, their typical tactic was to disrupt such dialogue.

At a variety of public meetings on the environment, I personally watched the lobbyists organize employees from large companies, urging them to spread themselves around the room to make sure one of their own was in each discussion group, at each table, to disrupt and make sure that none of the discussion groups came to any conclusions adverse to their position. Another tactic was to make sure industry representatives made every other statement at public hearings, which, of course, resulted in meaningless hearings. You know, one person comes to the microphone saying a specific chemical is bad, then the industry representative comes to the mike saying that chemical is good, and on and on. No dialogue, just conflicting statements.

So where is the extreme? Is it with those in the environmental movement who say everything about a specific substance is harmful to wildlife, humans, and the entire ecosystem? Or is it with industry, which says nothing about a persistent toxic substance is harmful and never was? It seems to me that both positions tend to be out there on the fringe of irresponsibility. Why not come to a common table and, through dialogue, prove your point? Bring your facts with you. Display your research. Substantiate your position. Let the first criterion be protecting unsuspecting members of the public from harm and the second criterion the rights of industry to operate freely in the marketplace. These two criteria should be one, the right to a free market as long as those actions do not harm the physical or mental well being of others.

But let's think about all that. Why should industry want to be on either extreme? As a bulwark of our free society, it should be the epitome of the center. I have concluded that it is the lobbyist mentality that drives industry to the extreme. It is the fallback position of denial, diversion, and delay that pushes industry to the fringe. It is a failure to recognize the truth, as many people see the truth. It is the lobbyist tactic of fear and paranoia in denouncing all efforts to prevent adverse effects to human and ecosystem health by claiming that every action of pollution prevention or remediation will cost "zillions" of jobs. The reasonable position would seem to be one that would provide environmental protection and economic growth, yet not take away job opportunities or health options from citizens of Canada or the United States. Not a pie-in-the-sky position but an option that is real. The cynical position is the one that promotes the thought that environmental protection and economic growth are mutually exclusive. They are not.

For the *Seventh Biennial Report*, I drafted the following thought which became commission recommendation number 17:

> Senior officers of business enterprises in and near the Great Lakes basin conduct environmental audits of their procurement, production and marketing activities in relation to the goals of the Great Lakes Water Quality Agreement; develop and announce corporate environmental stewardship policies which include the concept of sustainable development; and prepare annual reports relating to that policy for public review and regular review by the enterprise's senior management body.

Business will argue that trade secrets will be exposed should such a policy be enacted. That need not be. Trade secrets can be protected. The critical point is for society to move toward an open dialogue about chemical discharges and away from denial and secrecy at all costs.

My fear, as a supporter of industry in a free market, is that its very obdurateness might lead to its ultimate undoing. It is much like the unreasonableness of the health care industry in the United States, which has caused such problems for the profession and to our ability to pay for the services it provides. Throughout my decades of political activity, Americans have warned their doctors that unless they returned to a time when total care and real concern for the patient were primary factors in their practice, the public would not oppose the socialization of their profession. Instead, for thirty years, physicians generally became more remote from their patients and health costs escalated beyond reason. Physicians never really tried to police their own profession, never considered the ramifications of not knowing, or caring, about the patient's total personal needs. As a result, during most of 1994, the specter of socialized medicine no longer seemed remote.

My own profession, the law, is quickly falling into the same trap as did the health care profession. The reputation of the legal profession is suffering, to say the least. Both Canada and the United States are nations of laws. Some think that is wrong. A nation of peoples, they say, is what we should be. However, unless individual freedoms are based in law, we can never hope to be nations of peoples, at least free peoples. In law school, I found that two basic interests motivated my fellow students. All found fascination in the law, and properly so. Our common heritage, in the United States and Canada, is based upon the rights of individuals under the law, going all the way back to the Magna Carta. But beyond that, some law students were motivated by the desire to use their knowledge to earn a good living, while others were motivated by the desire to use their learning to perform a service for others. There is nothing wrong with either desire, and I recognize that it is quite possible to simultaneously do them both.

When Vice President Dan Quayle, a lawyer, proposed to the American Bar Association that lawyers take a look at a profession going astray, the first reaction of the legal profession was denial. The second reaction was denial, and so on. But Dan Quayle was right about this, as he was about so many other issues. The needs of the client must be the first priority of a lawyer. The needs of society come in at a close second. The needs and wants of a good lawyer are down the scale a ways. If a lawyer gives preference to the needs of the client and the needs of society, the lawyer will prosper personally. If the needs and wants of the lawyer are first on the scale, he or she may earn a good living, but it is that kind of unreasonableness that will bring the whole house of cards tumbling down at some point.

My own state bar association in Indiana, to deal with the declining reputation of the profession, has created a foundation to publicize good works done by attorneys. Most lawyers give time, talent, and money to help those in need, and it is fine for the bar association to recognize those who do. But that's not a way to recover the reputation of the bar. The way you do that is to put the needs of the client first, with the needs of society a close second. Honesty in all endeavors also would be helpful.

So yes, new thinking is in order all around. As a political leader I always found that times of change provided the opportunity to do great things. I thought a very positive change in the Great Lakes Basin would be the creation of the Council of Great Lakes Industries. My reason for so thinking was the obvious. If industry is not a part of the dialogue, progress in preventing pollution will not occur. Unfortunately, the spokespeople for the new industry council became agents of denial and diversion instead of agents of dialogue.

One of the early meetings I had with international industry in my role as United States Chairman of the International Joint Commission was with the Committee on Canada/United States Relations of the Great Lakes Chamber of Commerce in Toronto. The meeting was on January 17, 1991. That date doesn't mean much, I guess. It is not planted in our memory as are other dates of war, such as December 7. But that was the date that the Gulf War began with heavy U.S. air activity over Baghdad. The night before, I had been in the White House as a friend of mine was being sworn in to an important responsibility by the Vice President of the United States. I did notice that Pennsylvania Avenue was barricaded in front of the White House. I also noticed those guys dressed in black, like cat burglars, with automatic weapons on the roofs of that bastion of power. So I had a suspicion war was imminent.

The next evening I caught a plane from Washington to Toronto so I could attend the Chamber of Commerce meeting the next day. As I normally do on airplane flights, I was reading some nondescript book, intent on keeping my brain occupied but not challenged for a few hours and succeeding in doing so. I had forgotten about the prospects of war when the pilot's voice came over the loudspeaker saying he would keep us abreast of the war news. None of the passengers knew the war had started and, of course, the pilot never came back on with any news. Did you ever wonder what pilots are thinking about when they announce unintelligible messages at midflight?

But anyway, we finally landed at the Toronto airport, and in looking back at my remarks to the International Chamber of Commerce, I see that I said to the gathered representatives of business and industry from two nations:

> I want to be blunt with you today. It is not enough to say that current industrial practices and processes that result in pollution, particularly the creation of persistent toxic substances, simply reflect what society wants. That argument, if you will excuse the Great Lakes pun, will no longer hold water. Business and industry can no longer hide behind the guise of market forces which were in no small part created by its own advertising. Nor can fanatical environmentalists any longer hide behind the allegation that the profit motive is the cause of all ecological evils.

And I said:

> I think business and industry are at a crossroads with regard to their environmental stance. You are going to have to choose between being seen as the societal entity constantly waging a rear guard action to delay environmental progress, or as a positive initiator of specific efforts reflective of the kind of environmental care and sensitivity that will make the world a better place for those who come after us. I think you would be well served, I think you would be protective of your own best interests, if you were to choose the latter course.

I believed those words to be wise. Many businesses have adopted policies of pollution reduction, and some have opted for pollution prevention. They have success stories to tell, but it is hard to filter those positive stories through all the other rhetoric. I have observed some industry representatives keeping representatives of industries that have achieved success in finding alternatives to dangerous substances out of the public debate, because they say it would be anti-industry for them to proclaim their successes. And, sadly, their colleagues who are doing the right things accept that logic of the denial crowd to avoid unnecessary controversy. That scenario occurred during the planning of the 1993 biennial meeting of the International Joint Commission. Just another lobbyist tactic.

Those same industry lobbyists can spread any word they want to spread, true or not, and business executives always seem willing to believe them. Those same lobbyists can tell executives of small and large companies in their industry that science is overwhelmingly on their side. The executives tend to believe the lobbyists, evidently without ever looking at such alleged science, or never even asking to see it. Those same lobbyists can tell their people, and others, that an international commission has bad science or no science on which to base any of its recommendations, and their clients seem to believe such statements without question or doubt. Those same lobbyists can tell their clients that a commission recommended an *immediate* ban on chlorinated drinking water and chlorine use in the pharmaceutical industry and be believed without the believers checking any of the facts. Those same lobbyists can tell their business people that probusiness conservatives, like me, are antibusiness liberals, and the business people seem to blindly believe what they are told.

I ponder why that is. Are those business leaders too busy in their small world to check the facts? Are they uncaring? Is their thinking perspective too narrow? Has our education system failed them too? Are not those attitudes and blind acceptance of tactical misstatements more dangerous to business opportunity than some small international commission? Does not such behavior create a clear and present danger to the perpetuation of the American dream?

Let's spend some time talking about the lobbyist mentality exercised by the chemical industry in the summer and fall of 1993. As mentioned earlier, in the Great Lakes Water Quality Agreement the United States and Canada decreed it to be their policy that the discharge of persistent toxic substances was to be virtually eliminated. For years the governments have successfully tried to ratchet down the discharge of such onerous substances. In 1992, the International Joint Commission recommended to the governments that regulation alone would never achieve such virtual elimination. To meet their policy objectives, we recommended that the governments must set times certain when these onerous substances would be taken out of existence. No manufacture! No distribution! No use! No storage! We suggested a sunsetting process with industry at the table where decisions are made. The process would need to be orderly and allow enough time so as to not seriously disrupt social and economic activity. Since many of these onerous substances, DDT, PCBs, dioxins, furans and so on, have chlorine as a common precursor, we recommended a sunsetting process for chlorine as an industrial feed stock.

The chemical industry officials decided they were under attack, so they attacked back. They hired a public relations firm. They created a council made up of lobbyists. The purpose of the council was to convince their industry members, elected officials, the media, and others that six conservative commissioners on the International Joint Commission were either socialists or stupid. They told everyone that our motive was to put jobs in jeopardy, not to protect human health. The lobbyists did not mention, I feel quite sure, the commission's formal duty under the Great Lakes Water Quality Agreement, as assigned by the governments of the United States and Canada.

They, with a reported five-million-dollar budget, distorted our recommendation. They told all who would listen that we had attacked the manufacture of pharmaceuticals, the process of treating wastewater, and procedures for purifying drinking water—all statements they knew to be false. Probably the goofiest lobbyist untruth was that the commission was opposed to table salt. The lobbyists employed tactics that, if successful, would divert blame off the shoulders of the chemical industry and onto the backs of six obscure commissioners and their advisors. They used tactics that clearly displayed their naivete. And, yes, it does scare me that such naive tactics might work when applied to elected officials.

I had a fax machine in my home while serving on the commission. It was in my grown son's old bedroom, which I now use as an office. Into that office, strewing themselves all over the floor, using up all of my fax paper (purchased with personal funds), came letter after letter. Hundreds of them. All with the exact same wording. Some letter writers were so lazy they even sent along the form letter and instructions sent to them by the lobbyists. The letters would come from well-meaning employees of large companies who had been told some international commission was after their jobs. The letters would come from small and large business people who had been told that I personally was on a mission to destroy their ability to make a living. Letters would be sent to local officeholders who would then fax their own letters to the floor of my grown son's old bedroom. All of the letters had the exact same wording. Hundreds of letters from people who are supposed to be somewhat intelligent as business and political leaders. In one case those same lobbyist words came to us as a resolution from the City Council of Niagara Falls, New York. In other cases those same lobbyist-prepared words came to us as newspaper editorials.

In all my years of politics, I never worried too much about lobbyists. I knew them. They gave money to campaigns I supported. Some gave to my opponents. Some rode the fence and gave to both sides. Some of them I liked as individuals, some of them I did not. Some could be relied upon for good information. Some could not. But the candidates and officeholders with whom I worked did not change their votes or opinions based upon the suggestions or pleadings of a lobbyist. In fact, much of my time as a campaign manager and party chairman was spent in keeping lobbyists away from my candidates and officeholders. Knowing the lobbyists as I did, and knowing the quality of my candidates and officeholders, I never worried too much about the lobbyists having undue influence on decisions of importance.

But here I was as a front-row witness to elected officials doing whatever was asked of them by lobbyists, even a formal governmental resolution using words written by the lobbyists, being read in person by Andrew M. Walker, a councilman from Niagara Falls, who evidently did not realize that we knew the words were not his. The politicians evidently did such things because they had received letters, telephone calls, and personal visits from local business people conveying untruths transported to them through form letters written by lobbyists.

And then, I hear, in the 1994 Senate Foreign Relations Committee confirmation hearing for my successor, those very same lobbyist-generated words came spewing out once more. Several United States senators, one a former Republican state chairman colleague of mine, submitted identical lists of questions obviously written by the chemical industry lobbyists in their continuing effort to eliminate any potential search for the truth. Why would such normally good people, as I know my former colleague from Georgia to be, blindly fall prey to such lobbyist tactics? Did they think about it? Did they question the meaning of what they were doing? Or was it just the bad judgment of a staffer? It would seem to me that if you did not know what you were doing, the best course would be to do nothing (at least until you researched the facts).

Some members of the media also fell prey to the work of the lobbyists, but fortunately not many. Even though news conferences with local business people were organized by the lobbyists and held in U.S. cities around the Great Lakes Basin, the resulting news stories tended to dwell more on the dangers of the chemicals the lobbyists claimed to be pure or controllable.

In October 1993 the commission held a biennial meeting in Windsor, Ontario. Business and industry had traditionally ignored meetings and workshops that considered environmental issues relative to industrial chemicals or processes. In 1991, a few representatives of industry attended the International Joint Commission biennial meeting in Traverse City, Michigan. They heard a public concern that they had previously not heard. And then in early 1992, the commission recommendation on chlorine use certainly caught the attention of the chemistry industry.

By 1993 industry was paying a lot of attention to the activities of the International Joint Commission. Industry encouraged many of its technical people to attend the biennial meeting. The results were interesting. The technical people from industry found a commission involved with the best scientists in the Great Lakes Basin, along with eminent scientists from around the world. They found many industry representatives who had moved beyond denial and were promoting their successes in finding alternatives to the discharge of harmful pollutants. They found respected political leaders supporting commission activities. Most important, these good people who are proud and serious industrial scientists and engineers found a strong gathering of a concerned and informed public that will not just go away.

Industry held a workshop at that same meeting, bringing in two hired consultants and two serious scientists. But the lobbyists seriously underestimated the audience. The panel gave little science to back the points of view expressed. Even industry technical people went to the microphones to challenge conclusions of the industry science panel. Before the four-day meeting ended, however, representatives of industry were deeply involved in the dialogue of the meeting, as they must be in all such discussions. The battle to prevent pollution will fail if industry is not a full player at the decision-making table.

Coming into the meeting, the industry representatives' view was narrow, as if horse blinders kept them from seeing what was going on around them. One industry technician said he had been trying, in his work, to do the most good for the largest number of people. He was immediately confronted by representatives of the people who are most frequently exposed to dangerous chemicals. Hopefully he broadened his thinking a little as a result of that confrontation and will give some thought to the people we sacrifice, and in what ways, as we try to do the most good for the largest number.

The former mayor of Toronto, David Crombie, made several pertinent points as the keynote speaker. He pointed out that it was not enough to just claim that the goals of environmental protection and economic growth are not mutually exclusive. He encouraged the audience, consisting of representatives of governments, industry, environmental groups, and the public, to understand that "economic health and environmental health are mutually interdependent." He was correct, of course, and it seems obvious to me that such interdependence requires industry to put a precautionary environmental ethic into its decision-making process. It is equally obvious that environmentalists need to understand that a decent quality of life and individual freedom are reliant on a strong free enterprise system.

As I left the commission in 1994 I had a lingering question for my friends in industry. What's wrong with precaution? I also feared that the chemical manufacturers might be working against their own interests by building a wall of denial. Should the science continue to mount and should government decide finally that immediate action is called for, such as the immediate banning of a feed stock, then gigantic socioeconomic disruption could occur. A little precaution could prevent such a disaster.

Crombie said some other words that stuck with me. Words that explain why the environmental movement is growing. Why so many people are stepping forward demanding action. People not organized by anyone; not just Democrats or Republicans, both liberals and conservatives. Just many, many people who have an environmental problem in their community and who are frustrated because they cannot get the attention of the polluter or the government to prevent additional pollution or to clean up past mistakes.

Crombie said something like this: "When people start asking questions about nature, they are, in reality, asking questions about their God. Their activities and their concerns are based in their religious beliefs. And for that reason, they have staying power and will not be going away soon. In all probability, their numbers will continue to grow." This view of what motivates those who are concerned about environmental problems was, I think, another startling realization for the industry people present in Windsor, across the fouled Detroit River from the City of Detroit.

Hopefully, a prescient dialogue is about to begin. A dialogue with environmentalists, industry, and governments at the same table. For the dialogue to work, the industry participants must be executives, not merely hired lobbyists. If that dialogue works, governments could be excused from the table and industry could do what it should do in a voluntary fashion, with the monitoring and assistance of the public environmental community.

Why should government be excused? The first reason is simply because governments don't do these kinds of things very well. Second, the ingenuity of entrepreneurs can solve any problem once they become properly motivated. Ingenuity, you might be surprised to learn, is not a common bureaucratic characteristic.

8

Reactions of Organized Environmental Groups

RUSH LIMBAUGH IS RIGHT! Most of the leaders of organized environmental groups are very liberal in their political philosophies. Many I have come to know are true socialists. Occasionally, as one of them will be speaking about the real ills of the environment, he or she will drift off into dream-world words, describing how the ills of society could be solved once and for all, if only we had a benevolent government, if only we had someone in charge who would take all the excess wealth away from the producers in society and give it to those who mysteriously know best what is best for all of us. It is similar to the one-man-can-solve-all-problems attitude of those U.S. voters, of a different philosophy, who wanted Ross Perot to take charge of all our problems, get under the hood, and fix it.

It is also similar to the attitudes of those who promoted the philosophies of Marx and Engels eighty years ago, or the attitudes of those who supported Mussolini seventy years ago. Different philosophies maybe, but providing the same results for the people: an end to democracy, an end to individual freedom. What can be frightening is to consider the thought that Americans may be tiring of democracy, impatient with it, ignorant of its responsibilities. Déjà vu, those people might say who remember such impatience with the European democracies following World War I. My philosophical observations (along with 1994 vote results) cause me not to worry too much about those few politically misguided souls of organized environmentalism, because most of the people worried about an environmental problem are not motivated by political philosophy. They are motivated by a specific environmental problem in their community and by the desire to correct it. A sick child is often at the center of their worries. Such individuals are not the environmentalists we read and hear about in the news media, but that is another problem for another chapter.

There are thousands and thousands of such environmentally concerned people around the Great Lakes and throughout North America. They are not organized by the large environmental groups; in fact, they are hardly organized at all. They might just be a group of steel workers, or the families of steel workers in northwestern Indiana, trying to stop the discharge of an onerous substance into the local stream near where their kids play. They may be businessmen in northern Ohio who cannot obtain needed supplies by ship because the river, laden with contaminated sediments, cannot be safely dredged. They may be members of a community where most everyone suffers from asthma and where scientists from the local industry and from government either ignore them or tell them their problem is simply a figment of their imagination. They may be in a leukemia cluster or a high-incidence breast cancer locale, trying valiantly to get someone in authority to take notice.

The environmental movement I observed is made up mostly of modest groups of ten or twenty people, seeking information from some level of government and getting none, or seeking redress from the local plant and being ignored, or being told by some authority that they are off base and just don't know what they are talking about. These people normally crave information but have no resources to obtain scientific advice or to effectively communicate their concerns. As a politician, I see a great force, made up of many small groups, that could be recruited by a party or candidate, if anyone would take them seriously. Democrats and liberals normally get their votes, because they say the words these people love to hear. Liberals pledge to treat the woes of the environment seriously. They talk about the problems. They say all the right words. But when in office, they spend the money where it will do them the most good for reelection. Their actions do not follow their words. To those concerned about adverse environmental effects, their words seem to have no meaning.

But environmentalists love those words, which are the staple of liberal orations. Environmentalists live by those words. The words get notice to their problem, they think. The words give some kind of perceived power.

Even a year or so after Clinton and Gore came to power, the environmentalists were still excited by the words being said. They know the administration reneged on promises about timber and mining subsidies, government purchase of chlorine-free paper, grazing rights, water use, elevation of the Environmental Protection Agency to cabinet status, and on and on. But oh, the words still sound so sweet to the ears of the environmentalists. "Surely," think those dedicated to a clean environment, "liberals would not say those words if they don't intend to back them with actions."

Republicans and conservatives, on the other hand, just do not say the right words. When they speak of the environment it is normally in terms of aesthetics: "the river is so beautiful," or "the trees are so pretty, we should save them." Most of the folks concerned about the environment are not so much into aesthetics as they are concerned about the safety of their family, the health of their children, and ultimately the preservation of species, including the human species. Those aesthetic conservative and Republican words sound cynical to the environmentalists whom governments and industrialists have taught to be cynical. Such words connote only a perfunctory knowledge or concern about the real environmental problems facing their community and our society.

In the late years of the twentieth century, environmental problems to the general public have a health connotation; not so to Republicans, who immediately think of conservation when they hear the word *environment*. Too many of us have not yet learned that there is a difference between "conservationists" and "environmentalists." That split began to occur at the end of the nineteenth century. Conservationists at the time split into those who wanted to utilize nature and those who wanted to preserve it. Utilitarians wanted to protect nature so it could be used by humans for hunting, hiking, birding, fishing, and other *Homo sapien* pleasures; sort of setting humans above, or outside, of nature. The preservationists were more ecosystemic, including humans within the total mix of things, but sometimes they went to the extreme of trying to exclude humans from natural settings, creating unnatural settings. I have made it my duty to encourage my Republican friends to consider the connotations of the words they use; to catch up with a split between conservationists and environmentalists that began one hundred years ago unbeknownst to most North Americans. A good book to read on this whole subject is *John Muir and His Legacy: The American Conservation Movement*, by Stephen Fox.

As we consider the political leanings of the environmentalist community, it is important to remember that some of the most dramatic government actions to clean the environment have come during Republican presidencies: Richard Nixon with the creation of the Environmental Protection Agency and the signing of the Great Lakes Water Quality Agreement; the Protocol to the Great Lakes Water Quality Agreement creating areas of concerns and remedial action plans in the Reagan years; the Clean Air Act and the Air Quality Accord with Canada under Bush. It was George Bush and Bill Reilly who made the Great Lakes a national priority. I should mention that the Canadian Green Plan came to life under the Conservative leadership of Prime Minister Brian Mulroney. In my own state, a Republican governor, Bob Orr, created the first environmental department. And people still seem confused about me, a known conservative seriously promoting ideas about environmental protection.

I did come away from my experiences on the commission worried that to environmentalists, words often seem to be much more important than actions. One would think that if they care so much, they could see through the phony words of politicians patronizing their concerns in an effort to garner votes.

And some of the organized environmental groups do, I think, give preference to their political philosophy over their ecological philosophies. A personal example of such an attitude comes from the 1990 United States Senate race in Indiana. The Republican candidate had, as a congressman, provided the leadership to accomplish a good environmental result for a community in northern Indiana. I (and his advisors) thought it was a good story. It illustrated the concern a conservative could have for environmental matters. It made a good television commercial. Once aired, one of the major national environmental groups criticized the commercial heavily and demanded it be taken off the air. The group did not criticize the substance of the commercial; nor did it suggest that the environmental result of the action illustrated was anything but good. The Sierra Club and other organized environmental groups demanded the commercial be taken off the air because a conservative Republican had no right to pretend that he cared for the environment.

Such environmentalist arrogance surely would cause a conservative office-holder to think twice about caring for the environment, if, like the environmental group, his or her first concern was politics. The end result of the actions of the environmental group was damage to the cause of environmental protection. The candidate won reelection and, as he acts on matters of national concern, he probably is not too keen about the demands of these environmentalists. They were willing, it seems, to jeopardize environmental good for liberal politics.

As a campaign manager, should my advice to my Republican candidates be "Sweet talk those environmental folks. Lie to them. Tell them we have the cure to the problems of poisonous chemicals and contaminated sediments and that we will find the money, without raising their taxes, to destroy those sediments from hell lurking on the bottom of the streams and in the harbors of the Great Lakes"? I think not. Conservatives should set priorities for pollution prevention and remediation, make a promise, and then keep it when elected. The environment is a good issue for Republicans.

Obviously, conservatives need to do a better job of communicating their concerns and the priorities that they establish. They need not fib to voters concerned about the environment. The truth is good enough. When it comes to the environment, get the facts. Then act. We need to think more about society as a whole and how it can be sustained for each individual; how we can remove those substances that are adversely affecting the health of wildlife and humans, without destroying our social order while improving economic activity.

Some think such sustainable actions are impossible. I do not!

What's the answer? A good start would be a little more emotion by conservatives with a better understanding of what different words mean to different people, and then some serious encouragement to the environmental activists to broaden their thinking a little. Many environmentalists, such as Jack Weinberg of Greenpeace, are broad thinkers (I should mention that even though Jack's hairline is receding rather severely, he can still muster a ponytail). And while *conservation* organizations tend to be somewhat more sedate, *environmental* activists too often begin each day by shouting from the rooftops that everything is bad, everybody in charge knows it, and no one, but for them, cares. Is that an effective catalyst for action? Probably not. Environmentalists need to think more about their own conduct in promoting their cause. They need to question their techniques and tactics.

Does outrageous conduct stimulate reasoned response? Too many members of Greenpeace and other environmental activist groups still seem to think so, because they continue to do it at most all international meetings on the environment. Does dressing up like birds with hooked beaks or fish with cancers and then parading in front of the chief executive officer of a large firm, standing at a microphone trying to explain the position of industry, cause that chief executive officer to be more responsive to the wants of the people dressed up in costumes? Do those actions have a positive influence on a policy maker?

In my judgment, the answer to those questions is no. There was a time when no one paid attention to the environmental groups, so outrageous conduct did get them media attention. Now the issues about which they care are receiving more serious attention and are the subjects of more reasoned national and international debate. Today, outrageous actions tend to harm their credibility. Syllogistic thinking will cause many people to conclude: if your actions are not credible, how can your science or your cause be credible?

At the International Joint Commission biennial meeting in October 1993, spokesmen from industry baited the environmentalists in the audience with words the speakers thought were true but, in some cases, were not. When those businessmen heard the hoots from the audience, reacting to the bait, they thought they were being attacked by discourteous, ill-bred, uncivil people with marijuana-damaged brains. I received a letter from an employee of one of those chemical companies claiming I was destroying democracy by not shutting off one side of the debate. Most of the hoots were coming from just one person: a mother who testified before the commission that she had lost her one-year-old child to what she believed was the callous discharge of persistent toxic substances by the chemical industry. The industry folks, accustomed to the confines of their paneled and imitation leather offices, presumed she was just another hippie malcontent.

But still outrageous actions tend to discredit the science presented by the environmental groups. That is a shame, because their science tends to be in concert with that of private research, governmental research, and industry research. All, for example, report on the dangers of chlorinated substances. But, and it is another big but, only the environmental groups have been working to get the science into the hands of the public. Scientific studies resting peacefully in the libraries of government, universities, or business do little good in motivating needed positive action. Such restraints on the exposure of science, so important to so many, cause some people to claim that deceit is being intentionally practiced by those of whom they have such a strongly held preexisting distrust.

Environmental groups put their science out for public review. It is easy then for industry to claim bad science, or to suggest that conclusions are premature. But it is important to note that the science from environmental groups is on the table. And one has to ask: where is industry's science about which it talks so much? It certainly has not been on the table for public review. So these new tactics, by public groups, of bringing legitimate science to the debate is very much a positive turn of events for the North American public. Environmentalists should give serious attention to the concern that outrageous actions, by some of their members, detract from their science and from their positive contributions in raising public concern and societal action on such serious matters of debate.

Another observation of mine is that most any time governments make a proposal to improve an environmental situation, the organized environmental groups come out against it. The progress desired by these groups can be thwarted by an immediate negative reaction of those people whom governments would normally expect to be supportive. A proposal by the United States government, called the Great Lakes Initiative, has the promise to finally get after some of the really serious problems of persistent toxic substances in the Great Lakes. But it was slow coming out of the gate. Why? Because everyone was against it. Industry was against it because it was too tough on business. Environmental groups were against it because it was too lenient on business. Canadians were against it because it was an effort much more serious than what Canadians were yet willing to emulate. The folks in the Office of Management and Budget at the White House wondered why the U.S. government should fund an initiative that everyone was against. Finally one of the environmental groups obtained a court order forcing the initiative into being. But early on, because the first stage of the initiative did not cover everything wanted by the environmentalists, the environmentalists opposed it. A bad tactic, in my judgment. I would think a better tactic would be to take all you can get, then push for more.

In the continuing dispute that for some reason pits industry and public environmental groups against each other, environmental protection is slowed. Too many of these people just don't like each other. The extreme on one side believes no restrictions should be placed on business, and the extreme on the other side believes that business is the basis of all evil. One side believes that business is making life better by doing the most good for the most people; the other believes that some business practices are killing wildlife and humans. If either side is absolutely correct, some of us, maybe all of us, are in trouble. Surely there is room for reason. The best way to resolve this decades-long dispute is a serious dialogue on how the public, industry, and governments can work together to sustain our social and economic order within a healthy environment. The public environmental groups have been much more willing, in most cases, to enter an open dialogue on stewardship of the environment. Industry has just begun to open the door.

In the final chapter of any public controversy, the public can be the winner. Our system is so designed. Industry will produce what the public wants to buy. Officeholders will respond to the demands of the public. The public, to win such battles, must know the facts, be organized, and state its demands clearly. Hopefully, those public demands and actions will be responsible. I agree that the onus to eliminate persistent toxic substances from being discharged into the environment should be on those who want to manufacture, use, or discharge them. I agree that the onus should be on governments to be more diligent in enforcing laws and regulations and in funding research to determine what dangers are faced by humans from environmental contaminants. But in the final analysis, to make those things happen, the onus is ultimately on the public; on you and me.

9

Reactions of Scientists and Health Care Professionals

Scientists

I HAVE NO IDEA HOW MANY PEOPLE will actually read these words, but if you are, by chance, looking at these reflections of mine, could you, would you, ask yourself the questions I am preparing to ask? Will you consider my concern and consider whether or not it should be a concern of yours?

Before expressing that concern and my questions, let me state what we all know: that it is difficult indeed to get through even one day without hearing a friend, a family member, a colleague, or even a stranger bemoan the poor job our schools are doing in educating our children. Parents are in the forefront in making such complaints. Business leaders are distressed over the quality of employees available. Our position in world commerce is threatened by the declining achievements of our young. We blame governments. We blame school boards. We blame universities for not properly training teachers. Liberals blame society for the number of kids who drop out of the educational process and enter a career of crime. Conservatives blame the do-gooders for spending more and more money on public education but demanding no accountability in return. The poor blame the rich. The successful blame the poor. Blacks think it's because whites are uncaring. Whites think it's because blacks are lazy. Sounds like a daytime television talk show, right?

I meet kids all the time who are brilliant, but still we see factual indications that our children are not learning to the extent they should be learning. A dulling process may be occurring. Now I know I have touched on this before, but it is important. So here come the questions. What if, just what if, the learning problems being experienced by our kids are not systemic? What if the problem is not how much tax money is being spent? What if the quality of education our teachers receive is not the problem? What if the problem is not just the absence of values in the teaching process? What if the problem is not long bus rides out of the neighborhood and liberal experimentation with the minds of our youth? What if our children are not learning to the extent they should be learning because some of the persistent toxic substances we have discharged into the environment have diminished their ability to learn? Those would seem to be important questions for scientists to ponder, even though many pundits claim it is just a fad these days to espouse apocalyptic visions of the future. But there is science that supports the dulling process as a potential effect resulting from exposure to persistent toxic substances. Should that science be ignored?

How do scientists react to such news? Unfortunately, too often they react as their employer would have them react. We quite often think of scientists as a group of very intelligent, deliberative people, looking for answers to the woes of society, unrestrained in their search for new problems and new solutions. But reality tells us a different story. Scientists are seldom unrestrained. They work on research matters assigned to them. They work for government with specific duties assigned. They work for industry with specific work assignments. Academics have more freedom to expand their thinking, but only if they can find funding for their research, and such funding grants almost always have restrictions and boundaries within which the scientists must operate.

Keep in mind, however, that if scientists are not given boundaries or frameworks to work within, they will probably create their own boundaries. Scientists love to talk about spatial considerations. The first thing a scientist does when designing a study is to restrict the areas of consideration. Scientists tend to be reductionists, just the opposite of what I, as a layperson, would have expected scientists to be. The Great Lakes Water Quality Agreement calls for an ecosystem approach. It was a revolutionary concept at the time, and one that is still difficult to bring into scientific and regulatory reality. The ecosystem concept is to consider everything at once, look at it all, unshackle the boundaries. But even today, scientists are trying to frame the ecosystem with which they are concerned.

In defense of the scientists, they love to be on panels sponsored by organizations such as the International Joint Commission, where they serve in their personal and professional capacities and not as representatives of their employer or cause. In such a setting their minds can run free, and it is there, in those settings, where you can hear consensus on the problems of chlorinated organic substances that are persistent and biocumulative. Not restrained by the rules of their employer, they can expand their thinking and come to a consensus on the potential harm humans face by exposure to such onerous substances. But having come that far, then what? The scientist when unharnessed from the dictates of the workplace may come to a conclusion that PCBs have adverse effects on the immune systems of our children. But will the scientist then recommend that PCBs be banned? Maybe. Maybe not.

For science to be pure, scientists say, science must be value neutral. OK, but does that mean that scientists must be value neutral in their conclusions? Is proposing a sunsetting process to get PCBs out of existence a value judgment, or is it the end result of a scientific conclusion? If scientists are value neutral, what good is their work? Without taking the next step to spur action, what is the meaning of their work? Is not the decision to be value neutral a value judgment? Is being value neutral a wall behind which scientists can hide? A wall that protects them from criticism and lost opportunities for advancement? Or is it just an indication of the inability of scientists to communicate their findings to decision makers or to the public?

Are scientists inherently the vast thinkers we think them to be, or are they trained to live in worlds that demand narrow thinking? An example of such narrow thinking might be the industry scientist at the weight-of-evidence workshop at the International Joint Commission's biennial meeting in 1993 who asked a question that was perplexing to him. The forum was in a discussion about taking precautionary actions to avoid potential for harm. Most regulators and technical people have been taught to act only when there is some absolute proof of harm. Preventive action sounds simple, but it is a new way of thinking for most technical people, who can have serious arguments about whether or not zero, as a number, exists. That one industry scientist, who obviously was dedicated to his work and convinced it was beneficial to humankind, asked: "What about relative risks? I thought our goal was to do the most good for the most people."

It was not an unreasonable question from a scientist working within a confined framework, but it was, of course, narrow thinking. His thinking left out people who need an inexpensive food supply, such as native peoples, or minorities, or the poor. How many fish eaters must be adversely affected, or their children adversely affected, in the attempt to do the most good for the most people? How many children with learning disabilities are we willing to accept in an effort to do the most good for the most people? How many cancers? How many reproductive failures? How many immune systems destroyed? How many deaths? Who, except God, is keeping score on what adds up to be the most good for the most people? Those, for some reason, were new and different questions for someone who wants to do good for humankind to consider.

So how do we get scientists out of their shells? How do we get them to sound the alarm when it is time to do so? How do we get them to communicate their findings, with recommendations to policy makers? Well that's going to be difficult, because scientists are not good at coming to closure on an issue; nor are they good at communicating conclusions when they do get that far along. Consider this. In October 1993, in the *Report of Special Presidential Commission on Cancer*, it was determined that there had been a 53 percent increase in breast cancer since 1950. The commission predicted that two million women will be diagnosed with breast cancer in the 1990s and that 460,000 will die. The chairperson of the commission said, "Two things we don't know about breast cancer: (1) what causes it, and (2) how to cure it." And we learn from an interesting series of stories published in *Maclean's* in July 1994 that "a majority of breast cancers occur in women with no known risk factors." Those are the kinds of uncertainties that scientists often offer as findings, even though there is now some science that ties breast cancer to chlorinated substances. It is reminiscent of the old Danish proverb, that "advice after injury is like medicine after death."

The good news is that some in the scientific community are now moving toward consensus on how science deals with uncertainty. More are communicating not only the results of their science but also their beliefs and conclusions as to what the science means and how society should react to it. And more and more effort is being made to bring various disciplines of scientific thought together so that findings can be shared and compared and conclusions formed. A world leader from the scientific community in arriving at this good news segment has been Dr. Theo Colborn.

Reticent Scientists

At various meetings of the International Joint Commission, I would often find myself sitting in a room of scientists, hearing a consensus that dioxin (as an example) could have adverse effects on humans and their progeny, born or unborn. The scientists might be from industry, government, academia, or public environmental organizations, but the basic conclusions tended to be similar. As a layperson I would always wonder, why is it, if a consensus exists among whatever group of scientists with whom I was visiting, that they don't sound the alarm? Why not take your evidence to the public, to your boss, to the legislature?

I have not arrived at a suitable answer to that question, unless it is that these scientists fear being "burned," as they were when scientists sounded the "cancer scare" alarm a decade or so ago. As we now know, that alarm was warranted. At the time, however, many careers were jeopardized as those scientists were labeled premature by the more traditional scientists and labeled quacks in the media.

Or is it just a fact of human nature that individuals with such deliberate, searching minds are always willing to wait until all the evidence is in, knowing that it may never all be in? Or do people who make good scientists not make good spokespeople to put out front trying to make a case that their science is real and needs to be dealt with? The debunkers of science tend to be better communicators. Maybe one of the problems facing scientists, in their unwillingness to express their concerns, is their training in singular disciplines. They may be trained in chemistry, physics, or whatever. So when looking at a problem, they tend to see it narrowly, only from the perspective of their discipline, rather than from a more integrated, holistic view.

In the commission's *Seventh Biennial Report*, we said:

> Institutional science in particular has tended to divide knowledge into specialized compartments based essentially on reductionist thinking. For hundreds of years, it has been believed that phenomena can be explained by improved specificity and certainty in distinct areas of enquiry. It does not, however, provide a model to understand the "big picture," or to provide the basis for questions that are meaningful only with complex and dynamic systems characterized by uncertainty and disequilibrium. The Great Lakes (especially under the influence of humans) must be understood in this way.
>
> Scientists who attempt to work in the broader context tend to face non-supportive institutional reward systems and other barriers. While there are notable examples of scientists with international reputations—including our

own advisers—addressing Great Lakes issues in an integrative way, most scientists tend to focus within specific disciplinary fields and research streams.

This situation is reinforced by an educational system that channels students at all levels into specialized rather than integrative programs. From primary grades, students are not taught to explore and think across subjects, to link common threads, but rather to focus on narrow topics and established methodologies. Universities reward professors and students on the basis of expertise and publishing within narrow fields. Even where institutes and faculties are mandated to pursue cross-disciplinary studies, their intellectual roots tend to exist in separate academic departments.

How to nest the highly sophisticated, intensive research that advances knowledge of specific ecosystem components into an integrated, ecosystemic model concerned with the relationships among the components should become a major preoccupation of research managers and scholars.

That last sentence was long and complicated, but I think we were trying to say something relatively simple. Just as one-medium laws and regulations (those addressed singularly to water, or air, or land) are barriers to pollution prevention, and just as single-medium departments in our environmental protection agencies become barriers to cleaning up problems of the past, so do single-disciplined scientists create barriers to seeing, understanding, and communicating the multifaceted problems that could now be infecting the human race. Too many specialists. Not enough scientists who can see the big picture and work to resolve multifaceted problems. We need to think anew about the training of the more integrated, cross-disciplined, ecosystemic scientist.

Health Care Professionals

Physicians are trained to cure and heal people. They are not trained to advise patients on how to prevent disease or injury. But when physicians do learn of a major health problem, they, as a profession, go to great lengths to teach prevention. They taught themselves about the need for sterile procedures. They taught the public and government how to avoid or prevent such diseases as cholera. Obviously there are many more examples. If you can pull medical practitioners away from a life-style that is demanding and hectic, to look at and consider a major but subtle problem that their patients might encounter, they will react, because by their very nature they are caring people. But prevention is hard to get a handle on. It is not common in the instruction they receive in medical school or in their continuing medical education programs.

A personal physician asked me, "If a toxic substance gets into a human body, can you get it out?" My answer was that I didn't know, but the damage may be done at the point of entry. I told him I did know that mothers can pass on their PCB loadings to their babies. But I am a lawyer. He is a physician. Why was he asking me that question? Finally, in an effort not to look too stupid, I replied that prevention is the better solution. But prevention of injury from environmental causes is really a tough one for physicians. What is it that needs to be prevented? What is the potential for harm? What are the potential generational effects that could maybe not surface as a harm in one of their patients, or in their patient's family, for thirty or forty years?

If the potential harm is a reproductive deficiency in the offspring of a mother who was exposed to the toxicant twenty or thirty years ago, or if it is a learning problem, or if it is a reduced penis size or reduced sperm count, what does the physician recommend? On what does the physician base the preventive recommendation? Is the causal agent easily identified? Can you see it, smell it, feel it, taste it? Where is it? What is its pathway to humans? Well, a starting place might be the fish consumption advisories issued by states and provinces. In 1993, 164 such advisories were issued by governments around the Great Lakes alone. Those advisories indicate whether or not a young female should eat the fish, or if a young child should eat the fish, or if anyone should eat the fish and in what quantities. Surely primary care physicians could easily receive and transmit those warnings. They would be good starting tools for the practice of preventive medicine.

The International Joint Commission had some very positive interactions with health care professionals in several Great Lakes states and the Province of Ontario in 1992 and 1993. We encouraged those interactions because we recognized that medical professionals are perhaps the most trusted sector of our society. The public looks to them for advice and information. We felt it was important, therefore, that they receive the latest and best information available on the health effects of pollution, and we began a project to bring them that information. The potential effects on human populations are important matters to debate, and for the debate to be successful representatives of all the public, which certainly includes the medical profession, must be at the table where decisions are made.

What kind of damage are we talking about? The remarkable thing is that we know far more about what happens to fish and wildlife than we know about the effects on humans. The most pronounced effect from Great Lakes research is on the development of fish and wildlife embryos, but all vertebrates have strikingly similar physiologies. In particular, human embryos are subject to the same programming during development, which is controlled by various hormones. Persistent toxic substances can disrupt the timing of such programming, resulting in subtle but devastating effects for society. What happens to fish and wildlife embryos can also happen to human embryos. We also realized that while the results of studies on the effects of persistent toxics to fish and wildlife may alarm and concern us, the results of studies on human health are what will enrage us and lead us to change. Because health care professionals are one of the most trusted sectors of society, it was essential that we share our information and findings with the medical profession, so they can begin to reach their own conclusions and effectively inform and advise their patients.

That is why the commission made human health a priority and why we focused on gathering additional information through an ecosystem health work group. We also joined with physician and health care organizations to sponsor a physicians' roundtable in Wisconsin and another in Toronto. Several physicians and medical researchers came together to help us learn how medical professionals communicate with one another and how to design a continuing medical education course on the human health effects of Great Lakes pollution. When I left the commission, courses had been sponsored by the Medical College of Wisconsin and the Michigan Medical Society. The Toronto session was interdisciplinary. It involved, maybe for the first time, discussions between physicians, nurses, public health inspectors, and students about what was needed to better inform health professionals relative to preventing the potential effects of persistent toxic substances. A task force was formed in Ontario, with U.S. linkages, to develop a network for referral and for an environmental information exchange process between professionals.

Also undertaken was a survey of Wisconsin pediatricians, obstetricians/gynecologists, and family practitioners to assess the current views and experiences regarding the clinical significance of environmental pollutants. More than 86 percent of the physicians considered themselves to be somewhat uninformed about the risks of mercury and PCBs to human health. Yet those same physicians in overwhelming numbers (90 percent) felt that it was appropriate for physicians to be a source of information for patients about environmental risks. Seventy-eight percent responded that physicians should also take public positions about issues that affect public health. The results of the study told us that we have to do a better job of getting the information out to the medical community.

It was the hope of the commission that the two-year effort with health care professionals would be the stimulus for continuing medical education throughout the Great Lakes Basin toward the goal of physician-assisted prevention of human health effects from Great Lakes pollution. I had the opportunity to speak to state medical associations around the Great Lakes and to be questioned by physicians asking what they could do to help prevent the adverse effects of exposure to such onerous substances. It was an exhilarating experience for a lawyer.

It was in this effort, and in our effort with educators, that I felt we commissioners, as a catalyst for widespread action, had done not only the most good but a lasting good. The members of the health and education professions reacted more seriously to the discussion of potential adverse effects on the environment, which includes humans, than any other members of society with whom I interacted.

10

Reactions of the Media

Thomas Jefferson once said, "Advertisements contain the only truths to be relied on in the newspaper." That may have been a wise thought a couple hundred years ago, but what about now? Are even the advertisements true? If not, should we carry forward the words of Jefferson in trying to determine what in the newspaper (or electronic media) we can believe and what we cannot believe? Many, many people no longer read a newspaper. Is it because they don't believe what is being reported, or that they disagree with the reporter's interpretation? Is it because they are too lazy and uncaring, preferring a mindless absorption in televised fare? Is it because our public educational system has not taught them to read well enough? Or is it because people believe the newspapers report stories from a predisposed viewpoint?

Maybe it is the reporting profession that has languished owing to biased preconceptions, lack of preparedness for or understanding of subject matter, or just plain laziness. Let me use remedial action plans in the Great Lakes to illustrate my concern. When the International Joint Commission came up with the idea of suggesting remedial action plans, there were those who thought the effort would not be worthwhile. They lived in areas they thought were hopelessly impaired and would forever appear on some official-looking list but never be the subject of any serious effort.

But enough people believed, and enough people cared, and enough people thought that remedial action plans made a lot of sense. Thousands of people stepped forward, not willing to ignore the problem, but willing to be part of an effort to plan and implement solutions. What a great public interest story for the news media to grab onto. People caring. People in action. But in reality it has been extremely difficult for the hard-working remedial action teams to get publicity for their good works. When they do get publicity, it normally reflects the negative, not the positive: failures to obtain sufficient funding or needed technology, or the lack of government support tend to be viewed as newsworthy. The positive actions of citizens working to restore a resource tend not to be thought newsworthy by those who decide what is news worth reporting.

In addressing a forum on remedial action plans in the fall of 1993, I suggested the need for broadly communicating the problems being addressed, their potential effects, and the proposed solutions. I said communicating what was under way in an area of concern and why it was under way was essential to a successful remediation. I suggested bringing in local news reporters and briefing them so they could understand what was going on, so they could write better stories, stories that just might result in increasing the cadre of volunteers and uncovering latent funding sources.

I said, "Whatever you do, don't make reporters attend meetings where they don't know what you are talking about. Most reporters will be on the side of the people trying to do good work, if it is made clear why you are about the task you are about." I told about a remedial action plan review meeting in Sault St. Marie, Ontario. A reporter was present and had been listening intently. At the end of the meeting he asked if he could ask a question. He informed the government officials and Citizen Advisory Council members that he had been listening for four hours and "I don't know what the hell you are talking about." He just was not up on the acronyms, nor familiar with the bureaucratic and scientific buzzwords. That is not surprising. After more than four years of trying to understand government talk, I still had to ask for definitions "in English."

I then gave an example of another reporter at another review meeting in Erie, Pennsylvania. The reporter sat through the entire meeting. From the story he wrote in the *Erie Morning News* on October 15, 1993, it was obvious that he understood what was going on. He was familiar with the words and the work of the Presque Isle Remedial Action Plan. But the headline writer wasn't. The front-page banner headline had a subhead that was printed above the headline. The subhead said, "Sport Fish Still Healthy." The headline right underneath said, "Bay Sediments Blamed for Cancer in

Some Fish." A photographer for *USA Today* picked me up early that morning to take my picture out by the water. One of the first things he said to me was that he was glad the fish in the bay were safe to eat. The headline writer had given him two choices; he believed the one that implied no problem. All the good efforts and all the words of a knowledgeable reporter were negated by the headlines.

I told the hundreds of people in attendance at the forum, who were trying to clean up their own local waterfronts, that those examples simply meant they should try harder. But I am not sure that will work. Again the questions. Did the headline writer in Erie have a different prejudice about environmental contamination and the effects thereof than the reporter had? Was the headline writer just lazy? Was the person assigned to that task qualified to make such judgments? Or was he or she just doing what newspapers often think they must do if they are to appear to be objective: give both sides of a story? They call it balance.

As a paperboy during World War II and after, and as a watcher of television since its introduction into our society (which was the late 1940s in Indianapolis), and as a newsmaker in my state, and now nationally and internationally, for thirty years or so, I have some very firm opinions about the motives of those who provide us with the news.

First comes the question of balance—reporting the story that is on the daily agenda, but then finding someone to give the other view. An example might be that a news conference is held where eminent scientists from public and private sectors announce that cigarette smoking is bad for your health. The "newsie" takes notes and gathers up all the scientific papers and then, in a normal practice for reporters, calls a tobacco industry representative to get its side of the story for balance. Industry doesn't let a reporter talk to its scientists, but rather to a lobbyist or public relations person. The PR person says, "Look, those people who say smoking is bad for you have bad science. Our science overwhelmingly indicates that there are no adverse human health effects from smoking." That follow-up interview is normally done by telephone. No scientific papers offered or asked for.

How does the balanced story come out? Normally, something like "X, Y, and Z say smoking is harmful to your health, but A says that it is just a lot of nonsense based on bad science." What does the reading public believe when the news reporting implies that both sides of an issue are equal through balanced reporting, a matter of choice? The reading public believes that whatever is being done is the right thing to keep on doing, especially when there is no weight of evidence presented in the story for or against either side. Balance, in this instance, is another way of attempting to be value neutral, as scientists attempt to be value neutral, as the politically correct now say we should all be. And the attempt to be value neutral normally is a value judgment that gives undue weight to the *other* side. In environmental reporting the *other* side is often the *wrong* side. The dangerous side.

The *Indianapolis Star* ran a series of environmental stories during the first weeks of 1994. In my judgment, it was a banner event, the first time Indiana's environment, other than for waste matters, had received any extensive coverage. The reporter, Kyle Niederpruem, did a good job of exposing state government for environmental inefficiencies. One of the stories was extremely serious and received prime front-page space in the Sunday paper. It had to do with the governor of Indiana deciding not to fund the program that administered the fish consumption advisories. No longer would Indiana government warn fishermen that what they ate or fed to their children could adversely affect them and their children and their grandchildren for generations.

I mention elsewhere that state and provincial governments do not do a very good job of warning people that the fish those same governments stock into the waters are unfit for human consumption. But to threaten not to warn at all is unconscionable. The methods used by governments for testing are based on exposure to carcinogens (cancer-causing substances), but cancer is no longer the only worry. Reproductive problems, immune suppression, and all the other maladies I have mentioned so often, such as a child's learning difficulties, are more subtle but maybe more serious in the long run. The primary exposure route for these adverse health effects are by ingestion, mostly from eating fish.

But the story in my local paper suggested only the voluntary risk of cancer and quoted one person as saying that no one had ever shown him a fish-eater who had died of cancer. That one quote took the story out of the serious category and left the reader with a mental option, an excuse to ignore the seriousness of the original intent of the story. That quote made the risk appear to be a voluntary risk. The risk, however, is not voluntary to the small child fed the wrong kind of fish by an unsuspecting parent. The risk is not voluntary to the unborn child who may not do as well as she or he would have done in school, in health, and in life had the family not eaten the wrong kind of fish. An angler today may still think the risk is voluntary, without ever considering whether or not it will ever be possible to be a grandmother or grandfather.

Since most reporters are generically proenvironment, you would wonder why they still report environmental stories in that way. Is it the caution of the editors? Is it the probusiness, antienvironmentalist views of the ownership? I cannot imagine that was the case with the reporter for *Indianapolis Star*, who is talented and conscientious. That certainly does not seem to be her reputation when dealing with other issues. It more likely was just the fallacious search for balance.

Religion provides a good example of media mistreatment of a subject through the guise of balance. Normally the national media are dead set against saying anything good about people who take literally the words of the Bible. National news readers parrot such phrases as "the religious Right" or "fundamentalist Christians" with aspersion evident in their voices. The values of Christianity, Judaism, Islam, or whatever are usually reported with sneers by news reporters, and that is especially true of Christianity. When interviewees express their own personal beliefs, the dominant liberal media types challenge them with such questions as "Who are you to tell me how to think?"

Prejudice and intolerance are common traits among the national reporting fraternity. But still reporters and news anchors claim they try to be balanced. When reporting a story about why religion is failing, they always bring on a well-dressed, well-spoken antireligion guy, along with some goof (once I remember a guy wearing a buffalo head hat) as the representative for religion. In so doing, the media argued that they were balanced; they interviewed someone from each side of the issue. As we approached the 1994 midterm elections, however, most attempts at media balance had been forgotten as national reporters overtly joined liberals in the defamation of those people who proclaimed themselves to be Christian.

In television news the three older networks try so hard to be balanced that they not only report the same stories but also report them in the same order. They even run their commercials at the same time. If you don't believe me, sit down in front of your television with your clicker and push the buttons from station to station during the network news or during the network morning shows. It is amazing. They are so balanced that one has to wonder whether all networks pick their news stories for the right reasons (news value) or are so fearful of being different from their competition that they report the same things, from the same point of view, in the same way, at the same times.

But back to environmental reporting. I live a little over a hundred miles south of the Great Lakes. These lakes and their environs form an ecosystem that contains 20 percent of the world's freshwater. The Great Lakes are of major importance to the economy of my state, and in 1993 the lakes had a traumatic year. Record precipitation caused high water sufficient for the International Joint Commission to take actions that caused the St. Lawrence Seaway to be closed for two days a week during the peak shipping season. That unique action could have had serious consequences for the Indiana

Harbor and for commerce in Indiana. Was it mentioned in the news media in the state capital? I don't think so.

An interesting thing about the Great Lakes states is that most of them have capitals (Springfield, Indianapolis, Columbus, Harrisburg, Albany) that are quite distant from the lakes. Legislators in those state capitals rarely see or hear news stories about problems of the Great Lakes that should be of concern to them.

What else made 1993 a year of concern in the Great Lakes that should have been of interest to editors and news managers throughout the Midwest and Northeast? Well, how about the zebra mussels and their cousin the quagga mussel filtering away and potentially changing the very basic nature of Lake Erie, where so many water-loving midwesterners boat and fish on weekends? If what appears to be happening is happening, the food chain and fish community of Lake Erie could be in danger. I didn't read or hear much about such a potential calamity on or in the news media away from the immediate Great Lakes Basin.

Remedial action plans were finishing phase one and moving into phase two in many areas of concern around the Great Lakes, but not much was reported about that. Some fines for the continued industrial discharge of prohibited substances were reported, but little or nothing was reported relating to concerns about the continuation of discharges, either in general or specifically. Ah, but chlorine was a matter of interest. Why? Because lobbyists did the work for the reporters. They wrote the stories for them. In place after place, lobbyists dragged out chief executive officers of local plants that employ many workers in specific communities to engage in denial of the problems and in name calling. Reporters covered that story, because it was easy to cover.

But that coverage basically came a year or two after the International Joint Commission recommended the sunsetting of chlorine as an industrial feed stock. In the summer of 1993 that recommendation brought considerable attention from national magazines, mostly of a technical and scientific nature, but not from the mass media. Then the lobbyists started their campaign to influence the public through the mass media. Their strategy was naive and did not work. The reporters for the most part, as I said before, took time to get the other side of the story, and the other side of the story seemed to prevail. There were editorials, such as the one in Detroit, which accepted the misinformation of the lobbyists and suggested that the International Joint Commission, not chlorine, be sunset. An interesting thought.

And then there are the words that can and cannot be used that become a barrier to communicating a message. For example, when reports are issued detailing adverse effects on humans and wildlife, one of the most serious of those effects, reduced penis size, is often deleted from the printed story. I wrote an op-ed piece for the *Indianapolis Star* which ran on February 8, 1994. The reference to reduced penis size was omitted.

So I am back to an old conundrum, one that I used to debate with reporters relative to my political campaign activities. Whose job is it to educate members of the public about the issues facing them? Reporters used to say it was their job to report the news as they saw it, not to educate the public about the pros and cons of issues or the rightness or wrongness of various elements of an issue. As a campaign manager or party chairman, I would always claim that financial supporters gave me money to help elect a candidate or candidates, not to educate voters about how our constitutional system works. We would argue that it is the responsibility of the schools to educate our children. It is the responsibility of voters to educate themselves.

Later, in a debate of sorts sponsored by the Bowen Institute at Ball State University after I was no longer a political party chairman or campaign manager and after a veteran political reporter was no longer on the job as a reporter, we both agreed that we should have accepted that responsibility. It had become obvious that our schools were failing in their value-neutral educational climate and that voters in general were just not willing to make the effort to educate themselves. We decided that perhaps some educational element injected into the television commercials on which I had spent millions and millions of dollars could have tempered the current climate of voting irrationality. Perhaps a few words injected into the reporter's stories about what government could and should do in our constitutional system could have aborted the false hope that a benevolent dictator, perhaps a Ross Perot lookalike, was a viable option.

But one of the interested parties in the public-awareness debate is not so timid. Industry makes a constant effort to educate the public. It spends millions and millions of dollars annually to educate the public through advertising. It has for fifty years told us that white is clean, pure, and desirable at all costs: ninety-nine and forty-four one hundredths percent pure. Think about that. Is white any cleaner than any other color? Does the chlorinated bleaching necessary to make things white harm wildlife and humans? Could not industry commercials convince the purchasing public that gray or even brown toilet paper could accomplish its task as well as bright white? Yes, it could do that. But some might ask: is that industry's responsibility?

I have come to the conclusion that the responsibility to educate members of the public about things they can do to sustain a high standard of living without harming wildlife or humans is the duty of all: your responsibility and mine. It is the responsibility of industry and of each member of the public. It is the responsibility of scientists and technical people, of teachers, of doctors, of lawyers, and especially of the news media, which are in daily communication with the public. Some members of the media are doing it, some from a national standpoint, some from a local or individual reporter standpoint. Some as a matter of policy, some as a matter of individual interest. Editors, publishers, producers, and managers need to encourage these few to continue, and others to begin.

We live in a time when cable television brings us thirty, forty, fifty, or more channels, satellite disks even more. With all these choices, many viewers never watch television news. How do you deal with that? Even if the reporters try to educate, the viewers are somewhere else. It means running thirty-second commercials that sneak up on the viewing audience somewhat subliminally, as successful television commercials do. Well, then, who pays for those commercials? Do networks and local stations do it for free? Why not? A few of the cable networks are beginning to do a good job of environmental education under the guise of entertainment. Still, I wonder, why do we need to be tricky to get messages across to Americans who should be demanding such information?

Always more questions than answers, but the time for answers is upon us.

II

Reactions of the Public

ONE THING I FOUND SURPRISING about most people was their reluctance to expose themselves to facts about the environment. That was also true of elected officials, Republican or Democrat. I say it was surprising, but I guess I should not be surprised. I reacted the same way before taking on an international responsibility dealing with the environment. That responsibility exposed me to science to which otherwise I probably would never have been exposed.

My conservative friends still like me, even though I am concerned about the long-term effects of toxic substances. They just think I have been duped somehow, and they continue making sure that they are not exposed to the facts that duped me. Most of my friends are open-minded, inquisitive, seeking new information on most every issue, except the environment. Why is that? It is a resistant attitude that is seemingly woven into the fabric of our ethos. It seems as if most of us don't want to know about anything we are doing that might somehow interfere with the mysteries of life and our abilities to learn, to reproduce, and to fight off sickness. It is one of those difficult barriers that must be overcome.

But just how does the general public react when it learns of a problem that may, or may not, adversely harm someone, perhaps a family member? How do people react when they cannot get the attention of their political leaders about a major concern? Anger? Blind vengeance? Shoot the messenger? Blame the mayor? Too often, lately, citizen reactions have been something less than reasonable or responsible. Hardly noticeable might be a better description. And why is that? Are citizens too lazy to dig up the facts? Too busy to read? Unable to read well enough? Don't care? Care too much, but don't know what to do?

Will Rogers once said, "One of the evils of democracy is that you have to endure the man you elected, whether you like him or not." That was long ago, and the thought was based upon mistaken judgments by voters, evidently not a new phenomenon. But over the past several years, people in the United States and Canada have been voting for candidates they don't want to win, because they don't want to vote for the ones they already have, the incumbents. Party or philosophy be damned; let's just turn out the top people we have in. 1994, on the other hand, saw voters isolating their anger toward a single party.

It is important to understand what voters in these two great nations have been saying, as they continue to vent their anger on election days. The message they are sending is not just directed toward politicians and officeholders, as some would like to believe. The message is clearly directed to all who are in charge in our society. To politicians certainly, but also to business people who are perceived as leaving ethics and stewardship out of their decision-making process. The message is directed to the moguls of television who bring blood, fire, and misery into our living rooms under the guise of delivering information (if it bleeds, it leads). To the entertainment industry, which never gives up trying to distort morality. To cops on the beat who are so consumed by the misfits of society that they find it hard to treat decent people decently. To leaders of our religious institutions who seem to find it not so difficult to moderate the word of God in the face of societal pressures to accept life-styles they should abhor. To industrialists who continue to discharge onerous substances into our environment.

Voters do not always aim their anger in the appropriate direction, but how do we motivate a society to demand morals from their leaders, or ethics in the decision-making process of industry, or stewardship among the users in our society? Maybe the Golden Rule should come back into fashion. As a boy, I remember my mother saying, almost daily, "Remember the Golden Rule: do unto others as you would have others do unto you." Today's application might be: if you don't want me to discharge a poisonous substance in your backyard, don't do it in mine.

A former mayor of Toronto said in Windsor, Ontario, at the International Joint Commission's biennial meeting in October 1993, "We can no longer tolerate those who move in, use up, throw away, and move out." David Crombie was right about that, as he is about so many things. But how do we enforce the ethic that he so clearly enunciated? Who can enforce it? How do we get the public to care?

Again, communication is the answer to this concern, as it is the answer to most everything. If the problem reaches the ears or the eyes of the average family, they will be moved to some kind of action, if they believe what they heard or saw. And that's another problem. So let's look at the average family.

Wake up in the morning. Struggle with the kids. Dad gets off to work. Mom takes the kids to day care or Grandma's and then goes off to work. After work they pick up the kids, try to have some meaningful family time, eat a pizza, watch Barney or Power Ranger tapes on the television, get the kids to bed, worry about the mortgage payment, take a few deep breaths, go to bed, wake up in the morning, and start all over. If you notice, my scenario didn't leave time, or desire, to read the newspaper or watch television news. That is not an unusual scenario in the 1990s. So how do we get the environmental message to an average family?

And if they hear it, do they believe it? Natural occurrences or disasters such as fire, flood, and earthquakes are easy to see and believe but hard certainly, and maybe impossible, for average people to prevent. What about contaminated substances lying on the bottom of a lake? How does that affect normal people? Well, the truth is they don't even think about contaminated sediments, because they have probably never heard of them. Since the invention of tea bags and instant coffee they probably don't even know what sediments are. I remember, as a teenager in war-ravaged Korea, boiling water from a small mountain creek with coffee grounds in my "steel pot," as our helmets were called. My bayonet was a convenient tool for stirring. I would then strain the brew through an old T-shirt before drinking. I know what sediments are. I spit out my share of sediments with my morning coffee for month after month in the coldness of the mountains in the middle of that frozen peninsula.

If a landfill (dumps, we called them when I was a kid) is proposed for a neighborhood, the average resident might hear about it, go to a meeting or two, make disparaging remarks about those stupid politicians, and go on about one's business. If a municipal incinerator is proposed for a big city, the average family probably won't even hear about it. If they do, they probably think it is a good idea, so long as taxes do not increase. They have no way of knowing that incinerators burning chlorine-containing trash and hazardous wastes send toxic organochlorines into the environment worldwide. They can visualize the vermin creeping around the landfill. They can sample the odoriferous breeze wafting through their backyard from the dump. They can easily conjure up images of the rotting process. Most people don't like those things and do not want them in the neighborhood. But what about the incinerator? Who cares is the probable response of my average family. Can't see it. Can't often smell it. Can just visualize all that garbage burning up and disappearing. But maybe they should worry a little more about the inputs of toxics into our air from incineration. In the *Seventh Biennial Report*, the International Joint Commission reminded governments that "any strategy towards virtual elimination and zero discharge of persistent toxic substances must address the significant inputs from incineration."

We all know that fishing is a good thing. It's a back-to-nature kind of thing. Our grandfathers told us about it, about how many fish were in the lake, about how much fun they were to catch, about how good they tasted. But now, if we can ever get away from our hectic schedule, the fish we catch have sores on them. What does that mean? Should we take them home to feed the kids?

There are fishing advisories everywhere. Don't eat the large salmon or trout in the Great Lakes, the catfish in the Ohio River, and on and on. But do those who fish know about those official advisories against consuming certain fish? I personally visited some bait shops around Lake Erie during Walleye tournament time. I asked a bait shop employee if it was safe to eat the fish. His answer: "It's up to you." After numerous questions, he found me a copy of the *1989–90 New York State Fishing Regulations Guide*. It gave me very clear information about how to obtain a license, about definitions of words such as *angling*, about how to catch the fish, what size of what kind of fish I could keep or had to throw back, the dates of various seasons, whether I could fish at night or could not fish at night. All of that information was given straight up, easy to read.

But the health advisories in the fishing regulation book are given in code. For Lake Ontario, the St. Lawrence River, and the Niagara River below the falls, in print so small you need a magnifying glass, it says: "American eel, channel catfish, lake trout, chinook salmon, coho salmon over 21", rainbow trout over 25", brown trout over 20" •." That's right, it says •. Down at the bottom of the second page of advisories, if you look, you can find an explanation of what • means: "• means 'EAT NONE.'" So, if you are a proud parent who just caught a nice channel cat or a salmon or a big trout, are you going to take it home to feed to your young daughter, or are you going to read further back in a little book that gives you a code to decipher and learn that the

State of New York, based upon good science, recommends to all humans that they eat NONE of those fish?

Why do governments do that? Are they intentionally making it easy to do the wrong thing? Why make it easy to find out how to catch them but then make it so hard to find out that there is a potential for harm not only to the adults but also to their kids and unborn grandkids? Where is the ethics in all that? And how does that sort of activity by government make it easier for the public to become informed? And if members of the public find out that governments are treating them this way, how will they react? Anger in the election booth, or apathy?

In the *Fifth Biennial Report* of the International Joint Commission, issued in April 1990, we dealt with the questions of fish consumption advisories and recommended that governments which stock fish into the Great Lakes and then issue warnings to humans not to eat those same fish should reconsider their policies. To me it sounded like a reasonable suggestion, but it created a furor. I had to show up at congressional hearings to defend such a thought, and I endured the outrage of many angry fishermen, governments, tourism agencies, and on and on. We need to keep in mind the reason why governments stock fish into the Great Lakes. The primary reason seems to be that persistent toxic substances discharged into the water affects the reproductive system of the fish, and they are unable to reproduce in the fouled waters. Is the stocking necessary, as many experts say, to protect the ecosystemic balance, or is it necessary to fool the fishing (and paying) public into thinking the lakes are healthy? Much, if not most, of the public grabs on to the latter thought.

In the *Fifth Biennial Report*, we said:

> Catching Great Lakes fish is the passion of many thousands of Great Lakes residents and others, and this activity is encouraged by governments to develop and promote the sports fishery. For this and other reasons, governments stock fish in the lakes.
>
> The consumption of Great Lakes fish, however, is the principal source of human exposure to a number of persistent toxic compounds. Consumption of certain fish species poses a special threat to women of child-bearing age, who pass these toxic substances on to their offspring. As a result, fish species that are the subject of consumption advisories by one government agency may continue to be stocked by another. Because of these inconsistencies in advisories and other fisheries management policies among jurisdictions, conflicting messages are sent to anglers.
>
> These two facts seem strangely inconsistent and troublesome. Indeed, they have been branded an exercise in contradiction. The commission concludes the Parties and jurisdictions should review and strengthen Great Lakes fish

consumption advisories as necessary and re-evaluate stocking programs for those fish which pose a threat to the health of animals and humans when consumed.

We then went on to encourage the governments to be catalysts in providing "greater awareness in helping people avoid personal use of and exposure to persistent toxic substances."

But people still do not know what dangers lurk in the waters, or in the ground, or in the air. Not only do they not know; they are not trying to find out. Oh, some are, of course. The environmental organizations are spreading the word to the extent their private resources will allow. Governments on the other hand are still trying to balance the needs of the people with the wants of the lobbyists, looking always for another compromise position.

But in my own state, Indiana, we don't even get that much concern. There the governor announced the abolishment of the agency that does fish testing and human consumption advisories, for budgetary reasons. I guess the reasoning must be that if fish advisories are not dealt with seriously by the governments that issue them and the same governments that stock those fish to begin with, you might as well save the money and not go through the hypocritical charade. It seems to be the old "what you don't know won't hurt you" attitude at a time when we do know that those toxic substances we cannot see, feel, or smell can hurt us and our unknowing progeny. What greater responsibility does government have than to warn its citizens of such dangers? How could Indiana's governor abdicate that responsibility? An analogy might be to take down all the stop signs, dismiss all the state troopers, and announce that traffic laws will no longer be enforced.

Even some members of the public will say, "Look, if you were so worried about human safety, you wouldn't let people drive cars. More people are killed in cars than by eating fish." Obviously the statement is true. The fallacy with that argument is that it tries to liken voluntary risk with involuntary risk; it's an argument that won't hold water. When people decide to smoke cigarettes, they pretty well know now that they are taking a voluntary risk. We might die a year or two earlier from lung cancer, but we don't give much thought to what the quality of life might be like in those last few years, just that it is a personal decision, and by God each person can make it on his own. "Besides," they often say, "I just read an article the other day saying cigarette smoking isn't as bad for you as people say." But what about their little son and daughter with asthma and ear infections? Did they take a voluntary risk, or did they just get sick because old Mom and Dad were only thinking of their own risk when they decided to go down to the basement to light up, and, by the way, let the smoke travel through the forced-air heating system throughout the house?

And what about persistent toxic substances that we cannot easily see, feel, smell, or taste? What about children who don't do as well in school as they might have done had their parents or grandparents not lived where they lived, or ate what they ate? When did the young child get to make a choice? These are tough questions. And I worry that most people in North America don't even know the questions are being asked, or that they should be asked. It is easy to believe that the government does not care or that government is inept in this area, because people now think that about government generally. People certainly have no thought that the local manufacturing plant is concerned about their family.

So what's next? How do these problems get resolved? It will take effort, but members of the public can move governments and industry to action, if only they get off their butts and do it!

Industries say they cannot change their manufacturing processes or their product lines because of market pressures. They say consumers will only buy paper that is pure white, not 85 percent white but pure white. But in reality, most people just don't give a damn. They don't care if their toilet paper is white or gray. They buy the whitest of whites because industry advertising tells them to do so, and because they have little choice. Industry obviously has the greatest ability to reeducate the public to buy newer, more environmentally friendly products, because only it has sufficient resources to pay for television advertising. Of course, the television industry could do the same free of charge, if it cared and was not worried about alienating advertisers.

Government doesn't like to act unless it is pressured to act. And the public is not really very good about pressuring governments, other than in highly profiled situations. On the other hand, lobbyists are good at that. Elected officials and their appointed staffs often misconstrue lobbyist pressure for public pressure. And, of course, we all recognize that government actions often cause more problems than solutions. In a representative democracy, governments should at least be catalysts for information distribution when populations are at risk.

Only the public can truly pressure governments and industry to stop the discharge of persistent toxic substances into the Great Lakes, or any other ecosystem. Only the public can pressure the governments to get serious about the remediation of various hot spots. But how do you motivate an apathetic public to do so? How do you get members of a public that wishes a pox on all the leaders to realize that they and their children are at risk? If we cannot rely on industry to be a good steward without public pressure, and if we cannot rely on government to act without public pressure, and if the public is not paying attention to something so serious but so subtle as indications that its own species may be slowly losing its ability to reproduce, then what in heaven's name do we do? I have thought about that question a lot. I still don't know the answer. Maybe I should react like everyone else. Maybe I should just close my eyes and my mind.

12

Education

IN A COLUMN CALLED "Young People without a Conscience," William Raspberry made an interesting statement: "Who can blame people for not learning what they haven't been taught?"

As is true in so many other areas, the public education system in the United States has failed to instruct our children as to why it is important to protect the environment, let alone how to protect the environment. Universities do not adequately provide prospective teachers the fundamental information needed to teach our children how they can include pollution prevention in their daily lives, and therefore most teachers do not feel competent to do so. School administrators do not, in most cases, provide a place in the curriculum for environmental matters, and, maybe more important, if a dedicated teacher has the motivation, the necessary funds will not be available.

Even so, many teachers have been identified in the United States and Canada who are bringing environmental education into their classrooms on their own initiative, without funding and without formal training. In some cases, however, industries, such as Ford Motor Company, are providing some of those dedicated teachers with funds for student testing of polluted rivers. Kids generally are more environment conscious than are their parents and grandparents, but some would argue that today's kids are being taught more by emotion and less by fact. Whatever the stimulus, however valid the instruction, industry had better get ready. These kids will soon be the "market force" that industry leaders say causes them to do what they do.

Surveys of public opinion continually report that the American people believe that the educational system is failing but, on the other hand, that the school attended by their own children is just great. Similarly, such surveys reveal that vast majorities of voters believe the United States Congress to be totally inept, out of touch with reality, incapable of making decisions in the best interest of the people it is supposedly there to serve. However, those same people often think their own member of Congress is quite all right. As a politician, I know that pollsters and politicians have attempted to deal with the latter misconception for decades. Not necessarily trying to correct it, but trying to figure out how to use the "dulling" of the electorate for the best electoral advantage of their own candidate. We would say something like "Congress is bad. Your congressman is bad. So vote for the challenger." Or we would tell them, "Your congressman is as dumb as all those other guys, so vote for me." But, until 1994, American voters seemed to believe that their own member of Congress could straighten out all those other bad apples. Obviously, that has not been a cogent theory.

If something has not worked for twenty years, maybe change is in order. Right? Well, in 1992 voters thought they were demanding change. They wanted a new Congress, but again they reelected their own incumbent. A few new members showed up in January 1993, but the leadership (the only members who can make a difference) remained exactly the same. The voters got no change in Congress, but they lost the checks and balance on Congress that they previously had in the White House. To vote against an inept and scandalized Congress, those same voters changed their votes for president, thinking that would bring change. Fifty-seven percent of the voters got a president they didn't want, along with policies they still don't want. But congressional leadership remained the same.

Why had that happened? Why had voters become so unaware of how democracy works, of the responsibilities attendant to maintaining a republic? Why did voters (and nonvoters) not know the basic rudiments of our constitutional system? Why didn't they know that we, in the United States, have three coequal branches of government? Why didn't they know that they cannot change a Congress by voting for a Ross Perot? Why didn't they know that an unrealistic impatience with democracy can destroy it? The answer to all of those questions, I believe, has to do with the decline and failure of the public educational system. I think maybe it is the same reason why environmental problems do not get on the agenda of most folks. Oh sure, the media, especially television, deserve a major share of the blame, but I deal with that in another place, in another way.

What does the public know about DDT, PCBs, dioxins, or other substances that are toxic, and persistent, and biocumulative? What does it know about the effects of such substances on the environment? What does it know about the effects of those chemicals on humans? Why don't people know more about something that might have a direct effect on them or their children or grandchildren now, or maybe thirty or forty years from now? Here, I think, it is not just the liberal manipulations of the public educational system, but also that system's unwillingness to stay abreast of contemporary science along with today's realities and uncertainties. It is my judgment that public schools today are focused not on the best education for our children but instead on the social engineering of little humans. They are laboratories testing how children will act and react when they are torn away from their neighborhoods to be schooled with strangers, where teaching techniques are employed not to educate but to test social reactions of those being subjected to such quixotic testing; where memory is thought to be a false tool of learning; where, in an effort to be value neutral, negative values are taught as a way of proving they are not trying to teach positive values; where the liberal social agenda of the National Education Association is becoming more important than the future of our children competing in a world market.

And what about pride? I remember, in my schooling, how proud I was of my nation and of all those people two hundred years ago who set us free and created our republic. I remember the pride of singing "God Bless America." I remember praying in school on Armistice Day and Decoration Day (of course the names of those holidays have now been changed to make them more politically correct, but I will leave it to the reader to find out what they are now called—sort of a test to see if you care). That pride, taught at home and fostered in school, and the values of the Ten Commandments, not ignored in schools then, one-half century ago, gave me (and my schoolmates) the motivation to be the best I could be, for myself of course, but also for my country, my community, my school, my family. My learning responsibility was not just for me. I also carried a burden for those people and places of whom and for which I was taught to be proud. It was a burden of responsibility; a burden to preserve what they had created, fought for, and kept.

I have met many, many bright schoolchildren in my travels on both sides of the international boundary between Canada and the United States. I have seen really exciting environmental learning activities along the Rouge River and on the vessel *Nimby* (not in my back yard). I know there are dedicated teachers and brilliant students. The problem is that they now appear to be the exception, not the norm.

Today's kids are left with the thought that "if they do it, it must be okay," and "if it feels good, do it." In my early school years, if I did something just because it felt good, or just because I wanted to do it, the result would probably have been a ruler across my knuckles. If I did it again, I would probably wait in the principal's office for the custodian to come up with his paddle, under the supervision of the principal. Oh, I have heard all the debate about the evils of corporal punishment (because of his expertise with a paddle, I think my grade school custodian must have been a general); however, then and now, discipline can be an effective learning tool.

It is not my intent to brag on my public education in the 1940s and 1950s, because it left a lot to be desired. I found myself in schools that taught "down to the average." "Down to the average" was a phrase used by my innercity high school principal when he visited me during my freshman year in college. He used that phrase in answer to a question of mine about why I was not as well prepared for college as were some freshmen from rural high schools.

When I went to school, things were just different. Kindergarten was a private, voluntary type of thing. In those pre–World War II days, at age five, my friends and I walked a half mile or so to kindergarten, which was held in a storefront on Shelby Street, next to the dry goods store, across the street from the dentist, who ran his drill by pedal and foot power. Most every day, walking to and from kindergarten, we five-year-old boys and girls would play along Bean Crick. More than fifty years after graduating from the storefront preschool, where taking naps on braided rugs is about all I can remember, I met one of the girls with whom I used to play along the shores of Bean Crick. She lived then between Willow Run and Southern Avenue, on Manker Street. She walked right up to me, not having seen me for more than forty years, called me a "little shit," and showed me the scar on her forehead where I had hit her with an ice ball from the shores of Bean Crick at age five.

It wasn't always cold. Snowballs and ice balls were not always available for throwing, but a very thick foam was always there, floating on the waters of the little stream. It could be molded into something almost as good as a snowball. The foam, which ran into the crick through a pipe from the dry cleaning store on Shelby Street, could almost satisfy the roguery of a five-year-old boy. I wonder what it was, from the dry cleaning plant, that made such neat foam?

But then the Japanese bombed Pearl Harbor, and I was ready for the first grade. At that time each grade was divided into semesters. One B and one A. Or 6B and 6A. In looking at some old photographs, it appears there were

nineteen of us in grade 1B, at P.S. 72, in January 1942, with twenty of us finishing the eighth grade and moving on to high school in January 1950. Of
course, three of the kids in my class (15 percent) spent most of their time in
the dumb room. Yeah, you read that right. We would walk to school together
and be together in gym, music, and shop classes. But while the majority of
us were in our rooms dealing with science or math or English, two girls and
one boy were off in the dumb room doing whatever it was that the dumb
kids did at School 72. Other kids would come to me and say, "What room
are you in?" I would answer "Room Seven," or whatever the appropriate
number might be. When those three kids were asked about their room, they
would proudly respond, "I am in the dumb room."

So no, I am not here to claim that my formal public schooling experiences
are to be emulated as the paradigm for educational efficacy. Things were
just different then. And certainly I never once, in twenty years of formal
education, had a course dealing with the environment or environmental protection. It was not much of a concern in those long-ago days. I didn't know,
then, words like *ecology*. I did know the word *environment*, but not so much
in its connotative relationship to nature. Occasionally, though, in studying
Theodore Roosevelt we would read of his interest in conservation.

But that was then. What do we do about all this now? The Great Lakes
Educators Advisory Council had some good ideas. Some of them are para-
phrased here for your consideration. Schools, especially institutions of higher
education, should develop environmental literacy programs to ensure that
graduating students are, at least, environmentally literate citizens. University education departments should create necessary courses and programs to
ensure training in environmental literacy and environmental education
methodology for prospective teachers. Governments and school systems
should demand specific goals for environmental education at various grade
levels. Another good idea would be forming partnerships of educational,
business, and media organizations to expand the quantity and quality of information available on television about environmental concerns.

The first thing that needs to happen is for the public to get serious about
its concerns. The onus is on us (the people) to prod governments, public
education systems, and industry to center in on the real problems. Whether
those problems be the loss of the "neighborhood school" and the support it
used to receive from the local business community or a capitulation by
school administrators and teachers to offbeat ideas against discipline, competition, pride, values, learning through memory, we need solutions. We need
to consider whether it is possible to have environmental protection without
pride in self and community. We need competition to develop new ideas and

better ways of doing things. And sadly, we also need to consider whether a dulling process is slowly and subtly creeping through our population, at both the teaching and learning levels, because of alien chemical substances supplied to our environment by other humans. Obviously, solutions must be found and acted upon.

But keep in mind one terribly important fact. When we call upon governments or school districts or teacher organizations to solve these serious problems of educational failures, we need to remember that they are the ones mostly responsible for educational decline in the first place.

We need to understand that the real problem with our educational system is OUR SCHOOL.

As we began to understand in 1994 that the real problem with Congress is OUR MEMBER OF CONGRESS.

Change has to start at home. As the environmentalists say, "Think globally, act locally."

13

Future: Great Lakes and Beyond

The Message Is Not Getting Through

SOME REALLY SERIOUS HEALTH PROBLEMS face the forty million or so people living around the Great Lakes as a result of the discharge of persistent toxic substances into the waters of the Great Lakes Basin. The problems are global, but the data base in the Great Lakes is copious. Information is sufficient to know that future generations are at risk. If policy makers in the United States and Canada, including policy makers in government, industry, and other walks of life, even slightly suspected that their child or grandchild might have learning difficulties, immune suppression, or reproductive deficiencies just because of what the policy makers ate or where they lived or how they conducted their business, I am sure policy regarding the discharge of persistent substances would change immediately. I am convinced that is true, but somehow that message is not being effectively communicated.

The weight of scientific evidence supports the conclusion that what we are doing to the Great Lakes, we are doing to ourselves and to our children. Most all Great Lakes scientists acknowledge the dangers of chlorinated organics to future generations. But laws don't change very quickly. Industry does not substantially change processes and it continues to discharge persistent toxic substances into the water and air of North America. And, obviously, individual citizens do not easily change life-styles. Again, it is my belief that all would change their way of doing things if they had even a suspicion of the potential dangers to present and future generations. So what is the problem? It dawned on me that the problems we can see with the naked eye, in person or in photographs, clearly receive more attention than the more serious problems of persistent toxic substances that normally cannot be seen or pictured without elaborate laboratory equipment.

Consider this. The International Joint Commission receives several hundred thousand dollars each year from the taxpayers of Canada and the United States to deal with the problems caused by the discharge of persistent toxic substances. That is true even though there is solid evidence of what adverse effects those discharges are having on future generations, such as the ability to learn. On the other hand, even though the weight of technical evidence clearly demonstrates that water levels in the Great Lakes are overwhelmingly caused by precipitation and evaporation, the governments of the United States and Canada eagerly gave the International Joint Commission $12 million U.S. ($15 million Canadian) to study fluctuating water levels. The two federal governments gave us that money for a study, the principal conclusions of which were pretty well known in advance. Who among us could not guess that the controlling factor for water supply is nature? No matter what we say or how we act, most all of us know that we cannot control nature. What we humans don't seem to realize is that we can alter nature, often adversely. Why is our knowledge so limited?

Of the forty million or so people living around the Great Lakes–St. Lawrence River, eighty to one hundred thousand of them live or work near the water. That makes you wonder how it is that such a small part of the population (one fourth of one percent) can move their concern (water levels) up on the agenda of policy makers, while the other 99.75 percent cannot get governments to sunset the discharge of those substances so onerous that the two governments decided in the Great Lakes Water Quality Agreement that it was their policy to virtually eliminate? Either the 99 percent have not adequately communicated their concern about dioxins, furans, PCBs, et al., or those in the know have not communicated the dangers and the risks to the 99 percent. I suspect the latter is the problem, because I again say that any individual who learns that his or her progeny may be deficient or suffer because of something he or she innocently did (such as eating large trout or salmon from the Great Lakes) will communicate with the proper ears to get action.

The riparians could take pictures of their eroded shorelines, damaged cottages, and storm-ravaged communities, show them to members of Congress and parliamentarians and communicate an adverse property condition in living color. The effects of persistent toxic substances are somewhat more difficult to picture. They cannot easily be seen, felt, smelled, tasted.

Why don't scientists clearly communicate the dangers of persistent toxics to governments and the public? First, it is important to point out that scientists have, in fact, communicated various messages setting out the effects of persistent toxic substances on the environment, which includes humans. But scientists (and most all technical people) have difficulty communicating outside of their own professional community. They tend to use words such as *2,3,7,8-tetrachlorodibenzo-p-dioxin* and such statements as "Definitions are not correct in and of themselves, but some are more useful than others." What does that statement mean? I don't know, but I found it in a report submitted to the International Joint Commission. Scientists often need interpreters to carry their messages on to those who need to be convinced. Scientists would surely doubt that statement. They tend to think the problem is that the people in the middle, such as IJC commissioners, do not interpret and deliver the message properly to those in charge; otherwise policy makers would act.

It sometimes seems that everyone is right and everyone is wrong. The problem is still one of learning how to properly communicate some very serious messages. We are not getting the message through. We still don't know how to deal with danger within the reality of scientific uncertainty. All of our statements are qualified with a "may" or a "might," implying a lack of urgency. We don't even speak with sufficient clarity to spur precautionary actions. It makes one wonder where policy makers do get their information on environmental matters. From scientific reports? From the news media? From staff reports? Where do staff members find their information? Do those who work for members of congress tell their bosses there is no problem, because they think that is what the bosses want to hear? Do research and development people in industry tell the CEO that no environmental problems exist with the use of a particular feed stock or industrial process because the boss wants to hear about ways of saving money instead of ways to spend more?

The communication necessary to result in pollution prevention must take place at the top level. The midlevel discussions are not moving us forward. Decision makers from differing forums must come together and communicate with each other to decide if real problems exist and to ponder ways to resolve such problems. When the governor of my state decided to stop warning citizens that some fish, in some locations, if eaten, could cause death, cancer, reproductive problems, etc., the response was silence. It was a front-page news story, but few people, including legislators in session, seemed to think it was a problem serious enough for concern. Hoosier environmentalists seemed to be tongue-tied. The resulting silence was ubiquitous.

In communicating problems and risks to the general public, remember the discussion about deficiencies in our public education. An apathetic state of unawareness does exist. Too many citizens do not read printed materials about environmental problems. Too many citizens do not read newspapers or news magazines. Too many do not even watch television news. The conclusion from those statements, if you accept them, is that the message to the general public must be very, very clear. No ambiguities. But it is that clear, unambiguous message that scientists fear, because the issuance of such a statement will bring the charge that they are merely being alarmists, or that they are coming to closure on an issue prematurely. Sometimes alarms do need to be sounded. There can be alarms warning of imminent danger and there can be precautionary alarms. And, I continue to wonder, when is precaution premature?

There are truly many barriers to communicating the message about the effects of the discharge of persistent toxic substances in addition to the trepidation of many scientists. Those barriers might include the use of technical language, fear of rejection or damage to reputation, extreme caution, communicating with the wrong listeners. To me, the strangest of the barriers preventing widespread communication of environmental concerns is the demand for absolute scientific certainty. How did we, as a society, come to the conclusion that unless a chemical substance could be proved bad beyond any shadow of a doubt, that it is good? Why did we decide that no precautionary measures should be taken to protect ourselves from a substance that science fears may be having an adverse effect on humans and their unborn progeny, unless we had absolute certain scientific proof that the substance caused the effect without any inkling of doubt? Why no communication of concern?

What other aspect of human life demands such certainty before exercising caution? Not the law; we convict people on the subjective judgment of just twelve individuals. Not education, where 70 percent can be a passing grade. Not religion, where there is always room for forgiveness and atonement. Not health care; take two aspirins and call tomorrow. Certainly not the media, reporters never being accountable for what they said yesterday. In accounting? Engineering? Architecture? All have margins for error.

But in the regulation of the manufacture, use, and disposal of persistent toxic substances, we demand scientific certainty that the substances cause harm. Not certainty that they are safe, but certainty that they cause harm to humans and wildlife. Is it intellectually honest, in this uncertain world, to demand such certainty on one side of a proposition and not the other? In my congressional testimony on May 24, 1994, I said:

> As a campaign manager, I tend to think in terms of strategy and tactics.
>
> In the debate over persistent toxic substances, I see one side applying a strategy of getting good science on the table and then using the tactic of educating the public about that science. The theory being that the people will act, if they are subjected to the facts. On the other side of the debate, I see a strategy of keeping information off the table; out of public view. The tactic is to squash any legitimate attempt at fact finding, such as that proposed by the President of the United States in a study to determine whether or not the fears about chlorine as a class are real. I wonder if what we don't know will hurt us. We can all have differing views about what the role of government should be relative to environmental concerns, but surely, fact finding and informing the public is a responsibility of government that most all of us can agree upon.

It sounded logical to me, but my words only stimulated glazed stares by federal legislators who hear so many words that it becomes difficult for them to distinguish between words of wisdom and words of nonsense. It is easier for them to keep on doing what they have always done. Somehow, such barriers against communicating environmental concerns must be overcome!

A Communications Agenda

As I finished my tour as chairman of the International Joint Commission, I was asked to write an article for the commission's newsletter *Focus*. The article was to pull from my supposed wisdom, being the senior commissioner and all. It was to be something of a legacy, advice I could leave behind that would be of value in future work of the commission. I struggled with that thought for a while, as I pondered all the important things the commission could be doing.

Trying to understand how pollutants get into the water. Where they are coming from. How to safely get them out. That's a big job. Likewise, understanding the relevance of everything to everything else is a big job. You know, what you do in British Columbia affects some folks in Wyoming.

What I do in Indiana affects some folks in Maine and New Brunswick. What some farmer does with DDT to increase his crop output in the Indian subcontinent creates problems around Lake Superior. Environmental problems are global and it is a big, big world. So what is the most important thing that could happen if our goals are to prevent pollution from happening in the first place, or to figure out how to avoid it, or, in the end, to clean up the problems of the past? What catalytic role could the International Joint Commission play, to really move things along? I pondered all of that and wrote the following, which I titled "Ruminations."

It seems like a lot of people care. Nearly 2,000 people came to the IJC's Biennial Meeting in Windsor last October, the most ever. Approximately 14,000 individuals and organizations have been identified as being interested enough in what the commission does that we have included them on the mailing list for this newsletter. But please do remember, there are 40,000,000 or more people living in the Great Lakes Basin. And it is true. I have more than twenty years of formal education and a doctorate degree, but math was not much of a factor in my education, qualitatively or quantitatively. Even so, I have calculated that somewhere between 0.005 percent and 0.035 percent of the people care, even in the slightest, about the work pursued by the commission. The weight of evidence would imply that perhaps whistling in the dark would be a more fruitful use of our time and taxpayer resources.

But let's think about that. What is the IJC agenda, as it relates to the Great Lakes? The duties are clearly set out in the Great Lakes Water Quality Agreement. The United States and Canada assigned to the International Joint Commission the responsibility to monitor and assess progress made pursuant to the Agreement, in particular the adequacy of actions by the two federal governments, the Province of Ontario and the States of Illinois, Indiana, Michigan, Minnesota, New York, Ohio, Pennsylvania and Wisconsin.

The commission was assigned a duty to assist governments in implementation, given a review function for Remedial Action Plans and Lake Wide Management Plans, and it was also given a public information responsibility, . . . ergo this newsletter.

And what did Canada and the United States agree to do in their agreement? They said the purpose of their Agreement was to restore and maintain the chemical, physical, and biological integrity of the Great Lakes Basin ecosystem. They agreed it was their policy that the discharge of toxic substances in toxic amounts be prohibited and the discharge of any and all persistent toxic substances be virtually eliminated, pursuing a philosophy of zero discharge. All of those words, *ecosystem, virtual elimination, zero discharge,* are words of the two federal governments, formally adopted in their Agreement, an Agreement which was finally given the force of law in the U.S. by the Great Lakes Critical Programs Act of 1990. Too often, those who might disagree with the goals of the Agreement tend to think the Agreement and its words are the creation of the commission. Not so!

So, the work is important. Progress has been made. Plans for remediation in Areas of Concern are well along, in some cases. Governments have spent large sums of money, with many positive results. But the work is far from done. The commission has been given important duties; to assist, to review, to monitor and assess, to provide public information. It is that latter responsibility where I believe the commission can best be a catalyst for future success. It is also the area where the commission, the governments, the public groups, and others have experienced their greatest failures.

Serious problems exist because of the discharge of persistent toxic substances into the Great Lakes environment (and the global environment). Cancers, reproductive failures, immune suppression, neurological problems, learning deficiencies, behavior abnormalities are just some of the possible adverse effects to wildlife and humans. All exist in an era of scientific uncertainty, as problems continue to expand faster than science can confirm them.

But still, we have not adequately informed the public about the possibilities of what "we" do know, if I may use the collective "we." Most people do care about environmental quality, but most people don't think about it every day of their lives, as do "we," the Choir, to whom I am preaching, and most people really are not aware of the potential problems. Most don't know what chemicals are good or bad, which ones are being discharged (albeit legally) into the water, the air and the ground. Most people still believe they can trust their government to protect them from such toxic substances, although faith in government is a diminishing tenet.

Our failure is that even with all that we now know, we have not clearly told the residents of the Great Lakes Basin (and the world) that precaution just might be in order. Fish consumption advisories are not apparent and go unnoticed or ignored. People do not suspect their health is at risk, primarily because "we" have not made it clear to those who fund cleanups and research, or to those who with a process change could prevent future discharges, or to those in the general public who should be made aware of the involuntary risks to which they might be subjected. That failure to inform is why I am excited about one of the priorities set for the next two year cycle of the IJC. I will look forward to the 8th Biennial Report to see how it comes out. The priority would anticipate a grouping of staff and non-staff communications experts to work at the task of:

1. *Defining the appropriate Great Lakes message.* Included, I would think, would be the value of the Great Lakes to industry, recreation, riparians, education, preservation of natural systems, and just the personal enjoyment of nature by individual citizens. A second area might be all the reasons why the system should be restored and maintained as called for by the Agreement. A third area would *need to be* a summary of the most serious problems facing the Great Lakes, . . . persistent toxic substances, and a listing of potential effects.

2. *Defining the audience* to whom the message is to be delivered. Is the audience the people who make the laws and fund research and clean-up ac-

tivities? Is it the people who could most easily prevent such onerous discharges, if they would? Is it the educators, the physicians, the engineers, the municipal leaders? All of the above. Should audiences be prioritized?

3. *Defining the most effective methods by which the best messages, to the appropriate audiences, can be delivered.* I have sat at tables with scientists, regulators and others, all agreeing upon a message of import that would, unfortunately, never find its way to the ears or eyes of legislators, administrators, educators, industrialists, or the average person out there just going about her business. Quite often, how the message is delivered is as important as the message. Certainly an undelivered message is of little use.

Essentially, the task is to determine the message, define the audience, and then come up with an effective delivery scheme. The commission could then recommend that package for use to governments, industry, educational institutions, public groups and whoever else might be identified.

Technical people, I suspect, will not think this matter deserves priority status. And some will worry about blame being attached to the messenger. However, as a person who has spent a lifetime concerned about messages and their delivery, I am convinced that a widespread public awareness is the first step toward solving societal problems. As an outgoing commissioner, it is my hope that this priority just might be the catalyst that does truly make a difference for all who are concerned about achieving the goals of the Great Lakes Water Quality Agreement.

I believed those words then and I do now. Too many technical people involved in the Great Lakes work presume that what they know is common knowledge. And if anything was ever not true, it is that. The future environmental well-being of the Great Lakes, and the world, is in the hands of people willing to take a stand. If we tell them the truth, they will take their stand.

14

Late Words on Chlorine

As EARLIER MENTIONED, a few significant declarations were made by governments toward the end of my service on the International Joint Commission. For more than four years, my colleagues and I had made a valiant attempt to draw attention to the role of organochlorines as common precursors for many of the persistent toxic substances. We had some degree of success, but as I have said, the United States and Canada formally replied to the commission that orderly actions to sunset chlorine as an industrial feed stock were premature. The United States and Canada rejected a specific chlorine recommendation from the commission in October 1993. In January 1994, however, both governments, especially the United States, began acting positively on that very same recommendation.

Organochlorines are a class of industrial chemicals made from chlorine and carbon-based organic matter. They have been around for quite a while, but they only came into heavy use following World War II. Such chemical substances as PCBs, DDT, and dioxin fall into that class. Most chlorine use is in the manufacture of vinyl and other plastics, in pesticides and industrial solvents. Pulp bleaching is also a major use.

Organochlorinated substances stay in the environment for a long, long time; for decades, maybe for centuries. They have found their way into the bodies of probably all humans on earth, and they can result in the adverse health effects set out in the United States–Canada definition of toxic that I have mentioned so often in this book, not the least of which is the inability to reproduce. The effects of these chlorinated substances on wildlife have become pretty well known. Their effects on humans are less well known, though they are highly suspected to be the same on the human mammal as on other mammals.

A chain of events began at the very beginning of the last decade of the twentieth century that could sound the death knell for organochlorinated substances.

- The calls from environmental groups, notably Greenpeace, in the Great Lakes were loud and clear but were not given serious enough attention by the decision makers of the time.
- The 1990, 1992, and 1994 reports and recommendations of the International Joint Commission on persistent toxic substances, specifically chlorinated organics, were at the forefront of intellectual debate and international leadership.
- Industry was still leaving the matter in the hands of its lobbyists to deny, attempting to divert attention from itself and onto a bunch of econuts, and working to delay any potential action.
- But it was the leadership role played by Dr. Theo Colborn that was undoubtedly the defining factor in turning the corner on this debate. Dr. Colborn was instrumental in bringing together eminent scientists from around the world, crossing disciplines, forming conclusions, all of which resulted in a major conference on hormone-mimicking chemicals in Washington, D.C., in January 1994.
- The *Washington Post* covered the conference, and on January 25, 1994, ran a major story on estrogens in the environment.
- On January 28, 1994, the Clinton Administration sent to Congress its proposals for changing the Clean Water Act. Those proposals operated on the premise that "some pollutants are extremely harmful in small quantities and/or build up in the food chain to produce adverse and long-term effects to human health and the environment. Emerging evidence links certain pollutants not only to cancer, but also to neurological, reproductive, developmental and immunological adverse effects. . . . Some pollutants may also persist in the environment for decades, posing a continuing threat to humans, aquatic organisms, birds and other wildlife.

It was also about that same time that the government of Canada was deciding that chlorinated wastewater effluents, discharged from municipal wastewater treatment plants, were toxic and harmful to health. But the Clinton proposals were more on point. They would give the Environmental Protection Agency discretionary authority to prohibit multimedia environmental releases that cause or contribute to a water quality impairment, but such authority would not apply to pesticides, for some reason. I suspect the agriculture lobbyists were a little better organized and more alert around the White House than were the chemical industry lobbyists.

On chlorine and chlorinated compounds, the Clinton proposal was: "To develop a strategy to comprehensively protect human health and the environment and to move towards the national goal of the Clean Water Act of eliminating the discharge of toxic pollutants, the Administration will develop a national strategy for substituting, reducing, or prohibiting the use of chlorine and chlorinated compounds. . . ." To create a task force within six months. To collect, within eighteen months, all data "on the use, and environmental and health impacts of chlorine and chlorinated compounds. . . ." And then within thirty months to "(1) Review the information collected by the task force; (2) develop a plan for any appropriate actions, including the exercise of existing statutory authorities, to restrict or prohibit the use of chlorine and chlorinated compounds. . . ." The plan would then be put out for public review and implemented. A yearly budget of two million dollars would be provided for the study and strategy development, if the proposal is included and passed in the Clean Water Act. It is the beginning of the very orderly process recommended by the International Joint Commission in 1992.

As I said earlier, it was fun to be a commissioner on a small, low-budget, independent international commission and to see the development of my work as it became policy in Canada, the United States, or both. The President made a proposal nearly 100 percent in agreement with the reports and recommendations of the International Joint Commission, even though just three months earlier the United States had formally rejected the idea. Interesting. It is true, I have noticed, that Clinton doesn't always do what he says he is going to do, but he did pass his proposal on to the Democrat-controlled 103rd Congress, which adjourned after passing only one environmental bill (regarding a desert in California). The remainder of the chlorine proposal is in the hands of the Environmental Protection Agency.

Just a few weeks later, on March 21, 1994, the government of Canada announced a similar undertaking. In the House of Commons debates of that date, a member cited the recommendations and statements of the International Joint Commission on the industrial use of chlorine as a feed stock. The government acknowledged the health concerns relative to chlorine use and the parliamentary secretary to the deputy prime minister announced,

"Through the Great Lakes action plans and programs in place already and through close interaction with other countries, especially the United States, we need to establish strategies along with our neighbors to the south to reduce, prohibit and substitute for the use of chlorine and chlorinated compounds." And he said further, "Currently the minister of the environment is convening a consultation process of multi-stakeholders to do exactly this, to try and define an action plan to reduce, prohibit and substitute the use of chlorine. This action plan should be ready by the late spring of this year." This announcement came just five months following Canada's rejection of the IJC recommendation.

Also included in President Clinton's Clean Water Act proposals was the following:

> Within three years of enactment, the National Academy of Science should complete a study for the Congress on the current knowledge of chemicals that exhibit endocrine, immune, and nervous system health effects in humans and wildlife, including evidence that they increase the incidence of breast cancer, decreased sperm count, or impaired reproduction. The study should include recommendations for any appropriate actions which are based upon scientifically defensible findings for reducing or prohibiting the production and/or use of such chemicals. There should be $500 thousand appropriated per year to fund this study.

A new study was to begin at Laval University in Quebec in the fall of 1994 to test a widely held suspicion that organochlorines may play a role in causing breast cancer. And then finally, on June 30, 1994, the Michigan Environmental Science Board's Chlorine Panel released a report somewhat different from what I had expected it to be. It would seem to be some more good news for preventing pollution. On November 18, 1993, Governor John Engler had asked a panel of scientists to evaluate the IJC chlorine recommendation and to evaluate for him the status of Michigan's regulations relative to chlorine. Governor Engler is to be commended for his attention to the concerns about chlorine use, and for pursuing an orderly process as recommended by the International Joint Commission.

The body of Michigan scientists, although representative of a good mix of disciplines, was still a body of scientists. For that reason, I feared that absolute certainty of harm would be a criterion before recommending any precautionary actions. I was wrong. The panel concluded that "insufficient evidence does not prove lack of potential for harm." Another concern I have mentioned is the folly of trying to consider chemicals one at a time, rather than looking at classes of chemicals. The Michigan panel, even with some qualification, took another big step forward for society and concluded that "the grouping of chemical substances for regulatory purposes on the basis of physical, chemical and biological characteristics is scientifically defensible whereas consideration of a single property (e.g. chlorine) alone is likely to be inadequate for the intended purpose. Thus, persistent toxic chlorinated and non-chlorinated compounds released to the environment can be treated as a group for the purpose of regulatory control."

The Chlorine Panel also recognized the need for an orderly process as recommended by the IJC by saying, "The known toxicity of certain chlorinated compounds, particularly those exhibiting persistence, and the possibility that unknown products of similar toxic potential are now reaching the environment, or may do so in the future, makes it necessary to evaluate current and future uses of chlorine and chlorinated compounds." So even though the Michigan scientists occasionally fell into the trap of saying not to worry about some substances because others substances were more problematic, and even though they did not fully agree with the recommendations of the IJC while I was the United States chair, they did move science a few steps closer to reality, a few steps closer to real pollution prevention of the most onerous substances. Although the strides may seem to be just baby steps to laypeople, for scientists those few little steps were huge.

The governments are beginning to talk the talk pretty good. Will they walk the walk? Will they seek the truth and communicate it to the public? I hope so, but I am not holding my breath.

15

Time for a Change

Reflections on the International Joint Commission

THE INTERNATIONAL JOINT COMMISSION has not been a highly profiled entity, when one looks at the entirety of government. The commission is much better known in Canada than it is in the United States. The reason, obviously, is that life along the international boundary, and especially near the Great Lakes, affects a much greater percentage of Canadians than it does their U.S. counterparts. I say this with the realization that folks from the Western Provinces have little empathy for the concerns of eastern Canada. Politicians in the United States, and some nonpoliticians, if they know about the commission, tend to think of it as a place where political hacks can make a good salary without doing much work. After each presidential election, those in the know, who have supported the winning candidate, clamor for a chance to be on the International Joint Commission.

No matter how hard commissioners might work or how successful the commission might be during their tenure, they still hear from media, friends, even family, about the soft job. No work and big pay, they continue to think. Hopefully, that is not the attitude of any who might actually become commissioners. The plate is pretty full. The staff is minimal. The budget is small. The travel is incessant. The work is challenging and important. The opportunity to make a difference is great. If all the commissioners do not work at the job, failure will be their reward.

The commission has offices in Washington, Ottawa, and Windsor, but the travel is normally to where the work is. It might be a remedial action plan review meeting in Erie, Pennsylvania, or Sault St. Marie, Ontario. It could be in Toronto or Rochester. Maybe Estevan, Saskatchewan, or Devils Lake, North Dakota. It can be to really neat places such as Victoria out there on Vancouver Island or Niagara-on-the-Lake or Kingston. During the fifty-two weeks of 1993, I made thirty-five trips, some of them to combinations of events and places. Of course, each of those trips required hours, and sometimes days, of mental preparation. More than a hundred days on the road in 1993, in and of itself, is not a soft job. Air travel is tough and very dehumanizing. The loading and unloading process has an ovine characteristic to it. I am glad to be off that air travel circuit, where, on the average over four years, one flight out of every five had problems. When flights are canceled so often, you might think the ground crews would be prepared. They never are. It is always a mess. But one of the really good things about being a United States commissioner on the International Joint Commission is that you need not move to Washington, D.C. What a relief that was. Flying out of Indianapolis International was much more tolerable than time spent at Washington National Airport.

The primary responsibility of the commission under the Great Lakes Water Quality Agreement is a watchdog role. The commission monitors and assesses how well the two federal governments, the eight state governments, and the Province of Ontario are doing in meeting the environmental requirements of the agreement. Living in Washington amid the insular thinking that occurs there (within the beltway, as they say), would make a watchdog role very difficult. Governments are easier to monitor and assess from a distance. Carrying out the watchdog role requires a myriad of meetings, briefings, scientific roundtables and workshops, reading and understanding vast quantities of words on reams and reams of paper. The watchdog role, under the Great Lakes Water Quality Agreement, accounts for a majority of commissioner time, as much as 90 percent at times. The 1987 protocol to the agreement added much more work for commissioners.

Water quantity concerns can also be time consuming, as they were in the spring of 1993, when high waters threatened the residents of Lake Ontario. And to understand the decisions they are required to make, commissioners must travel, from time to time, to the various meetings of commission boards all along the boundary between Canada and the United States. And new air-quality concerns have been deposited on the work plate of the International Joint Commission under the United States–Canada Air Agreement. There is, in fact, more work assigned than can be handled by commissioners and a small U.S. staff. And as a good conservative, I did not fill employee vacancies as they came up; but in reality, those vacancies were only three in number. The Canadian staff in Ottawa, on the other hand, is nearly double the U.S. staff in Washington. My experience and prejudices indicate that smaller is better. But that also means commissioners are required to work, if the work is to be done. During my time, we had hard-working and dedicated individuals as commissioners.

People with Whom I Served

In four and one-half years, I served with ten commissioners on the International Joint Commission. When I first came aboard, Pierre-Andre Bissonnette was the Canadian chairman. He was ill and passed away within a few months of my beginning. Commissioner E. Davie Fulton, a revered figure in Canada, then became the Canadian chair. Davie Fulton is a brilliant man. A man of deep convictions. Serving with him was an intellectually challenging adventure. Together we pursued great thoughts, devoured new ideas, and made major decisions and innovative recommendations to the governments of Canada and the United States. Many became law or policy in our two great nations.

Robert S. K. Welch, Q.C., is a man of intellectual common sense, with many talents, many accomplishments, and, most of all, a good friend. Gordon Walker, Q.C., is an activist, a man on the move, a guy who wants to get things done, the right way. The Canadian nickname for Gordon is Gord, not the more gentle Gordy, as I was known in my younger years. Hard to get used to being called something that sounds like gourd. James Macaulay, Q.C., is a quiet man, but highly motivated and highly successful, always well prepared.

And then there is my good friend Claude Lanthier, ing. Have you ever noticed how Canadians like to have little initials behind their names? Some, such as Davie Fulton, have numerous initials, all representing meritorious service to their nation and the resulting high honors received. Claude has "ing." behind his name. I think it is the French abbreviation for the word *engineer*. That's what he is, an engineer, and a darn good one. He also is an expert arbitrator. For the last two years or so of my service, he was my counterpart as the Canadian chairman of the commission. Claude Lanthier is on constant alert for conflicts of interest. He insisted upon a squeaky clean operation, and should any of us begin to drift astray, he would quickly bring us back within the fold. While Davie Fulton concerned himself with the why, Claude was more attuned to the how. The discipline of an engineer, no doubt. Davie was serious, Claude was fun. But when it came time to do the job, especially in drafting the final two major reports during my service, Claude Lanthier was on the side of the angels.

I knew about the work of the International Joint Commission, due to the service of my good friend L. Keith Bulen. Keith was a U.S. commissioner for eight years under President Reagan. He brought the first biennial meeting of the IJC to Indianapolis; I attended and listened to concerns about which I had not previously been exposed. Keith Bulen has succeeded in all his life endeavors simply because no one cares more, works harder, or thinks more broadly and deeply than does he. He tried to resign before I came aboard, but technically our times overlapped for a while. Another U.S. commissioner, Donald L. Totten, also served under Reagan but stayed on with us for a while under the Bush Administration. An engineer, an accomplished politician, Don is from Schaumburg, Illinois, and was a driving force behind the Great Lakes Fluctuating Water Levels Study.

My Bush colleagues on the commission were Hilary Cleveland from New Hampshire and Robert F. Goodwin of Maryland (originally Iowa). Hilary was only the second female commissioner with the IJC. The first had also been from New Hampshire. A no-nonsense, straightforward New Englander, Hilary could always be relied upon to get to the nub of any problem. She did her homework, she was always prepared, and when she spoke up she always had something meaningful to contribute. What a delight it was to have a colleague with no hidden agenda, with a true concern for her fellow human beings, with compassion for wildlife and nature, and with a willingness to be forward looking and hardworking.

Ambassador Bob Goodwin was another individual who could quietly assess a problematic situation and offer a constructive, well-thought-out solution. Bob is another one of those hardworking guys who has achieved success in most all of his endeavors, except one. He was confirmed by the United States Senate as ambassador to New Zealand shortly before the 1992 election. When Bush lost and Clinton won, the Clinton folks didn't want him to go. So Ambassador Bob stayed on the International Commission, while the ambassador's position remained vacant for at least a year. New Zealand's loss was my gain. Bob Goodwin was another great colleague.

I think that adds up to ten. Great people all. Dedicated and willing to give their time and talents, in work that, if properly observed, could make a real difference for humankind.

Future of the International Joint Commission

The future of the International Joint Commission depends entirely upon the commissioners who succeed me and my co-commissioners. When I came on the commission, Keith Bulen suggested it would be necessary for me to broaden my thinking. I had thought I was a broad thinker, a big-picture kind of guy. But Keith was right. I had not been chairman long before I was buying and reading books on the history of Canada—books on the ABCs of the human body, trying to understand how the reproductive process works—books on chemical terminology (what is a congener?)—failing to understand recorded cassettes in my car that were trying to teach me the French language—and reading a whole series of past reports from the commission, the governments, the universities, and the environmental organizations.

The learning curve is sharp for new commissioners, but it is up to them to make the job what they want it to be. They can quietly sit back, making no waves, issuing noncontroversial and nonconsequential reports. They can be receptacles of irritable governmental problems, hiding those problems from public view as they quietly spend years studying them. Or they can get ahead of the curve. They can be catalysts for governmental action at the state and provincial, federal, even international levels. That latter course has been the tradition of the commission, and I hope the tradition continues.

There is always a need for government watchdogs, and governments quite often need a catalytic prodding. A binational commission with no authority to act, just a responsibility to study, recommend, and inform, is something of an ideal watchdog. That is especially so when the binational commissioners are not bound by the policies of their own governments in carrying out their duties. We operated in just that way during my time on the International Joint Commission.

Then we heard that the Clinton Administration wanted a new group of U.S. commissioners "not as green as the current bunch." As conservative Republicans, we found that sentiment amusing, knowing that we were to be replaced by liberal Democrats. But it is consistent with what I have said throughout this book. Liberals may talk the talk, but they don't always walk the walk. My hope is that what we heard does not become reality. For if it does, it means the lobbyists may once again have an undue influence, not only on the operations of government but also on those who are to be the watchdogs of government. I have met with the new "Clinton commissioners" and I think the commission will be in good hands.

Bright people, caring about the well-being of their nations and their peoples, unfettered by restrictions of their own governmental policies and bureaucracies, can provide a shining light in a time when too many lights of freedom and progress in North America are being dimmed. As I left the International Joint Commission, the commission was a major player, a leader, in the worldwide efforts to find solutions to the most serious environmental problems. It should continue to be so.

Future of Environmental and Conservative Concerns

In addition to the International Joint Commission, what lies ahead for environmental protection? Is it an issue that should be co-opted by conservatives, since liberals, despite all of their soothing words, have failed to be serious stewards? Should not conserving our natural resources, our way of life, our quality of life, our health, be a conservative issue? Should not the prevention of adverse human health effects be a conservative goal, as opposed to the current regulatory efforts at the tail end of the industrial chain? I think so.

William E. Gladstone was four times the prime minister of Great Britain in the nineteenth century. Encyclopedias say he was an Olympian figure. I think that means he was a biggie. He started his political career as a Tory but later became famous as a Liberal. Even so, his statement which I used at the beginning of this book is important. He said, at some point in his career, "It is the duty of government to make it difficult for people to do wrong, easy to do right." Most North Americans would still agree: such is the duty of government. Most would also agree that somewhere, somehow, something went badly wrong. Now it seems that governments make it easy to do wrong, because wrong is not a politically correct concept. Nor is right. Quite often, those who do right, by the standards of most people, are treated as wrongdoers. Those who do wrong often seem to benefit by their acts.

I spent a lot of words in this treatise giving examples of government gone wrong. Such as:

- The governments say it is bad for industry to discharge poisons into the water or air, but, for a fee, governments will allow those discharges.
- Governments stock fish into the waters because persistent toxic substances, put there legally by government permit, prevent the fish from reproducing. Then governments warn people not to eat those same fish

that they put in the waters, because the poisons, permitted by government, are in the fish.

- In my own state, the Democrats in charge of the government decided they could save a lot of money if they didn't test fish for poisons or bother warning people what could happen to them or their children if they ate the fish. You remember, don't you, what could happen? Things like "death, disease, behavioral abnormalities, cancer, genetic mutations, physiological or reproductive malfunctions or physical deformities in any organism or its offspring," or at least that is what the governments of the United States and Canada say could happen, and it is what they agreed to in article one of their international agreement. Once more government is setting the spurious example; wrong is okay.

An independent watchdog, such as the IJC with the responsibility to alert governments to such failures, can, in the public interest, call attention to such governmental misfeasance. But what bothered me most is not that the governor canceled fish testing and fish consumption advisories but that there was no loud protest of his actions. No one seemed to care. Republican legislators did not say a word. Democrat legislators said nothing. The environmental groups were silent. So I guess public outrage was just too much to expect.

Leadership, in an instance such as the Indiana case, could make a difference. Conservative leadership could make a major difference. Republicans in Indiana were handed a major opportunity but did not recognize it. Any Republican legislator could have informed the public that the governments of the United States and Canada had agreed that PCBs, DDT, dioxins, furans, and other persistent toxic substances floating in on air currents could cause the adverse health effects listed above. That eating fish laden with those substances discharged into the waters could transfer those poisonous substances, in increased biocumulative amounts with their adverse effects, to you, your children, and your grandchildren. They could have informed the public that the Indiana governor had chosen not to test fish for those substances or to warn people of the dangers of eating such fish. But no one spoke up. Apathy reigned.

At the federal level, where until 1995 Democrats had been in effective charge of Congress for as far back as my fifty-eight-year-old mind could remember, government did not come to grips with environmental protection. Environmentalists believe liberals will eventually save the day. I don't. I have given up any hope that facts have any meaning to the previous leadership in Congress. To them responsibility has a different meaning than what it has for most of us. Words, to the beltway insiders, seem to be just tools to be used in gaining an advantage. Promises are not promises. Just words.

Those people played with the minds of our youth with social experimentation in schools and among the poor, and they have wreaked havoc on our society. Liberals have said all the words environmentalist love to hear but failed to provide the people with environmental protection. They have somewhat successfully taught us worship of self in lieu of worship of God. They have tried to resolve crime by empathizing with the criminal. In 1993 they took full control of the White House and Congress, where they seemed bent on wrecking the entrepreneurial system that has worked so well for so long, and they thought a bureaucratized and socialized health care system was within their grasp. Such philosophies have failed in America, as they have failed throughout Europe and the rest of the world. Each time they are tried, they fail. In November of 1994 the voters rejected those philosophies. In January of 1995 the Republicans took control of Congress. Conservatives will now have their chance. Will environmental issues be on their agenda?

It is now time to give conservatives a chance, but will they stay too long? Many Americans believe that putting a limit on how many terms an elected official can serve is an answer to a sleepy, fast-talking, slow-walking government. My own governor, and many state and county officials in Indiana, have term limits that work pretty well. I might become upset with my governor, but there is solace in knowing that come the end of eight years, he is out of here. Those term limits work well, but what about at the congressional level? Would they work there? The people in many states are beginning to think the answer is yes. Courts are beginning to say the answer is no.

I have long harbored another idea for our legislative bodies that receives a reaction similar to the term-limit idea. Whenever I mention it, people think it too simplistic to enact. But I don't mind such elitist criticism. Some of the best ideas, it seems to me, are the ones that are simple enough to work. My idea is a continuation of Barry Goldwater's thought from the early 1960s, that we don't need new laws, we need to get rid of some of the ones we already have, or at least make them compatible to achieving intended goals.

So here is my simple silly idea. Why not dedicate the first hour of every session day, in all state and federal (and provincial) legislative bodies, with discussion from a mandated agenda? The agenda might include:

1. How can we reduce government spending?
2. What taxes can be reduced or eliminated?
3. What laws do we have that we can make better?
4. What laws do we have that we can get rid of?

All of the rest of the legislators' time could be spent dealing with new laws, as they now do. The "ins" will claim such a mandate would waste time, but what other entity in our society wastes more time than do legislative bodies? Just like term limits or balanced budgets, right? Never happen, right?

So what do we do? How do we complete the change that began with the 1994 elections, a change that would foster individual freedoms with economic growth and environmental protection? The best opportunity to do that, it seems to me, is by electing a Republican president and Republican members to both houses of Congress. If voters really want change, try that. Make Republicans the majority party in Congress and let them work with a Republican president. It is a totally new concept. It is different. It is real change. It is something that has not been tried in the United States within the lifetime of most voters. It will work. It just might be the revolutionary change in government the Perot voters were demanding in 1992. It just might bring about the change most all Americans have been looking for.

Not since I was a boy, not since before rock and roll, not since before Elvis sang *Teddy Bear* and *Hound Dog*, not since television was an amusing new gadget, have we had a Republican president with Republican majorities in both houses of Congress. The Democrats have enjoyed that opportunity on numerous occasions. That just may be why our nation is in such trouble; why environmental protection has not become reality; why laws on the environment are nonecosystemic and conflicting one to the other; and why some of the effective environmental laws on the books are not being adequately enforced.

It is indeed time for a change!

16

Conservative Environmentalism

CAN A POLITICAL CONSERVATIVE BE an environmentalist? Can an environmentalist be a political conservative? Sure. Why not? Who says otherwise—besides those in the media, teachers of political science, non-thinking liberals, and unthinking conservatives? Let me tell you why I think those folks are wrong. When I attend meetings of the Wildlife Federation and other environmental groups, even Greenpeace, I have people come up to me after my speech telling me that they are Republicans and political conservatives. They thank me for giving them an excuse to come out of the closet, so to speak. Why are they at those meetings? It is simple. They have experienced an environmental problem; they, or someone in their family or neighborhood, have been an environmental victim and they are trying to learn more. Such environmental groups are often the only source of environmental information, especially information about adverse human health effects, available to average people. For them their political philosophy is not a barrier to learning.

It is important to stress that most environmentalists I have met, in the United States and internationally, are not organized by any large group. Most of them are environmental victims, relatives of environmental victims, or friends of environmental victims. Their numbers are growing in the same proportion as are breast cancer, testicular cancer, reproductive problems, learning problems, and juvenile crime. A lot of those environmental victims are conservative Republicans.

In past years, many Republicans were conservationists. Teddy Roosevelt is a good example; Benjamin Harrison is another. Charles Lindbergh, the "Lone Eagle" who first flew solo over the Atlantic Ocean, was a conservative conservationist. Lindy opposed big government and was protective of individual rights, though he was duped for a while by the promises of Hitler. His fame and his political philosophy opened many doors for the conservation movement. But then it makes sense, doesn't it, for political conservatives to promote conservation, to save what we have, to try to make things as they were?

Recall again that there are differences between contemporary environmental movements and the century-old conservation movement. Oh, they mix and mingle quite a bit, but the primary differences are stark. When I speak before environmental groups, I find an audience somewhat young, impatient, and angry. Conservation groups, on the other hand, tend to be older, less angry, and nearly as interested in food sources for butterflies as they are in adverse human health effects. The conservation movement which began in the late years of the nineteenth century originated more or less as a hobby for the wealthy and elite in our society. For folks with names such as Roosevelt. For academics. For people who wanted to conserve natural resources for their own use, to save wildlife habitat for hunting, fishing, photography, and other human uses.

Contemporary environmental movements, on the other hand, have tended to be born of anger. Many of the leaders of the civil protests in the 1960s became deeply involved in the environmental movement. Jack Weinberg of Greenpeace was a leader of one of the first protest marches in Berkeley, California. It was the uninvited and unknowing assault on the human body that enraged such people. They were solidified by the writings of Rachel Carson. They were people among whom conservative Republicans would feel ill at ease. They were people for conservatives to ignore and to discredit. In the 1960s, 1970s, and 1980s, it was easy to be a conservative conservationist, hard to be a conservative environmentalist. But times have changed, at least somewhat.

As a conservative appointee of George Bush, I stepped into the lion's den and found myself accepted with open arms, not snarling teeth. Oh, they were a little leery of me for a while, but listening to what they had to say and treating them with respect caused them to treat me likewise. An honest discussion, a baring of the facts, is what most environmentalists are after.

They will take all the help they can get. I would invite conservative politicians and business executives to attend environmental group meetings. The welcome and the learning possibilities will be surprising, I am sure.

A look at the contemporary connotation of the word *conservative* is in order. The average American has a different perception of what the word *conservative* means than do the so-called experts in the media, academia, or other perceived intellectual circles. I can make that statement with confidence because of the quarter century of public opinion research to which I have been exposed. The teachers of political science tell us all those things we find in textbooks: conservatives are adverse to change, adherents of Adam Smith, preferring profit over the needs of people. The news reporters tell us that conservatives are antiabortion, anti–gun control, antidiversity, antienvironment, antieverything. The entertainment media try to lead us to the thought that conservatives are prowar, coldhearted, and racist.

The average person sees it differently. Most people tend to think they are conservative if they see the value of a two-parent home (whether or not they are in one) and believe they are accountable for teaching their children self-respect, self-reliance, respect for others, and values that will enable them to get along as adults. Conservatives believe that they are accountable for their own actions, that they must pay for their mistakes. They consider themselves conservative if they go to work every day, try to better their circumstance, own their own home, dream of going into business for themselves, pay their taxes, and try to improve conditions in their own community. They are proud of their nation, of their heritage, and they are optimistic about the future. They believe the miracles of life (animal life, plant life, and human life) are proof enough of the existence of a supreme being. They believe they have the right to openly practice their religion without restraint from government. They believe in normal sex instead of abnormal sex. They believe that they are better able to make decisions for themselves than is any bureaucrat at any level of government. They want governments off of their backs and out of their lives to the greatest extent possible.

I realize that I have just described the majority opinion. That is why most any public opinion survey, in most any state, at most any time, will indicate that a majority of people consider themselves to be conservative, while very few indeed will admit to being liberal. It has to do with life-style more than it does with a narrowly defined academic philosophy. The normal American life-style is a conservative life-style, a fact often missed by media, academic, and political pundits (who quite often just don't get it). One of the primary reasons for the lack of popularity experienced by President Clinton has been his attack on the *normal* or *conservative* life-style accepted and practiced by most Americans.

Let's wrap up this discussion with some practical reasons why conservatives should be interested in, and leaders of, environmental issues, of issues relating to what we are doing to ourselves with the chemicals we use and the processes we employ.

I start with the presumption that all reasonable peoples want clean air and clean water, that such people are opposed to unknowing exposures of our children, our families, and our friends to various poisons. I pray those are reasonable presumptions. So where do we start? First and foremost, if we didn't put the toxic substances in the air, ground, and water in the first place, we wouldn't have to worry about taking them out. Prevention is the least expensive method of achieving an acceptable environment. Avoidance is also a good idea, and with a little communicating, governments could play a strong role in teaching people how to avoid exposure to persistent toxic substances. But once again, the best way, the least expensive way, the conservative way, and the least painful way to accomplish the goal of environmental protection from the most onerous pollutants is prevention. JUST DON'T DO IT in the first place.

Isn't it less expensive in the long run for industry to retool just once, instead of every time one of the many governmental jurisdictions changes its environmental standards? If a suitable alternative could be found for an industrial feed stock or process, industry could then have a long run at profitability. Certainly the current environmental practice of denial and delay has some industries on a stairway to nowhere. And we all know that governments, singularly or jointly, will never have sufficient funds to continue cleaning up onerous contaminants lying on the lake floor and elsewhere. We're talking big-time money, assuming all the appropriate technology exists (which it probably does not). So again, whether we are talking about a lack of money or an absence of technology, prevention is the answer, not just for economic conservatives but for all people.

Government regulation is something that most every conservative abhors. It is never really fair or reasoned. It often punishes those who should be rewarded. Regulations tend to be compromises between the wants of society and the nonwants of lobbyists (and other players). Safe, as it relates to humans, loses its denotation as a word and its definition becomes subject to political compromise. When industry executives come to visit the president, or the governor, or the premier (even socialist premiers), it's a big deal. "Eh, Governor, the giants of industry are here." They chat, they compliment the governor on his or her brilliance, and as they are leaving they say, "Lower the standard just a little." They are such good people; it seems reasonable. They wouldn't ask if it were a bad idea. They just want it lowered a little, just a few more parts per million, or billion, or zillion. Why not?

That example is just one more indicator of why regulation alone will never virtually eliminate anything. Evidence to the contrary is nonexistent. But as long as our mind set is on trying to ratchet down the amount of poison we are injecting into the air or the water or the ground, society will never get rid of the rotten stuff that most all agree must go. But thousands and thousands of people work for government as regulators. They have spent careers learning how to ratchet down. Will they favor changing their jobs from trying to manage the unmanageable to taking charge of preventing serious pollutants in the first place? Probably not, but that is where hope and future success lie.

Had my mother said, "Gordon, stay away from the acid pond or I will have your dad beat you silly when he gets home," it probably would have deterred me. It may have prevented me from exposing myself to those dangers. Maybe I would have avoided that place. Will governments need to use such language, enforced by law, with industry? Or will the giants of industry be smart enough to do it themselves? If they do, that would provide for a much brighter future for our economy and our environment than would simply relying on government to cure all of our ills.

Conservatives want lower taxes. Conservatives want smaller government, with fewer regulations and regulators. Pollution prevention, instead of all the high-cost bureaucratic mandates and regulatory harassment at the tail end of the pollution trail, can achieve those conservative purposes. If you don't make an onerous substance in the first place, you don't later need to regulate it, you don't need regulators or the increased taxes and fees to pay their expenses. If you don't discharge it, you don't need to buy a government permit with all the attendant red tape and bureaucratic nonsense to which businesses are now subjected. Pollution prevention doesn't just correct the physical health of our society; it promotes economic health.

Conservatives believe in individual rights. We believe in the right to own and use private property. Private dry lands should not be deemed to be wet by a remote government. Such actions violate our basic constitutional rights. But is not the insidious invasion of our bodies by harmful unsolicited chemicals the most flagrant violation of our individual rights?

We conservatives bemoan the decline in values that has besieged our society. We scorn government and media assaults on our constitutional right to freely practice our religion in a value-neutral, politically correct time. Why then should we not abhor the lack of morality involved in discharging untested chemicals into the air, ground, and water to alter and harm, to whatever degree, human life and wildlife? As a conservative, I do abhor it. If they think about it, I am sure my compatriots will agree.

We conservatives preach out against the decline in learning in our schools, the increased incidence of juvenile crime; we worry about abnormal sexual practices and the lack of respect that young people now seem to have for the property and person of others. Should there be evidence (as there is) that some of these things are being caused (again, to whatever degree) by chemicals tested and untested flowing into our environment, should we not add that concern to our litany of concerns? Yes, I think so. We preach self-reliance, but what if, unbeknown to us, mysterious chemicals are affecting our ability to be reliant upon ourselves?

We conservatives believe it unconscionable that government programs such as welfare are tearing at the fabric of the family. We are upset with the growing incidence of single-mother families, with children bearing children. Why then are we not so concerned with the causes of childhood cancer? Why not go to the local children's hospital and visit with those brave youngsters with ineffective immune systems trying to fight off the devastating evils of cancer? Observe their parent's pain. See how that circumstance tears at the family structure. Why not add childhood cancer to our concerns about the family, asking why the emphasis is still on how to cure it instead of on how to prevent it?

These are grim matters, but I am optimistic about the future. I have always been an optimist. I always believe things will turn out as they should. Oh, it might require an extraordinary effort by me and by others, but given the desire and a willingness to work, things in my life normally will turn out OK. I believe that about our environment. The symmetry of nature is loaned to us for human use over relatively short periods of time, seventy or eighty years each if we are fortunate. Each of us has a moral duty not to disrupt that balance. For centuries humans met that moral duty, but over the past half century we have become just too urbane to worry about such mundane things. We (generically) have unknowingly done with chemicals what we would not have intentionally done had we pursued the moral basis of the conservative philosophy I have described.

Daily we are being exposed to more and more information about the need for environmental stewardship. The quarter-century campaign to halt tobacco use is a good example to follow. It was not an immediate ban. The tobacco industry had time to involve itself in other endeavors. Hopefully, tobacco farmers found other things to grow, and the tobacco industry workers found other equivalent work. The same could be true in the chemical industry with good stewardship now: a reasonable timetable for change, concern about socioeconomic dislocation, research into safe alternatives. All of those activities could result in a safer and cleaner environment. And who knows, if we stop discharging the onerous substances, nature just might clean itself up much faster than what the experts now think is possible.

Unfortunately, so far the chemical industry is emulating the lobbying and public relations tactics of the tobacco industry by denial and delay and by diverting attention elsewhere. But I think business people will see the light. I think they are decent people. I think they care. I think they want to do the right thing. And I think they will do it. Oh, it might take a reminder from the public now and then or a prod by an international commission or a poke by government, but we are on the way to achieving serious pollution prevention. The time for toxic tolerance is past. It is time for us conservatives to sign on. We can be the leaders who make a major difference for our nation, our continent, our globe.

I like to think the positive because, in this instance, the negative is just too grim. The inability to reproduce is a pretty basic problem for a species to experience: no children, no grandchildren. Then what? The inability to learn at appropriate levels. The inability to fight off the simplest of diseases. Physical deformities at birth. Artificial alterations in sexual preference. All of those things, just too grim to accept.

As the new information comes in, as we hear more and more about the need to exercise precaution before putting harmful chemicals into the environment, I would just ask that you pay a little more attention to what is being said. Don't immediately dismiss worrisome words. Investigate the facts on your own. Don't be diverted by the formalized concentration of attention on trash. Don't demand 100 percent proof of harm before acting. Think about morality and the Golden Rule. Set priorities, make some decisions, then act on those decisions. I have done that, and I have come to the conclusion that we are unintentionally putting our children and our grandchildren in harm's way. I have concluded that we need a basic change in direction.

The future depends on you. Tell your neighbors. Tell your state legislator or your member of Congress that you want and demand appropriate environmental change. Tell the local industry that you want proper stewardship of the environment. The problem is global, but it is a problem that will be solved by your own actions in your own community. So get involved. Make some noise. Kick up some dust. Be optimistic. Know that your concerns, your words, your actions, do matter.

And one last word for my conservative colleagues: we should be leading this parade!

Bibliography

American Assembly, Columbia University, and Council on Foreign Relations. *Canada and the United States: Enduring Friendship, Persistent Stress.* New York: American Assembly, Columbia University and Council on Foreign Relations: Prentice Hall, 1985.

Ashworth, William. *The Late, Great Lakes: An Environmental History.* Detroit: Wayne State University Press, 1987.

Berton, Pierre. *Why We Act Like Canadians.* Penguin Books Canada, 1982.

Buffalo Environmental Law Journal. University of Buffalo School of Law. Vol. 1, no. 2, Fall 1993.

Caldwell, Lynton K., ed. *Perspectives on Ecosystem Management for the Great Lakes.* Albany: State University of New York Press, 1988.

Canada Government. *Toxic Chemicals in the Great Lakes and Associated Effects.* March 1991.

———. Ministry of Environment and Energy, Province of Ontario. *Candidate Substances for Bans, Phase-outs or Reductions—Multimedia Revision.* October 1993.

———. Ministry of Environment and Energy, Ministry of Natural Resources, Ministry of Agriculture and Food, Province of Ontario. *Restoring and Protecting the Great Lakes.* Progress Report, 1991.

———. *Priority Substances List Assessment Report on Chlorinated Wastewater Effluents.* Environment Canada, 1994.

Carnegie Commission on Science, Technology, and Government. *Science, Technology, and Government for a Changing World.* April 1993.

Conservation Foundation and Institute for Research on Public Policy. *Great Lakes, Great Legacy?* Washington, D.C., and Ottawa: Conservation Foundation, 1989.

E. B. Eddy Group. *A Question of Balance.* Ottawa, August 1993.

Fox, Stephen. *John Muir and His Legacy: The American Conservation Movement.* Boston and Toronto: Little, Brown, 1981.

Greenpeace. *Chlorine, Human Health, and the Environment: The Breast Cancer Warning.* A Greenpeace Report, 1993.

———. *Chlorine: The Product Is the Poison.* Greenpeace USA, 1991.

International Joint Commission. *Applying Weight of Evidence: Issues and Practice.* Report on workshop held October 24, 1993. International Joint Commission, Windsor, Ontario, June 1994. (U.S. address of the IJC: 1250 23rd Street, N.W., Washington, D.C. 20440.)

———. *The Fifth Biennial Report on Great Lakes Water Quality.* Ottawa and Washington, D.C.: International Joint Commission, 1990.

——. *The Sixth Biennial Report on Great Lakes Water Quality*. Ottawa and Washington, D.C.: International Joint Commission, 1992.

——. *The Seventh Biennial Report on Great Lakes Water Quality*. Ottawa and Washington, D.C.: International Joint Commission, 1994.

——. *The Boundary Waters Treaty of 1909 and the Rules of Procedure of the International Joint Commission*. Ottawa and Washington, D.C.: International Joint Commission.

——. *Great Lakes Environmental Education: Special Report*. Ottawa and Washington, D.C.: International Joint Commission, May 1991.

——. *Great Lakes/St. Lawrence Research Inventory, 1991/1992*. Ottawa and Washington, D.C.: International Joint Commission.

——. *The Great Lakes Water Quality Agreement of 1978*. Ottawa and Washington, D.C.: International Joint Commission.

——. *Levels Reference Study: Great Lakes–St. Lawrence River Basin*. Ottawa and Washington, D.C.: International Joint Commission, March 1993.

——. *Living with the Lakes: Challenges and Opportunities*. Ottawa and Washington, D.C.: International Joint Commission, 1989.

——. *Methods of Alleviating the Adverse Consequences of Fluctuating Water Levels in the Great Lakes–St. Lawrence River Basin*. Ottawa and Washington, D.C.: International Joint Commission, December 1993.

——. *Our Community, Our Health: Dialogue between Science and Community*. Ottawa and Washington, D.C.: International Joint Commission, 1993.

——. *A Strategy for Virtual Elimination of Persistent Toxic Substances*. Ottawa and Washington, D.C.: International Joint Commission, August 1993.

——. *Winds of Chance: The Effects of Air Pollution on the Great Lakes*. Ottawa and Washington, D.C.: International Joint Commission, 1992.

Journal of Toxicology and Environmental Health. Vol. 33, no. 4, August 1991.

Maclean's. Canada's Weekly Newsmagazine. Vol. 107, no. 28, July 11, 1994.

Michigan Environmental Science Board Chlorine Panel. *Impacts of Chlorine Use on Environmental and Public Health*. Lansing, Michigan, June 30, 1994.

National Research Council. *Pesticides in the Diets of Infants and Children*. Washington, D.C.: National Academy Press, 1993.

National Wildlife Federation. *Hormone Copycats: New Pollution Threat to the Great Lakes Environment*. Ann Arbor, Michigan, August 16, 1993.

New York State. *New York State 1989–1990 Fishing Regulations Guide*. Albany: Department of Environmental Conservation.

Raloff, Janet. "The Gender Benders." *Science News*. Vol. 145, January 8, 1994.

——. "That Feminine Touch." *Science News*. Vol. 145, January 22, 1994.

Reader's Digest Association. *ABC's of the Human Body*. Pleasantville, New York, and Montreal: Reader's Digest Association, 1987.

Roberts, Sam. *Who We Are: A Portrait of America*. Times Books, 1993.

"Science and the Environment." *Freeman: Ideas on Liberty*, September 1993.

United States General Accounting Office. *Need to Reassess U.S. Participation in the International Joint Commission*. GAO/NSIAK-89-164. Washington, D.C., June 1989.

——. *Pesticides: Issues concerning Pesticides Used in the Great Lakes Watershed*. GAO/RCED-93-128. Washington, D.C., June 1993.

——. *Reproductive and Developmental Toxicants: Regulatory Actions Provide Uncertain Protection*. GAO/PEMD-92-3. Washington, D.C., October 1991.

Walker, Gord. *A Conservative Canada*. Sutton West, Ontario: Paget Press, 1983.

Weiss, Rick. "Estrogen in the Environment: Are Some Pollutants a Threat to Fertility?" *Washington Post*, January 26, 1994.

Wingspread Conference Center. Statement from work session, "Chemically Induced Alterations in Sexual Development: The Wildlife/Human Connection." Wingspread Conference Center, Racine, Wisconsin, July 26–28, 1991.

———. Statement from work session, "Environmentally Induced Alterations in Development: A Focus on Wildlife." Wingspread Conference Center, Racine, Wisconsin, December 10–12, 1993.

Index

Bulen, L. Keith, 174, 175
Bush, George: appointment of author, xii, 21, 181; environmental legislation, 53; Clean Air Act and U.S./Canada Air Accord, 123

California, 72
Canada (environment): subtle problems, 40; U.S./Canada environmental work, 41; Great Lakes Water Quality Agreement, 51, 53, 60; Lake Superior, 54; definition of toxic, 57; sunsetting, 64; U.S./Canada Air Quality Agreement, 67; ecosystem approach, 103
Canadian Fisheries Act, 60
Canadian mining industry, 31
Canadian pulp and paper industry, 31
Cancer: author's family, 8; awareness, 47; pre-eminent among suspected effects, 75; dioxins, 78; exposures, 79; increased occurrences, 80, 86; thinking reoriented, 88; clusters, 94; chlorinated substances, 130; persistent toxic substances, 164; childhood, 185
Capons, 6
Carbon-generated energy, 49
Carcinogens: capons, 6, non-carcinogenic, 76; tobacco, 105; government testing, 139
Carson, Rachel, 181
Carter, Jimmy, 51
Castro, Fidel, 41
Cause and effect linkages: Council of Great Lakes Research Managers, 61; certainty, 75; weight of evidence, 88, 93, 94
Certainty/uncertainty: consensus decisions, 25; intellectually honest, 46, 161; regulatory decisions, 62, 88; a barrier, 75; governments and industry, 75; dealing with uncertainty, 94; training of scientists, 95, 130; qualified statements by scientists, 160; Michigan Chlorine Panel, 169; mentioned, 80
Chandler, James, 104
Change: an anathema, 99; good or bad, 110; to foster environmental protection and economic growth, 179
Chemical manufacturing industry: U.S. policy, 51; dioxins, 77; barriers to dialogue, 108; denying change, 111; fall of 1993, 115; chlorine recommendation, 118
Chemicals, classes of, 82
Childless marriages, 110

Chloracne, 8
Chlorine and chlorinated substances: anthropogenic use, 32, 33; human management, 46; dirty dozen toxics, 64; prove the negative, 75; sunsetting, 78; endocrine system, 79, 80; as a class, 82, 162; DDT, 85; banning, 93; drinking water and pharmaceuticals, 115; chlorine-free paper, 122; dangers, 125; news coverage, 141; incinerators, 146; communications, 158; definition and use, 166; Canadian decisions, 167, 168; Clinton proposals, 167; mentioned, 98
Cholera, 132
Christians, 19
City Council of Niagara Falls, New York, 116, 117
Clarke, Alan, 104
Clean Air Act, 53, 100
Clean Environment Act, 100
Clean Technology, 41
Cleveland, Hilary, 174
Clinton Administration: chlorine recommendation, 105; Clean Water Act, 167; IJC commissioners, 175
Clinton, William J.: environmental promises, 121; lack of popularity, 182
Colborn, Dr. Theo: multi-disciplines, 61; hormone mimickers, 79; leadership, 130, 167
Cole, Nat King, 9
Cole-Misch, Sally, 104
Columbia River, 70
Committee on Public Works and Transportation, U.S. House of Representatives, 104
Communicating/communications: slowness of, 4; aversion to, 34; IJC priority, 35; preach to the choir, 45; tools for success, 56; medical profession, 66, 118; hormone copycats, 79; government workers, 97; E. B. Eddy principle, 109; remedial action plans, 136; average family, 146; risk to human health, 158; barriers, 161; defining Great Lakes message and audience, 164
Communism: failed examples, 11; protesting, 16
Como, Perry, 9
Condoms, 9
Confounding factors, 92
Congressional testimony, 45
Consensus building: leadership tool, 33, 34; international experts, 51
Consensus decision making, 24, 25

GORDON K. DURNIL is a lawyer, diplomat, politician, and conservative environmentalist. From 1981 to 1989 he was Indiana Republican State Chairman and a member of the Republican National Committee. In 1989 President Bush appointed him as United States Chairman of the International Joint Commission, the U.S.-Canadian organization charged with maintaining the quality of the environment along the U.S.-Canadian border. Mr. Durnil served as chairman until 1994. In June of 1992 he was Head of Delegation for the International Joint Commission at the U.N. Conference on Environment and Development in Rio de Janeiro, where he addressed the Plenary Session.